WILSON HARRIS AND THE MODERN TRADITION

Wilson Harris, c. 1980. *Photograph courtesy of Wilson Harris.*

WILSON HARRIS AND THE MODERN TRADITION

A New Architecture of the World

SANDRA E. DRAKE

CONTRIBUTIONS IN AFRO-AMERICAN AND
AFRICAN STUDIES, NUMBER 93

GREENWOOD PRESS
NEW YORK • WESTPORT, CONNECTICUT • LONDON

Library of Congress Cataloging in Publication Data

Drake, Sandra E.
  Wilson Harris and the modern tradition.

  (Contributions in Afro-American and African studies,
ISSN 0069-9624 ; no. 93)
    Bibliography: p.
    Includes index.
    1. Harris, Wilson—Criticism and interpretation.
  I. Title.   II. Series.
  PR9320.9.H3Z62 1986   813   85-9874
  ISBN 0-313-24783-8 (lib. bdg.: alk. paper)

Library of Congress Catalog Card Number: 85-9874
ISBN: 0-313-24783-8
ISSN: 0069-9624

First published in 1986

Greenwood Press, Inc.
88 Post Road West
Westport, Connecticut 06881

Printed in the United States of America

The paper used in this book complies with the
Permanent Paper Standard issued by the National
Information Standards Organization (Z39.48-1984).

10 9 8 7 6 5 4 3 2 1

FOR JOSEPH SOMMERS

Contents

Illustrations

Preface

Writing this book has been an illuminating experience in ways I had not expected. I learned much about obstacles peculiar to considering an author in a relatively new field of academic inquiry—Caribbean literature—and about whom relatively little critical work has been published.

No accepted "canonical" truths about Wilson Harris have been established, either to be supported or refuted. There is no shared universe of discourse in the sense that it exists for authors such as Shakespeare or Joyce. This means that no terms have been established in which to think about the writer, which is especially difficult in the case of Harris, because his work eludes the confines of prevailing "generic expectations."

In one sense, the critic is presented with an embarrassment of riches. But where to begin, and how? My first intention was to deal with Harris's entire oeuvre—an oeuvre that, disconcertingly, increased even as I was working on this book. Increasingly, too, a more interesting critical approach suggested itself as I considered the question of why I was especially intrigued by his work, why he seemed to me an important writer. The focus and final form of this book reflect my answer: Harris is important because of what he does with language; because of his intellectual breadth and depth; because of his interest in connections between different cultures and traditions; because of his conviction of the possibility of a meaningful apprehension of truth and of knowledge, a conviction distinguishing him from many Western Modernists; and because of his sense of the necessity of revising the way the modern world conceives of its own history, especially the history of the last half-millennium, in terms of centers, origins, and identity—in short, because of the particular way his writing constitutes part of the Modern tradition, from the perspective of the Third World.

My first two chapters, then, address the historical relations of the West and the Caribbean, and the emergence of the Modernist tradition. The following six chapters consist of a close textual analysis of four of Harris's novels that are especially interesting for his treatment of Caribbean society, relations with the West, and the range of his literary style and sources. My final chapter explores Harris's theory of language and its relation to his ideas on the novel, the nature of the psyche, and historical experience.

The most salient characteristic of the modern world is that it is increasingly one world, for better and for worse, and this one world came into being with the Voyages of European Conquest in the Caribbean five hundred years ago. Modernism, the Modernist tradition, identified itself as such during roughly the last quarter of the nineteenth century. It is a movement with significant roots in the changing relationship between the Third World and the West; we are still in the throes of that process of change. This process is the working out of practical interests and resultant ideological and cultural paradigms developed since the onset of "modern times" with the Voyages of European Conquest.

Modernism cannot be understood as merely a Western phenomenon, either of attitude or of literary style, even if Westerners adopt an assimilationist stance and allow that some educated persons from the Third World who have adopted a Western point of view may participate. Non-Western paradigms also constitute part of the Modernist tradition.

To understand how Harris adapts non-Western beliefs—for example, the zemi, or African ideas of the relation between the living and the dead—an audience with a Western education may find comparison with some Modernist thought developed in the West more helpful than traditional Western ideas. This is the use I make of the work of such Western scholars as Derrida or Lacan, and must be distinguished from making a "Derridean" or a "Lacanian" analysis of Harris.

I have addressed two different audiences, and I have two different aims. The first audience consists of persons familiar with Harris's work and with the criticism already published. My aim in addressing them is to build upon that criticism and to contribute to a dialogue that is now at one of its most interesting as well as frustrating stages: a very important writer is just beginning to get the attention due him. I hope that my book will stimulate discussion, suggest directions for pursuing the study of Harris's fiction, and provide further impetus for such study. My second audience is composed of persons unfamiliar with Harris's work and the critical writing on it. I hope to interest this audience sufficiently so that they will read his fiction and his critical writings. In one sense, then, my book is unabashedly partisan. I consider Harris to be a very good and a very important writer who deserves to be read more widely than he is and who would interest a large number of people who have not yet had the good fortune to encounter his work.

Harris is never an easy writer. A reader could be forgiven the initial occasional suspicion that the convolutions of conception and of prose are unwarranted. And, as is the case with any author, he is not equally successful in what he attempts. But the more he is read, and the more carefully, the more evident becomes the underlying richness, rigor and consistency of his thought and the often remarkable beauty of his language.

Harris's breadth and what at times amounts to his idiosyncrasy present the critic with great organizational difficulties if one is to do his work justice and avoid the impression of an overexuberant eclecticism. Harris does draw on a wide variety of sources. He is not simply writing from a tradition of English fiction or mining the riches of a single Caribbean tradition, whether Afro-Caribbean, Indian-Guyanese, or Amerindian. The task he has set himself as a writer involves them all. Justice cannot be done him without reference to Arawak *zemis*; to the theological systems of India; to Anancy, the West African and Caribbean trickster-figure; and to the established literary canon and the culture of the West.

Because the field is relatively new and Wilson Harris is not widely known, especially in the United States, I had to assume that most of my readership consisted of scholars educated in traditional English and American literature but unfamiliar with the history, the culture, and the geography of the part of the world in which the fiction I discuss is set. Not only was this information important as background but it is fundamental to my discussion of how Harris relates to the Western Modernist tradition. In short, before I could get down to my central task of discussing Harris's work, I had to identify him, identify his critics, present the cultural and historical background of the region, and provide enough basic information on the books to provide a basis for intelligible discussion. Just providing plot summaries is an especially difficult task in the case of Harris!

Both Harris's poetry and his fiction reveal a high degree of what he has called in one of his essays the "subjective imagination" and a wide range of knowledge of European classical culture, Asian philosophy, and Western humanities and science. A reviewer of one of Harris's early novels, reacting to the comments of others emphasizing that he was a Caribbean novelist, wrote in the *Times Literary Supplement* in 1962 that he "should not be described as a West Indian writer in the narrow restrictive meaning of the words. He is a novelist writing in English out of a common perception, a particular experience, and a unique vision." I could reasonably expect most of my audience to be familiar only with the Western tradition. I have therefore devoted my least specific and detailed attention to the elements in his writing drawn from the Western canon. Thus I do not elaborate in greater detail upon his sources, references, and allusions to Yeats, Blake, Eliot, and Hopkins, among others. I have judged the greater need to be a discussion of the importance in his fiction of Anancy, Osiris, and *zemis*—that with which I cannot reasonably expect my readers to be acquainted. Harris's interest in the social function of art is obvious from his selection of incident and his treatment of character in the four novels discussed in this book: *Palace of the Peacock, Ascent to Omai, Tumatumari,* and *Genesis of the Clowns.* But his novelistic practice in these and other works, as well as in his critical writings, makes clear his strong conviction that the realist literary tradition has serious limitations not only from an artistic point of view but also as social criticism.

As Greenwood Series Advisors, Professors Henry Louis Gates and John Blassingame point out in their foreword to *The Womb of Space,* Harris's "primary concern would seem to be with the reality of language itself, rather than with reflecting directly material or political relationship." From the philosophical as·well as the literary perspective, "the Word," language, in all its polysemy, is centrally important to Harris. Indeed, as I seek to demonstrate, they are not separable in his view. Gates and Blassingame also note Harris's concern for "community"; he is concerned with the way the novel can "convert rooted deprivations into complex parables of freedom and truth," thereby contributing toward profound psychological changes. As they judge the matter, Harris believes that this "is a formidable but not hopeless task."

Many individuals and institutions assisted me with this book; I thank them all, and especially the following. The National Science Foundation administered the grant I received from the Ford Foundation and the National Endowment for the Humanities. Stanford University's Administration and Department of English allowed me a year's leave. Within the Department of English, Chairpersons George Dekker, Robert Polhemus, and Albert Gelpi have been considerate and helpful. The late Professor Charles T. Davis of the Department of English at Yale University, just before his tragic and untimely death, agreed to my affiliation, while on leave, with the Yale Afro-American Studies Program of which he was chairperson. Subsequently, on short notice, Dean Helene Moghlen agreed to my affiliation with Kresge College, University of California-Santa Cruz; and Professor Michael Cowan of the Department of English, Kresge College, agreed to sponsor that affiliation.

I thank those who read the manuscript in its entirety for their helpful suggestions: Professors David Halliburton, Herbert Lindenberger, and Lucio Ruotolo of the Department of English, Stanford University; Professor Michael Cowan, Department of English, University of California-Santa Cruz; and Dr. Elisabeth Boisaubin Moreno.

Thanks are due to Faber and Faber, Ltd., for permission to quote extensively from *Palace of the Peacock, Tumatumari* , *Ascent to Omai*, and *Genesis of the Clowns*. Quotations from Richard Macksey and Eugenio Donato, editors, *The Structuralist Controversy: The Languages of Criticism and the Sciences of Man,* are reprinted through the courtesy of the Johns Hopkins University Press.

A word of appreciation is due Professors Nathaniel Mackey of the University of California, Santa Cruz, who shares my scholarly interest in Wilson Harris's work; Louis Green, San Diego State University; Don E. Wayne, University of California-San Diego; and Bernth Lindfors, University of Texas at Austin.

My parents, Elizabeth and St. Clair Drake, and my husband, Raymond Meyer, gave me encouragement and varied and valuable assistance; Raymond Meyer also translated the passage from *Das*

Prinzip Hoffnung in Chapter 9. I thank those who helped produce this book. Lynn Flint and Susan Baker, my editors at Greenwood Press, were patient and efficient. Cindy King typed the first draft; Reese Cutler and John Baxter provided technical assistance. Kitty Vroom completed the final typing, and her intelligence, organization and good humor throughout a complicated project are much appreciated. Last chronologically but by no means least, I thank my brother, Karl J. Drake, for making his professional expertise available at a crucial point.

Wilson Harris himself I owe special thanks for his graciousness and generosity with his time during his visit in 1983 to the University of California-Santa Cruz and in subsequent correspondence.

Finally, I am grateful to Professor Henry Louis Gates, Jr., for the interest he has taken in this book as the Greenwood Press Series Advisor. Of Harris's *Womb of Space* he and his co-editor wrote that the book "will be especially useful for students and scholars of comparative literature." I hope that the same will be true of this book about Harris's fiction.

All of the above-mentioned have a share in what may be valuable in this book; errors and infelicities are, of course, my own.

Sandra E. Drake
Stanford University

WILSON HARRIS
AND THE
MODERN TRADITION

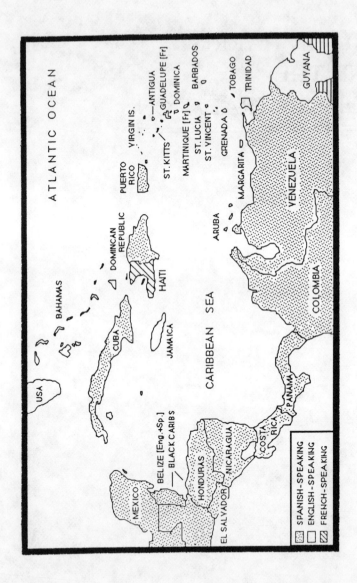

Fig. 1

West Indian Islands and the Caribbean Rimland

1

A View of El Dorado:
Nuestra América mestiza and the Modern Tradition

> Few Caribbean territories have exercised such a potent hold over the English imagination as Guyana, as the literature . . . sufficiently testifies. Ever since the Elizabethan exaggerations of Ralegh . . . who dreamed that he could subjugate the mysterious Empire of Guiana as Cortés had subjugated the Aztec Empire, the myth of the Guyanese El Dorado has enslaved both expatriate and creole. . . .[1]
>
> Gordon K. Lewis, *The Growth of the Modern West Indies*, p. 257

> Let us keep in mind that our people are not European nor North American, but rather a composite of Africa and America . . . the majority of the indigenes have been annihilated; the European element has mixed with the American and the African, and this latter with the Indian and the European. . . .
>
> Simón Bolívar, Message to the Congress of Angostura, 1819

World War I is still today the Great War, symbol of a crisis of faith and confidence that undermined the West before the catastrophe and has continued since. This crisis, adumbrated by Nietzsche, among others, was exacerbated by theoretical developments in a number of fields, all tending to erode the traditional structuring of an orderly and comprehensible universe. Freud, Jung, and others postulated that human behavior was dictated by drives and desires springing from a realm beyond the control or even the knowledge of the individual. Discoveries in physics and mathematics, especially Einstein's general theory of relativity, revealed the inadequacy of the traditional understanding of the nature of matter; they seemed to call into question the foundation of the physical world itself as well as the meaning of time and space. Painters such as Picasso and Modigliani and writers such as Joyce, Woolf, and Proust disturbed traditional sensibilities by exploring implications for the human psyche of altered relationships of time and space. Additionally, long-accepted conventions of aesthetics were found wanting.

Of the crisis of confidence that gave rise to Modernism, David Halliburton writes:

The rupture . . . is another name for a phenomenon brought to attention through Heidegger's reading of Hölderlin; it is the destitute time writ large, writ epochally.

We have seen its inscription (to borrow a Derridean term) in the poetic crisis of a Hoffmannsthal, and . . . we could trace it through the fabling *Angst* of Kafka, whose "In the Penal Colony" at once parodies and exalts the office of language, incarnate and lethal as it is there shown to be, not only to itself but to the colonial (read Western) historical tradition.[2]

As Halliburton's words indicate, the crisis of Modernism is related to the Western colonial tradition. In fact, the Great War signaled not only the West's cultural crisis but also the incipient decline of the West's political and economic hegemony, although the fact was not widely recognized until later. That hegemony was based on the European empires first carved out, half a millennium before, in Wilson Harris's native Caribbean. Western economic development, which provided the basis for Western confidence, had in turn been based on the fruits of imperial possession.

Derrida, for example, recognizes that the failure of traditional European philosophical constructs—and the resulting dilemmas, which have inspired his own reformulations—are traceable to what he calls political, economic, and technical "moments."[3] These moments, I argue, are rooted in the relationship between the Third World and the West, which until recently was conceived by the West as that of colonial power to colony.

The importance in Harris's fiction of unconscious psychic dimensions, nonlinear narrative structure, the awareness of a rupture in the correlation between language and an accepted reality, and a sense of cultural crisis indicate a Modernist understanding.[4] His fiction breaks with what the narrator of his novel, *The Eye of the Scarecrow*, calls the "dead tide" of realism. He radically undermines linear sequence, space, and time with a consequent alteration of conventional understandings of recollection, identity, and causality. The potent forces of unconscious memory and desire are crucial to his fiction, which has been aptly compared with that of Joyce and Woolf.[5] The critic Michael Gilkes has described Harris's work as being written in a "language of crisis."[6]

Each of the four novels I discuss in this book has a plot based on Caribbean historical, mythical, and social realities. This is important because Harris establishes the plots in these novels only to undercut them, thereby making an implicit critique of the "series of adventures," in Harris's words, which he thinks present a misleading and dangerous way of conceptualizing history.

Palace of the Peacock is Harris's version of the search for El Dorado, perhaps the quintessential myth of the post-Columbian Caribbean. The myth has a focal point in Guiana and interlocks with the conventional historical record to combine "reality" and "myth" in a single image. The historian Gordon K. Lewis points out that the urge to explore the interior, the obsessive conviction that wealth and salvation lie in its exploitation, has colored the attitudes even of sober government officialdom in Guyana.[7] Hena Maes-Jelinek observes in her article "The Myth of El Dorado in the Caribbean Novel" that "Guiana must always be discovered anew."[8] Harris's version of this Caribbean "Ur-myth" strikingly resembles accounts of actual expeditions, most importantly in tone. V. S. Naipaul cites one such account in his book *The Loss of El Dorado*. The greed, the hysteria, the self-destructive stupidity and brutality of the European crew abusing the Indian who is trying to answer their question; the wanton disregard of their own and others' welfare in the pursuit of fabled wealth and power; the suggestion of delirium and disorientation at the end of their terrible adventure—all of these echo throughout *Palace of the Peacock*. For these conquistadors, the pursuit of El Dorado amounts almost to a demoniac possession. As an element of the Guyanese historical experience, this pursuit has contributed to the Guyanese mentality even to the present day, and to a number of the dilemmas with which Harris is so concerned.

Tumatumari is the story of a marriage faltering under the stress of a hostile jungle encampment; a Heathcliffian husband, possibly insane;

an enigmatic Amerindian woman, probably his mistress; and a wife
whose family is crippled by emotional dishonesty and torn by racial
prejudices.

Ascent to Omai is set among the Black urban proletariat of Guyana's
Albuoystown. An abusive father has turned to drink and neglects the
child whose mother died at his birth. A factory strike, the father's
subsequent trial and imprisonment, and the reflections of the grown son
and the sentencing judge form the plot.

Genesis of the Clowns concerns the tensions and conflicts of a
surveying crew in rural Guyana. Its members, who belong to diverse
ethnic groups, fall victim to various stresses; sexual jealousy and
betrayal lead to murder.

These novels are concerned, furthermore, with the pervasive Guyanese
conflict between the idea of coastal society and the idea of the interior.
This dilemma is symbolic in Harris's fiction of mental expeditions into
the interior of the psyche and of literary expeditions into the hidden or
interior possibilities of language itself.

Chapters 3 through 8 consist of a close textual analysis of these four
novels; chapters 1, 2, and 9 present historical background, biographical
material, and a theoretical framework, all of which I hope prove
illuminating in considering the fiction itself. My discussion
throughout this study is organized around the importance of doubling in
three areas central to Harris's fictional vision: 1) his theory of language
and literary art, 2) his theory of the psyche, and 3) his theory of
history. I consider the characteristics of Harris's fiction that make him
a Modernist writer. I also consider those that make him, specifically, a
Third World Modernist writer: first, his sophisticated development of
concepts deriving from Third World cultures to represent a response to
the Modernist crisis; and second, his concept of hope for the
"individual" human psyche and for the psyche (history) of the human
collectivity, what he refers to as the "imperilled community."[9] His
hope, derived from his Third World perspective on the Modernist crisis,
differs from the attitude of many Western Modernist writers; he
expresses it in terms of his theory of language. Indeed, his hope derives
from the potential represented by the resistance of human language to
"obsessive centrality."[10]

Thus, his ideas of psyche and of history intertwine with his ideas of language and literature. I discuss this interconnection in detail in my final chapter on language.

The present chapter addresses the other two aspects: Harris's theory of psyche as it becomes a literary presentation of character in the novel and his theory of history as it becomes a literary presentation of plot in the novel. I consider both of them in terms of the key organizing concept of doubling.

Harris himself develops two ideas that are useful in understanding his writing: the "victim stasis" and the "novel of consolidation of character," sometimes called the "novel of persuasion." In the following passage, where he speaks of "the Caribbean novel as a whole," he indicates the connection between the two ideas:

> ... there are certain areas of the world in which one is aware that the people who live there are conscious of themselves as persons who have been exploited. ... The facts can all be listed, facts of injustice, facts of exploitation. ...

But, he continues, the novel of classical realism that documents these facts or these categories of facts is inadequate:

> The facts are true, but a syndrome occurs which in relating itself to the facts becomes something other than the facts. A certain psychological stasis is born, what I call the "victim stasis."

The juxtaposition of victor and victim in an exploitative society creates deformed persons and a deformed conception of reality and history. From this he draws the following implications for the art of the novel:

> An alteration needs to occur in the texture of the novel to allow these juxtapositions to play in such a manner that the creation of a vision through and beyond stasis, which I see as immensely pertinent to the late twentieth-century novel, may occur through an alteration in the settled fabric of realism that consolidates victor and victim . . . without that subjective alteration the community is doomed to perpetuate an endless reinforcement of conflict. . . [11]

The phrase "consolidates victor and victim" indicates the relation of psyche, literature ("novel of consolidation of character"), and history ("stasis of victor and victim"): The novel of consolidation confirms for the community (author and audience) the psychological experience of a certain kind of historical formulation. Here, Harris unites two ideas by combining parts of two different phrases, a characteristic way for him to establish connections in his fiction as well as in his nonfictional writing.

In his discussion of the dilemmas facing the thinkers in Europe who, faced with the challenges of the modern era, wished to redefine the premises of Western thought, Derrida writes: "We have no language—no syntax and no lexicon—which is alien to this history; we cannot utter a single destructive proposition which has not already slipped into the form, the logic, and the implicit postulations of precisely what it seeks to contest."[12]

Rather, it is, as Derrida views it, "a question of putting expressly and systematically the problem of the status of a discourse which borrows from a heritage the resources necessary for the deconstruction of that heritage itself."[13]

These passages illuminate Harris's literary itinerary and certain of his literary techniques that have baffled some critics, for Derrida addresses the same issue as does Harris when the latter writes: "an order which may have been a congenial value in the eighteenth- or nineteenth-century novel is beginning to set up an inner contradiction within itself: value becomes an implacable conceit of bias if it is to be maintained as a form which determines all content absolutely. . . ."[14]

This refers to what Harris calls the "novel of consolidation of character." This classical novelistic realism, rising to prominence in Europe along with the rise of the bourgeois class that presided over the Western empire—in the name of which América mestiza's subjugation was justified—relied on certain categories of narrative structure and on delineation of individual character.[15]

Harris uses a conventional plot with conventional events and characters, constructing the novel, to borrow Derrida's terminology, according to the syntax and lexicon of what Harris calls "colonial conventions" (*Palace of the Peacock*, p. 20), which are the literary expression of the "form, the logic and the implicit postulations" that Harris contests. He then undertakes the dissolution of these colonial conventions through the undercutting—with the very tool of literature itself, language—of the syntax and lexicon of the novel of classical realism.

Many important differences exist, however, between Harris's thought and certain Western ideas that I consider helpful to understanding his fiction. Derrida's *différance*, for example, implies the impossibility of a satisfactory relationship between language and the establishment of "presence," or "truth." As I discuss in detail in Chapter 9, Harris's assessment of the nature, possibilities, and effectiveness of language differs from Derrida's and is couched in terms closer to certain African and Asian ideas on the subject.

To take another example, some of Lacan's ideas are useful in considering Harris's fiction, as I will demonstrate in a moment. But Lacan is equivocal about how the "conscious subject" apprehends the "unconscious subject," the "truth of the barred a" (although he is not equivocal about whether such a truth may in some sense be said to exist). Harris's work presents the possibility of access to spheres of awareness ("below" the bar of the barred a) that is closer to mystical traditions, especially the Buddhist and Hindu.

Yet despite these divergences, Harris's conception of the psychological subject, so important to his fiction, is more accessible to someone educated in the Western tradition (as most readers of this book probably are) if considered from the Modernist perspectives of Derrida, Lacan, and Lévi-Strauss than if it is viewed through the lens of the traditional Western concept of the individual. In the traditional formulation, the individual is a center having a relationship of subject to object with the external world, especially nature, from which the individual is separate, and which the individual dominates, although ideally in a benevolent fashion.

Modernist theories, then, are useful in approaching Harris's work in part because Harris too is making a Modernist response to the modern crisis. But their usefulness is also attributable to Harris's sophisticated adaptation and literary expression of attitudes rooted in non-European traditions, Third World traditions that never formulated concepts of "man," "individual," "nature," "relation between subject and object" in the same way as the dominant European philosophical tradition did. Thus, when Harris writes of the figure of the West Indian slave as a model offering a "grassroots redemption" for the Western individual, he is suggesting a reformulation of the concept of "individual" in the light of both Caribbean historical experience and the philosophical constructs arising from it. These constructs derive not only from the West but also from the cultures of Africa, Asia, and Amerindia; and to some extent, they are more accessible from a Western Modernist perspective than from a traditional Western one.

Harris is a Third World Modernist. His identity as a Caribbean writer affords him a perspective on history and on Western philosophical developments that differs in important ways from those of his fellow Modernist writers, educated, as he was, in a Western tradition but not also rooted, as he is, in another tradition. Thus, he is able to use his Caribbean perspective on the "colonial (read Western) historical tradition," of which Halliburton writes to propose a different reading of the "office of language."

Similarly, Harris's ultimately hopeful voice, a far cry from Kafka's "fabling *Angst*," sets him apart from many Modernist writers whose work, in this "destitute time writ large," tends to be characterized by "loss, alienation and despair" and whose very gaiety seems to convey a brave but impotent stand in the face of such colossal cultural distress.[16] Harris's lack of *Angst*, in conjunction with as clear an awareness of crisis as any Euro-American writer possesses, derives from a view of the decline of Western hegemony not as the end of a centering tradition encompassing and grounding all meaning but as a welcome, albeit dangerous and painful, transitional period for the entire world. I examine this aspect of his writing in detail in the final chapter of this book when I discuss his concept of hope.

Harris's conception of character in his novels—the nature of the subject (which determines point of view and ultimately the nature of "event," which is for Harris, as for Derrida, a "suspect category")—is illuminated by the Lacanian concept of the subject as constructed by the linguistic system.

Lacan speaks of three psychological categories: The Imaginary, the Symbolic, and the Real. The Imaginary—the term is derived from "image," not from "imagination" as employed in popular usage—has to do with the image of the self that a human being develops. The Symbolic is the social order, and the individual entry into this order in the capacity of subject occurs through the acquisition of language. The Real is what is real for the subject and is not synonymous with an objective, external reality. Anthony Wilden writes that for Lacan, participation in the Symbolic order characterizes the human animal and derives from the linguistic system of organizing, and therefore experiencing: "The Symbolic is the primary order, since it represents and structures both of the others; moreover, it is ultimately only in language . . . that synonyms, ambiguities, and interpretations operate. . . ."

Other animals and prelinguistic humans experience emotional and cognitive states, but existence that is characteristically human develops from participation in the Symbolic order. Those exclusively human constructs, "synonyms, ambiguities, and interpretations," are a product of the linguistic realm, which includes the province of fiction. And the Subject is the nexus connecting the three realms: "Since the Symbolic, the Imaginary, and the Real co-exist and intersect in the subject . . . at the same time as they are functions linking the subject to others and to the world, any change in one order will have repercussions in the other."[17]

When the human being acquires language and enters the realm of the Symbolic, the Real is structured according to the rules of a linguistic system. To introduce things into the Symbolic realm, the human being attempts to make them function according to the rules of that system. But the sameness sought—the "thing" in itself and the "thing" incorporated into the system—does not lie in things but, as Lacan puts it, in the mark, the linguistic symbol that eliminates particularity, rubs out difference, and makes "repetition" possible: "the subject is the effect of this repetition inasmuch as it necessitates the 'fading,' the obliteration, of the first foundation of the subject, which is why *the subject, by status, is always presented as a divided essence* [my emphasis]."[18]

The psychological subject, or character, in Harris's fiction tends to be a self-image produced by "deluded" individuals, such as the members of the crew in *Palace of the Peacock*, engaged in trying to grasp the shadow of otherness, of a person or event that is linguistically and therefore experientially (but not necessarily "really") outside the self, and this subject is always a divided essence, a doubling and an otherness. In the arena of literature, this divided essence becomes a "doubling" of the "divided essence" of author and narrator.

Up to this point, my discussion has been concerned with the "individual locus" of the subject in doubling and repetition. I now address the question of that which, in Lacanian terms, the subject serves to join—others—and the relationships between them and the "world" that constitute the Real.

In this connection, certain ideas common to many schools of psychology, including the Freudian, are useful. The social psychologist R. D. Laing has constructed a schema that provides the transition to the level of the social implied but not explicitly developed in Lacan's theory. This level is crucial to an understanding of Harris's fiction.

In *Politics of the Family*, Laing is concerned with the family as a structural concept that patterns subjects (i.e., psyches) over generations. He distinguishes between the family as a biologically and socially defined entity and the introjected family—that is, the family as an *idea* of pattern of relationships held by each involved person.[19] In the introjected family, people belong to the same family if they have all incorporated the idea of each other as being part of that family. The two meanings of family do not necessarily coincide, and when they come into severe conflict or contradict each other, psychological disturbance is likely to ensue.

The introjected family becomes the prototype for the psychic incorporation of other social entities, such as religious, ethnic, and political groups. This conception of the family becomes important for understanding Harris's fiction, which is deeply concerned with the relations between such larger social entities—that is, with the "imperilled community." Cultural patterns may be frozen through time in the same way as the familial patterns are frozen in Laing's case histories.

Laing's theory is also useful for analyzing Harris's work because of its concern with "static" systems, specifically with why and how they persist as static, why humanity is enmeshed in what Harris calls "the stasis of victor and victim." In Laing's multigenerational system of complex knots of relationships, persons end up, through the psychological mechanisms of projection and introjection, acting out the behavior or the implications of the behavior of people who may have died long before they were born, but with whose existence the adults who raise them have, both consciously and unconsciously, acquainted them. The frozen, repetitive patterns outlast the "individual" human entity. In fact, the individual is a dancer executing a pattern of steps according to a choreography of which he or she very likely never becomes aware. Thus the river voyage taken by Donne and his crew in *Palace of the Peacock* symbolically reenacts the historical voyage of the people of Guyana. The "voyage" is the embodiment of the idea of a nation and a people "all in the same boat." In *Tumatumari*, the individual nexus of Prudence's psyche becomes the locus for dissolving the historical, sexual, and familial stasis of "victor and victim," for breaking out of the mass hypnosis posited by Laing as being at the root of both individual child-rearing practices and social practices aimed at cohesions on a larger scale, such as the ethnic or the religious.

The fundamental "action" in Harris's fiction consists in his characters' struggles in the coils of these patterns, all of which are manifestations of stasis of victor and victim."

Thus, Harris's literary itinerary is a deployment of the conceptual and artistic implements given us by our societies, by our Lacanian Real. The absolute validity of our "colonial conventions" is called into question. The purpose of this undercutting is to offer a glimpse into a reality not bounded by our conventional Real. Such insight gained from altering what Harris calls the "settled fabric" will constitute a resource for dealing with the psychological and cultural crises of the modern era.

In summary, the stasis of victor and victim is a frozen perception of *América mestiza* as conquered by the West. It finds literary confirmation when portrayed in the novel of consolidation of character, the novel of classical realism. This literary form does not permit the breaking of "colonial conventions" to allow for a new perception and interpretation of history that will permit the "imperilled community" to understand itself differently and break the historical cycle of violence and conquest.

The psychological "I," the literary character in Harris's fiction, may be grasped from the standpoint of the Lacanian nexus of the Imaginary, the Symbolic, and the Real. It may also be viewed through the Laingian lens of patterns that persist over generations, often without entering the conscious awareness of the individuals who perpetuate them. Laing's formulation is useful in considering Harris's fiction because it provides a transition between intrapsychic functioning and the psyche (Subject, in Lacan's terms) as locus of the community.

Some of M. M. Bakhtin's concepts on this point are also pertinent. He writes of "heteroglossia," or the rendering of the speech of different social strata, which in his view the novel is particularly well suited to do:

Thus heteroglossia either enters the novel in person (so to speak) and assumes material form within it in the images of speaking persona, or it determines, as a dialogizing background, the special resonance of novelistic discourse.[20]

He also states that:

even in the novel heteroglossia is by and large always personified incarnated in individual human figures, with disagreements and oppositions individualized. But such oppositions of individual wills and minds are submerged in social heteroglossia, they are reconceptualized through it. Oppositions between individuals are only surface upheavals of the untamed elements in social heteroglossia, surface manifestations of those elements that play on such individual oppositions. . . .[21]

Harris's fiction moves away from an emphasis on heteroglossia "personified." It is cast on another plane, where the "surface manifestations"—individualized characters—articulate with the underlying "untamed elements" of social heteroglossia.

Bakhtin's "individual human figures" are in a sense doublings and multiple repetitions of the underlying social elements of Harris's "imperilled community" as, for Laing, individuals double and repeat each other while playing out frozen familial and societal patterns of relationship.

Perhaps the single most important inspiration informing the fictional vision in the novels I discuss is provided by the land of Harris's birth, especially by the vast Guyanese interior where he worked as a surveyor for many years.

Guyana is a place of waters; the name itself, indeed, may derive from an Amerindian word meaning "the watery country." Its river system comprises part of the huge Amazon-Orinoco watershed, whose principal arteries deploy a network of tributaries that are themselves often larger than rivers considered sizable in Europe and North America.[22] The low-hanging foliage along the banks and the detritus from the unceasing growth and decay of the tropical forest combine to impart to their waters a shimmering array of colors at times intensifying to black. The elevated interior country is a wilderness of deep tropical forests, savannahland, broad rivers, and high waterfalls over steep escarpments, including Kaieteur, the highest in the world. Over the savannahs a light of perpetually shifting quality permeates great piles of cloud in a high, wide sky; it is not difficult to find the play of this light and shadow, these clarities and opacities, in the linguistic texture of Harris's writing and in the philosophy it expresses. The influence of the landscape is discernible, too, in his interest in painting as a metaphor for the perception of reality.[23]

Harris speaks of the importance of the Guyanese interior to him as an artist when he says that much of his fiction is

. . . related to a symbolic landscape-in-depth—the shock of great rapids, vast forests and savannahs—playing through memory to involve perspectives of imperilled community and creativity reaching back into the pre-Columbian mists of time.[24]

Perhaps the most striking evidence of the influence of the interior on Harris is his eloquent account of his near-death in a boating accident in river rapids. The vision that came to him at that moment of crisis seems to have been the source of many of his most effective fictional scenes, including the conclusion of *Palace of the Peacock* and Roi Solman's fatal accident in *Tumatumari*.

Another influence of the interior on Harris's fiction is found in his choice of relationships among crews working there as the medium for exploration of his central theme of "imperilled community." Much dramatic tension in the novels I examine lies in division among crew members, between the crew and its chief, or between all of them and the inhabitants of the interior. Sometimes these inhabitants are Amerindians; sometimes descendants of the maroons, runaway slaves who founded communities in the bush.[25] A further element of the dramatic tension is the response to the peculiar pressures of life in the remote interior and to the interior landscape itself.

The first Europeans to explore this region, which became at times Harris's crucible and later his source of literary inspiration, were Spanish conquistadors and English "sea dogs." In the sixteenth century, the name "Guiana" referred to the entire coast from the Orinoco to the

Amazon. The present-day nations of Venezuela, Cayenne (or French Guiana) and Surinam, and parts of Brazil, were known at that time as Spanish Guiana. Later this extensive area was contested by the British, the French, and the Dutch. The Dutch emerged triumphant and after the Congress of Vienna in 1815 sold the settlements of Essequibo, Demerara, and Berbice to the British, who united them in 1831 under the name British Guiana. For the following 135 years, until a delayed and contested independence in 1966, Guiana remained under English rule.[26] Then it became the Cooperative Republic of Guyana.

Guiana shared the economic system then basic to the Caribbean region: A plantation agriculture worked by slave labor imported from Africa. Slavery was abolished in Guiana, as in the British West Indian islands, in 1838; the majority of former slaves refused to work on the White-owned sugar plantations, preferring either to settle in towns or to farm for themselves. Plantation owners solved the resulting labor shortage by the mass importation of indentured servants from British India. This traffic did not end until 1924, and it contributed to the formation of a population deeply divided by ethnic group, language, religion, culture, and occupation. Slavery and indenture also resulted in a deliberate sexual skewing of the population so that for a long time it was disproportionately male. The ethnic divisions have been exploited politically by both indigenous and foreign interests, leading on several occasions to grievously bloody clashes that have made formation of a national consciousness very difficult.

Linguistically, culturally, and politically, Guyana has much in common with the British West Indian islands and, indeed, with the rest of the Caribbean islands; yet it also shares geographical situation and certain resulting social configurations with neighboring continental areas. The country's unique situation affected the Guyanese self-perception. Gordon K. Lewis has written:

This pervasive feeling, that Guyana is geographically and economically different from the other Caribbean lands . . . has tended to obscure the general truth that the historical development of the Guyanese society has been shaped by the same forces shaping the development of the [British] island colonies—colonization, slavery, sugar monoculture, the Crown Colony system.[27]

He also writes of the ambivalent Guyanese attitude toward the country's Latin neighbors and toward Guyanese society itself:

Guyana, indeed, is a fascinating complex of strident paradoxes: the paradox
between the over-developed coastlands and the underdeveloped hinterland; between
the continental dream and the "coastal mentality"; between the two sub-
economies, whose mutual isolation from each other is only now breaking down,
of an Indian agriculture and a Negro commercial urbanism; between the theory of
a Pan-American fraternal alliance with the Latin neighbours and the brooding
omnipresence of the Venezuelan threat to Guyanese territorial integrity in the
form of the famous boundary dispute. . . .[28]

Harris's fiction includes some elements that are shared with the
islands, others that are continental and shared, rather, with Latin
American literature. For example, in *The Secret Ladder*, when Russell
Fenwick, the technician from the coast, confronts Poseidon, leader of a
maroon community, the situation is not peculiarly continental; maroon
communities also existed on islands such as Jamaica and Cuba. In
Palace of the Peacock, however, Donne and his crew pursue the
Amerindians deep into the forest and along a boiling Guyanese river to
impress them into forced labor; this reflects the fact that Guyana, in
common with other South American countries, has what no Caribbean
island has: a genuine frontier and hinterland. Not unrelatedly, a
culturally identifiable Amerindian population survives there.
Furthermore, in continental literature, including Harris's, one often
finds a sense of spaciousness, different from the crowding so well
portrayed in novels from the islands such as George Lamming's *In the
Castle of My Skin*, C. L. R. James's *Minty Alley*, or Michael
Thelwell's *The Harder They Come*, set in Barbados, Trinidad, and
Jamaica, respectively.

On the continent, the possibility also exists for other social roles.
Among them are the "pork-knocker," the Guyanese roustabout seeking
a fortune in the interior—such as Adam in *Ascent to Omai*—and the
desperadoes fleeing or expelled from coastal society—such as Donne in
Palace of the Peacock. In fiction from the islands, equivalent characters
are likely to form a different social stratum; they work out a way of life
in an urban setting, either in the Antilles or abroad. The continental
hinterland also affords the possibility for precariously surviving
outposts and trading communities, set at great distances from each
other, the bonds between them as tenuous as a spider's web.

Thus, Guyana shares with continental South America certain geographical conditions and consequent possibilities and mental orientation. It is therefore interesting and significant that Harris's fiction is in important respects more similar to the fiction of Latin American practitioners of *lo real maravilloso*, broadly defined, than to the fiction of other writers from the English-speaking Caribbean. These similarities include systematic distortions of conventional novelistic parameters of time and space and an implicit or explicit insistence on the inadequacy of Western versions of the historical experience of *América mestiza*. The subject does not fall strictly within the scope of the present study, but a comparison would be rewarding between Harris's work and that of such writers as Gabriel García Márquez, Alejo Carpentier, and others for whom "most extraordinary things" are accepted as real in an American landscape and essential to an American self-definition.

Harris himself has expressed his own sense of continental *América mestiza*. He writes that he regards Central America as part of the landscape of his literary inspiration and responsibility, and that he once planned a novel set in Brazil.[29]

Despite the many differences, the ties binding the Caribbean region and the South American continent as a whole are strong, and—like the differences—rooted in the concrete specifics of a historically evolved situation. At the Congress Simón Bolívar identified prime Angostura characteristics distinguishing *América mestiza* from Euro-America, that is, the United States and Canada. (The Venezuelan city, where the Congress took place, is now called Ciudád Bolívar, in his honor.) Bolívar, known throughout Spanish America as "The Liberator" for leading the colonial struggle for independence from Spain, was reminding his compatriots of the unique character of what the great nineteenth-century Cuban poet-patriot José Martí called "*nuestra América mestiza*." Bolívar knew from his own experience the close connection between the South American mainland and the Caribbean islands; at one point in his long struggle he accepted an offer of asylum extended by the independent Black nation of Haiti. His statement that the aborigines have been annihilated is hardly too harsh when one considers the toll taken by slaughter, overwork, disease, and the shattering of cultures. Because of this depopulation and subsequent miscegenation with imported slaves and indentured laborers, the peoples and cultures of *América mestiza* are not aboriginal but include elements deriving from Africa, Europe, and in some places China, Java, Japan, and India. The principal socioeconomic terms of this America have been those of thoroughgoing participation in the modern capitalist economy that emerged in the centuries following the Voyages of European Conquest.[30]

In other words, Caribbean society is as thoroughly colonized, as thoroughly colonial, as any on earth. It differs from ancient, stable, coherent societies not only in the West but also in pre-Columbian America, in Africa, and in Asia. Thus the Guyanese-born characters in Harris's second novel, *The Far Journey of Oudin,* recognize the disdain the East Indian-born patriarch of the family feels for them and their "mekking-up and breaking up language."

Harris insists, however, that it is wrong and misleading to conclude that the Caribbean is culturally impoverished or sterile. The post-Columbian *América mestiza* that Bolívar and Martí describe possesses its own identity; what Harris's character in *The Far Journey of Oudin* calls a "mekking-up and breaking up" language and culture, the rubble of cultures that is a principal image of Harris's *Ascent to Omai,* possesses rich potential for cultural creativity exactly because of its confusion and broken forms.

To remain unaware of this and to perceive the nature and possibilities of the Caribbean only in terms of its colonial relationship to Europe is to limit oneself to "the stasis of victor and victim." A reevaluation is imperative. It must include a retrieval of Amerindia, displaced but not everywhere obliterated, and nowhere lost from memory; it also must include retrieval of post-Columbian African and Asian America to overcome the colonial conventions that define and confine the understanding of Caribbean realities and therefore of Caribbean possibilities. An important aim of Harris's fiction is to bridge this fissure, conventionally assumed to mark Caribbean origins, and put an end to a reading of the history of *América mestiza* as unrelieved victimization. Only an end of this reading will permit the emergence, from the brute facts of a violent and schismatic experience of genocide, slavery, indentured servitude, and pillage, of possibilities of rewriting the future as something other than a recapitulation of the past.

To avoid such a repetition of the past, an understanding is essential of the basic terms in which the relationship between Europe and the

Americas, especially *América mestiza,* was cast. I come now to the central issue of doubling, or repetition.[31]

The present book investigates the form of repetition that has marked this relationship, as Harris uses the repetition in the four novels I discuss. I argue that the deep cultural bias has been expressed in terms of doubling and a resultant hierarchy of domination. The attitudes of Europeans toward Amerindians and Blacks were not exactly the same and were not the same toward either group at all times and places. The degree of perniciousness varied by region, by colonial power, and by period. But in the end, the more benevolent interpretations of cultural contact lost out in the European scheme of things. Las Casas is a remarkable figure, but he himself could not effect the transfer of his attitudes from Amerindians to Blacks, and his benevolent attitudes did not prevail as the dominant attitudes of the West.[32] As the uncertainties and early relative variety of possibility for the course of relations hardened into the form of plantation economy worked by African slave labor, so hardened the Western ideological justifications in terms of inherent African inferiority and fitness for servitude. As the European immigrants advanced to wrest two continents from their aboriginal inhabitants, so the early suggestion of Amerindian prelapsarian virtue gave way to such a slogan as, "The only good Indian is a dead Indian."

Oriented to Europe as measure and norm, the European conqueror often seems not to have "seen" the Americas. This refusal of American realities is reflected in the naming not only of people but of landscape as well. In bestowing European names on a strange flora and fauna, Europeans both denied the American actuality and subtly reinforced a strong propensity, already present, to regard the Americas, especially *América mestiza,* as not just an imitation of Europe but a deficient imitation. This idea pervaded European intellectual life; a curious example is the way the belief that the life-forms of Southern regions were inferior to those of the Northern regions distorted the interpretation of paleontological evidence in the comparative evolutionary biology of marsupial and placental mammals.[33]

From its inception, Caribbean literature shared with other colonial literatures the difficulties that come from arising in a society that served only to supply "raw materials," was merely a subordinate appendage of the colonial power, and was not considered to have an independent cultural life. The cultural life of a colony often enough was imitation, as its educated groups were schooled in the metropole and adopted metropolitan values and literary models. The effect on a sense of identity is clear in *The Mimic Men*; Ralph Singh describes himself and his class as "we mimic men of the New World." As Naipaul's novel also demonstrates very well, however, the doubling and repetition were not simple mimicry. They have profound psychological roots that spring from the socioeconomic structural arrangements defining the relationship of metropole to colony—arrangements that created the imbalance of power.[34]

The process of doubling is revealed in the bestowing of names. Harris, for example, was born in "*New* Amsterdam," Guyana. All the Americas bear a linguistic record of the distortion or erasure of the most ancient traditions of the continent's indigenous peoples and of the repression of the cultures of the other major group to arrive at least as early as the Europeans, the African peoples.[35]

Naming is an index to identity and to power relations. "Who names, controls" is a widespread human belief, reflected in both religion and magic. It is one of the most fundamental aspects of "the power of the word." We see it exercized in one of the best known of all European novels, Defoe's *Robinson Crusoe*. The Cuban novelist Alejo Carpentier explores its significance for *nuestra América mestiza* in *The Lost Steps* and also in *Explosion in a Cathedral*. Naming is also a central issue in Jean Rhys's *Wide Sargasso Sea*, where in his relationship with Antoinette, his Caribbean wife, the Englishman Rochester stands for England in relation to the Caribbean. He tries to change her name to the English "Bertha." Antoinette resists; at one point she tells Rochester, who is terrified of "obeah," or witchcraft, that his changing her name is also "obeah."

Ranjit Kripalsingh, hero of *The Mimic Men*, also undergoes a significant difficulty with his own Hindu name. As a schoolboy painfully aware of his low status as an East Indian in a world where to be English is the highest value, he reduces his last name to Singh and changes his first name to Ralph. Discovered, he is ridiculed at school by the master and punished at home by his hurt, humiliated, and angry father. At the end of Naipaul's *The Mystic Masseur*, the Indian main character names himself "G. Ramsay Muir."

The aboriginal inhabitants of the Americas were named "Indians" through an error of the European conquerors; the erroneous designation persists to this day. Africans brought to the Americas as slaves were prevented from preserving their own diverse languages and were often required to adopt European first names of their owners' choosing; commonly, the owners' surname identified the slaves as well. During the social movements in the United States of the last twenty years, some groups, recognizing the significance of this history of renaming, substituted for the misnomer "Indian" the term "Native American"; and, among some Blacks in the U. S., notably members of the Nation of Islam, "X" was substituted for the unknown African name. Other Black Americans simply chose their own African personal and family names as an affirmation of a newfound and self-chosen identity.

In sum, then, rather than seeing the Americas in their own right, Europeans tended from very early days of contact to perceive them in relation to Europe. At best, the "New World" served as a screen on which to project European theories about society; for example, that the aboriginal Americans were possessed of primitive innocence, or that the Americas were a *tabula rasa* where Europe might begin afresh. Neither of these relatively benign views, however, accorded to the Americas an existence in their own right and because of this provided no defense against the more sinister and pernicious psychological use increasingly made of the Americas in the structure of European symbolism. At worst, the projections seem like a Freudian list of the European cultural unconscious's worst fears and most antisocial tendencies.[36]

In his introduction to *Stories of the Double*, Albert J. Guerard writes: "Few concepts and dreams have haunted the human imagination as durably as those of the *double*—from primitive man's sense of a duplicated self as immortal soul to the complex mirror games and mental chess of Mann, Nabokov, Borges."[37] Doubling is, at bottom, a repetition, an assertion of an existence that is at once the "same" as the original that is being copied and very often its "opposite." Thus in Dostoevski's "The Double," Goliadkin II is aggressive, assertive, and exploits the world, whereas Goliadkin I is self-destructively, almost pathologically, inhibited; Robert Louis Stevenson's Mr. Hyde is the embodiment of dissipation and evil in contrast to Dr. Jekyll's rectitude. Numerous other examples could be adduced. Yet the whole power of the concept of doubling derives from the awareness at a deep level of consciousness that this opposite and "other" is also an aspect of "self"—an aspect representing both profound wishes and profound fears.

As Harris himself has observed, doubling in European fiction has tended to take the form of the emergence of a "bad" self from the "good," socially acceptable, self.[38] Harris, as I demonstrate later, employs doubling and multiple identities as both benevolent *and* malevolent manifestations of psyche in his fiction.

The European pattern of doubling, however, followed the Dr. Jekyll-Mr. Hyde paradigm when symbolically depicting the relation between Europe and the Americas. The doublings and repetitions of identity so important in Harris's fiction, and the primacy of concerns about ethnic relations and racial miscegenation (an accurate expression of a Caribbean cultural obsession) thus have their source in the psychological history of the Caribbean.[39] Consequently, the inhabitants of the Caribbean were faced with the problem of how to experience themselves as something other than the "shadow half," the inferior and often grotesque Other, whose archetype is Caliban on his Caribbean isle, his name an anagram of Cannibal, his nature the "dark" side of the dominant European interpretation of reality and psyche.[40]

This Manichaean dualism is pervasive in European thought. Derrida, among others, suggests that one of its fundamental dimensions is the opposition posited between the symbolic rubrics, whose content varies, of "nature" and "culture"; he describes this opposition as "congenital" to philosophy in the West:

In spite of all its rejuvenations and its disguises . . . it [this opposition] is even older than Plato. It is at least as old as the Sophists. Since the statement of the opposition—*physis/nomos*, *physis/techné*—it has been passed on to us by a whole historical chain which opposes "nature" to the law, to education, to art, to technics—and also to liberty, to the arbitrary, to history, to society, to the mind. . . .[41]

In the terms of this ancient European philosophical dichotomy, *América mestiza* was placed in the category "nature." The compulsive denial and erasure of an Amerindian and an African past and presence, the rejection of these "dark Others," is duplicated in the social realm. Forms of this opposition are encountered repeatedly in Harris's fiction. It is central, for instance, in *Tumatumari*, where the struggle in the psyches of Prudence and her sister Pamela is the struggle of the

European component of Caribbean culture forced into a mind-breaking but spiritually essential encounter with that culture's Amerindian and African components.

The Caribbean political and cultural theorist and activist Frantz Fanon, who was born in Martinique and trained in France as a psychoanalyst, provides insight into some of the psychological mechanisms at work in this assignment of the "dark Others" to the "nature" half of the dichotomy. In his book *Black Skin, White Masks* , Fanon writes:

Jean-Paul Sartre has made a masterful study of the problem of anti-Semitism; let us try to determine what are the constituents of Negrophobia. This phobia is to be found on an instinctual, biological level. At the extreme, I should say that the Negro, because of his body, impedes the closing of the postural schema of the white man. . . . with the Negro the cycle of the biological begins.

Long before Lacan became known widely in the English-speaking world, Fanon perceived and developed the implications for the psychological relationship of Europe and *América mestiza* of what is, perhaps, Lacan's most famous theoretical contribution, the concept of *le stade du miroir*, the "mirror stage." Fanon writes: "It would indeed be interesting, on the basis of Lacan's theory of the *mirror period*, to investigate the extent to which the *image* of his fellow built up in the young white at the usual age would undergo an imaginary aggression with the appearance of the Negro."[42]

The "mirror stage" is essentially a theory of the emergence of the psychological subject or self, the I, as a process of doubling. As Lacan describes it:

Gestalt [the total form of the body] symbolizes the mental permanence of the *I*, at the same time as it prefigures its alienating destination; it is still pregnant with the correspondences that unite the I with the statue in which man projects himself, with the phantoms that dominate him, or with the automaton in which, in an ambiguous relation, the world of his own making tends to find completion . . . the mirror-image would seem to be the threshold of the visible world, if we go by the normal mirror disposition that the *image of one's own body* presents in hallucinations, or in dreams, whether it concerns its individual features, or even its infirmities, or its object-projections; or if we observe the role of the mirror apparatus in the appearances of the double, in which physical realities, however heterogeneous, are manifested. [43]

Of this theory, Fanon writes:

When one has grasped the mechanism described by Lacan, one can have no
further doubt that the real Other for the white man is . . . the black man. And
conversely. Only for the white man the Other is perceived on the level of the
body image, absolutely as the not-self— that is, the unidentifiable, the
unassimilable. For the black man, as we have shown, historical and economic
realities come into the picture.[44]

I would modify Fanon's observation in one respect only: "historical
and economic realities" come into the picture for the white person, too.
It is true, however, that the developments that heightened the anxiety
about these realities for the members of Euro-American culture were, in
the historical and economic sphere, largely incipient and poorly
understood when Fanon's book appeared in the early 1950s. It is in the
subsequent thirty years that the former colonial regions have clearly
emerged as a force on the world scene, a development in which Fanon
himself was destined to play no insignificant part.

The tendency, then, has been to cast the idea of the Caribbean in
European philosophical terminology and concepts that may be
summarized as follows: The European conquest was absolute. It was
not merely a watershed. It created a chasm. To the present-day
Caribbean, pre-Columbian reality is irrelevant. The Caribbean's only
history is post-Columbian, for the conquest created a *tabula rasa* and the
African-descended peoples who form the base of the Caribbean
population are without history as they are without culture. Thus, the
European defeat of indigenous, aboriginal America was a triumph of
Culture over Nature. Caribbean history (that is, what has happened
since the coming of the Europeans) constitutes an ongoing Manichaean
struggle of the forces of light against the forces of darkness, a struggle
to maintain culture (Europeanness) against savagery (Africanity and
Amerindianness) and also against "nature," that is, the American
climate, terrain, flora, and fauna. In fact, the idea of "natives" is really
a subcategory of "nature." The forces of light and culture are
represented by the "light"-skinned people.The "dark"-skinned people
embody the forces of darkness and nature.

The threat to light and culture (European domination) has had two
principal manifestations. One was the recurrent menace of Amerindian

attacks and slave uprisings. That is, the threat was political and economic, and fear of it was realistic, as attested to by the history of the Caribbean. This fear explains the tremendous shock waves sent throughout Europe and the United States by the successful revolution in Saint-Domingue, when the Africans rose, abolished slavery, and drove the French out permanently, becoming in 1804, the second people in the Americas to free themselves from colonial subjection and to establish a nation, this time a Black nation called Haiti. This accomplishment invested Haiti with great symbolic significance for Blacks and Whites alike.

The second principal manifestation of the threat to light and culture was miscegenation. Miscegenation which represented an encroachment of the "natural," the "fleshly," upon the "cultural," the "spiritual." The "threat" was also a real one, reflecting cultural behavior that literally created a population that might, as in Haiti where the mulattoes eventually joined with the Blacks, rise against the Europeans. The fear of the "threat" was all the more hysterical because it came about through the unacceptable behavior not of the "lesser breeds" but of the masters, who had fathered children by women "beneath" them in the "natural order." Thus it was a "self-betrayal," an eruption within the cultural sphere of "natural" impulses, a threat from the part of the "civilized" psyche that was still "savage."[45] The *mestiza* population of "nuestra América"—the European, Amerindian, African, and Asian mixture—became, then, a visible double. To the Europeans it stood literally as an unacceptable, unassimilable emanation of the psyche and body of the rejected, unacceptable aspects of the dominant, "rational," "culture-bearing," and "male" people of "light," an emanation that had to be repressed and denied.

This Euro-American conquest and doubling and a complex rejection of self-in-other, of other-in-self, lie at the root of characteristically Caribbean psychological tendencies. In the particular instance, the terms derive from the specificities of Caribbean history and socioeconomic relations. Caribbean realities have conventionally been understood in the dichotomized framework of conflict between Nature and Culture, victor and victim.

Harris's fiction dissolves this opposition of Nature and Culture. It does so in several ways, but most significantly by undermining the most fundamental of the Nature/Culture dichotomies, the opposition of mind and body, of spirit and matter. In other words, Harris dissolves the category of individuality, so central to what he calls "the novel of consolidation of character" and "novel of persuasion." This is the classic novel of bourgeois-imperialist Europe, the Europe that dominated *nuestra América mestiza* using the ideological terms of that Nature-Culture dichotomy. Harris's stylistic strategies, which have so frequently bewildered or frustrated critics, become not merely comprehensible but indeed elegantly appropriate when understood in this light.

Fig. 2
Mountains and River Systems of N.W. Guyana

2

Centers and Origins,
Watershed or Escarpment

... the mainstream of the West Indies ... possesses an enormous escarpment down which it falls, and I am thinking here of the European discovery of the New World and conquest of the ancient American civilizations. ... This escarpment seen from another angle possesses the features of a watershed, main or subsidiary, depending again on how one looks at it.

Wilson Harris, *Tradition the Writer and Society*, pp. 30-31

... the history of the Caribbean ... is one of beginnings or foundations.

Roberto González Echevarría,
Alejo Carpentier, The Pilgrim at Home, p. 252

... the conquest of America heralds and establishes our present identity. ...

Tzvetan Todorov, *The Conquest of America*, p. 53

In the previous chapter I discussed the historical and economic relationship between the West and the Americas as marking the beginning of the modern period. Todorov writes

... the discovery of America is essential for us today not only because it is an extreme, and exemplary, encounter. Alongside this paradigmatic value, it has another as well—the value of direct causality. The history of the globe is ... made up of conquests and defeats, of colonizations and discoveries of others but ... the conquest of America heralds and establishes our present identity; even if every date that permits us to separate any two periods is arbitrary, none is more

suitable, in order to mark the beginning of the modern era, than the year 1492.
. . . We are all the direct descendants of Columbus, it is with him that our
genealogy begins, insofar as the word beginning has a meaning.[1]

On the same subject, González Echevarría writes of the importance of
the Caribbean as the "proscenium" of Latin American history:

Colonialism, slavery, racial mixture and strife, and consequently revolution and
independence movements all occurred first in the Caribbean. . . . [It] was also the
site of the first Indian and maroon revolts and where Toussaint Louverture carried
out the first successful war of independence, other than the United States. . . .
the Caribbean was . . . the area where the most overwhelming historical
phenomenon in modern times—the conquest of America by
Europe—began . . . [2]

The passages quoted above—and more to the same effect by other
writers could easily be added—are striking for the emphasis placed on
this colossal and catastrophic cultural encounter as a dividing line and
signpost for all world history, and as marking the beginning of our
modern world.

Yet González Echevarría's study refers to the Caribbean's "origin-
obsessed history"[3] and analyzes Carpentier's treatment of it in his
fiction as characteristic of Caribbean literature in being factitious.
Todorov's statement ends with a caveat—"insofar as the word beginning
has a meaning."[4] And the passage from Wilson Harris's writing with
which I open this chapter explicitly concerns the question of why
Caribbean history should be "origin-obsessed." The same answer sheds
light on some of the sources of distress in the modern West, which is
not surprising given Todorov's assertion that "the conquest of America
heralds and establishes our present identity," for he makes clear in the
book that he knows that he writes out of the Western tradition.[5]

The central issue is identity. The modern history of the world as a
whole dates from the Voyages of European Conquest; modern identity,
including its dissatisfactions, derives from the relationships established
in the wake of that conquest between the West and the Third World. The
content of the dissatisfaction is different, but, for at least some modern
thinkers in the West, the role of Prospero does not suit so well. In
Chapter 1, I mentioned Fernández Retamar's use of this metaphor and
discussed it in terms of what Derrida identifies as an ancient dichotomy

of Western philosophy, the division between body and mind, Nature and Culture, and the way *América mestiza* and the West are conceptualized under those rubrics. I made the point that it becomes a form of doubling and of hierarchy. The West is superior, *América mestiza* inferior; Prospero and Caliban serve as a literary metaphor for this relationship.

In the present chapter, I first discuss the hierarchy established between the West and *América mestiza* from the point of view of a second Western concept that is related to the Nature-Culture dichotomy: Centered and decentered structures.[6] Second, I consider the relation of centered and decentered structures to ways of structuring history and identity. Third, I discuss the displacement of centered by decentered structures as part of the Modernist movement, and I consider the relationship of Negritude, one of the most important literary and cultural movements in the Third World in our time, to centered and decentered structures.[7] Fourth, I consider the relation of centered and decentered structures to the novel. I discuss what Fredric Jameson calls the artist-novel as an example of the novel of centered structures and identify it with the novel of classical realism, or what Harris calls the novel of consolidation of character.[8] I then discuss Harris's *Ascent to Omai*, subject of Chapter 8, as illustrating the principle of "decentering" in fiction that enables Harris to avoid what Jameson sees as the pitfall of the artist-novel, and I discuss the significance of Harris's style to the Western Modernist aesthetic. I conclude this chapter with a return to a consideration of the hesitation noted in the passage from Todorov: What is it about the modern identity that gives such pause? I then proceed, in Chapter 3, to a discussion of Harris's first novel, *Palace of the Peacock*, focusing on his treatment of the relationship between the conquistador figure Donne and his Amerindian mistress Mariella.

Centers and origins are organizing concepts of what Derrida calls centered structures. God is the guarantor of the centered structure Derrida describes. He is thereby the guarantor of everything, which is His creation. God, the center and guarantor, is untouched by all changes in the structure and validates both the natural and the social orders. A well-known paradigm of this system is the Great Chain of Being, as set forth in Arthur Lovejoy's work.[9] The following quotation from a work by the eighteenth-century French naturalist Charles Bonnet indicates clearly the relation between the Great Chain and the centered structure Derrida describes:

Between the lowest and highest degree of spiritual and corporal perfection, there is an almost infinite number of intermediate degrees. The succession of degrees comprises the Universal Chain. It unites all beings, ties together all worlds, embraces all the spheres. One SINGLE BEING is outside this chain, and this is HE who made it.[10]

In contrast with a centered structure, the logic and validity of a decentered structure are not guaranteed by God or by any other irreducible and unchanging center outside the structure. A decentered structure is not a given; it must be posited. And it must be maintained—or, in Derrida's terms, "repeated." "Modernism" includes the many manifestations of the critique that undermined the Western centered structure. It is this rupture, to use a Derridean term once more, that necessitates the repetition.

Since the terms of the decentered structure are not given and are of human and not divine origin, they have to "be thought," again in Derrida's formulation; and thought is a function of language. The repetition that characterizes Modernist thought may usefully be described in terms of the characteristics Lacan ascribes to a linguistic system. The characteristics of a decentered structure, from this perspective, are also those of a linguistic system where, as Derrida phrases it "the central signified, the original or transcendental signified, is never absolutely present outside a system of difference. . . ."[11]

Lacan's idea opens the way to a conception of human character that has the range of possibilities inherent in a system of signification whose elements are displaceable to any point in the system. The absence of a center gives rise to what Derrida has called "the anxiety of being implicated in the game" in a certain way.[12] In a decentered structure, one can no longer displace responsibility to King or God.

Centers and origins guarantee meaning by establishing beginning and conferring continuity. Center as meaning is identity. Origin as meaning is source, the beginning of a linear path that in modern Western thought becomes history. The colonial conventions locate the identity of *América mestiza*, in its relationship of Prospero and Caliban with Europe. Caribbean history was viewed from the perspective of Western history, which might well mean it was never seen at all.

Caribbean peoples are among those who in the words of the critic
Frederic Jameson have "fallen outside history"[13]—that is, outside the
history of those colonial conventions defined by the official cultural
norms.

It is reserved for those who die for good—the Indians and forgotten indigenous
tribes, the witches, the peasants slaughtered after uprisings not even recorded in
the history books, the torture and lynching of potential troublemakers from the
very beginning of time—to give the most anguishing glimpse of a death in
absolute despair.[14]

V. S. Naipaul offers a specifically Caribbean example of Jameson's
observation when he writes of a group that once inhabited a village in
his native Trinidad:

. . . more than four hundred years after Columbus . . . the people he had called
Indians had vanished. They had left no monuments; they were not missed.
Chaguanes was a place-name, no more. [The King of Spain had authorized the
governor of Trinidad to punish them because of their "bad disposition"; that is,
they were fighting the Spanish.] Naipaul continues: What was done isn't
known; but soon, in the place called Chaguanas, no one would know that there
was once a people called Chaguanes. The fact of their existence is recorded, so
far as I know, only in this document; and this document was disinterred from the
Spanish archives only in 1897.

Naipaul goes on to write of the way the Chaguanes fell outside of the
official scope of the Western version of historical reality:

People who write about Raleigh usually have to hurry back with him to the
Tower of London; they pay as little attention as Raleigh himself to what was
left behind. An obscure part of the New World is momentarily touched by
history; the darkness closes up again; the Chaguanes disappear in silence. The
disappearance is unimportant; it is part of nobody's story. But this was how a
colony was created in the New World.[15]

The colonial conventions seen from the Western point of view locate
the Caribbean entry into history as beginning with the defeat of the
Amerindian civilizations; if their existence is acknowledged at all, it
consists of the linear series of events occurring since their defeat.

The novel of classical realism is the characteristic genre of the triumphant European bourgeoisie that consolidated empire and adhered to the ideology that rationalized and justified the subjugation of *América mestiza*. *América mestiza* was subjugated in the name of ideological justifications supported by centered structures. The novel of classical realism is a novel of centers and origins, a novel of centered structures. Jameson's artist–novel is a good illustration of the novel of centers and origins. He writes:

> . . . it is notorious that descriptions of imaginary art works, of non-existent paintings or novels or pieces of music . . . fail to ring true. . . .the artist-novel always revolves around an absent center . . . but this center is . . . the empty place of that imaginary work of art which alone confers upon the novel's hero his right to be called an artist, a work of art whose absence stands as a kind of aesthetic imperative to the novelist him self, but one which he is necessarily and structurally unable to fulfill. . . . this failure is not accidental but inevitable: a work of art not being an object (which could be represented or used artistically) but a system of relationships.[16]

The artist-novel fails because it conceives of the artist's activity as an event that will produce an object rather than as a process. Meaning is ascribed to an absent center that must be filled by the work of art that the main character is trying to produce.

Ernst Bloch, writing of one mythical reconstruction of origins supposed to apply to us all, says, "all these various versions of the Oedipal metaphysic, above and beyond their mythological content . . . reflect, if not, certainly, any initial dreamed-up crime, then at least the very darkness or incognito of origins themselves."[17] A clear literary example is provided by the conventions of the detective novel: The answer to a present mystery lies in a determinable, isolatable past event. Bloch refers to the classical Freudian theory that explains the psyche of the adult almost exclusively by what happened to the young child (and Freud, indeed, explained human cultural origins, too, by primal patricide). The colonial conventions of Caribbean history accord similar status to the "Fall," the defeat of Amerindia by Europe.

The absent center in the artist-novel is an absence in space; the absent center in the search for historical origins that characterizes the Oedipal metaphysic is an absence in time. In terms of the Western interpretation of the history of the Caribbean and of *América mestiza* generally, the absence in space is the geographical dislocation of the colony from the metropolitan center. The absence in time becomes the dislocation of the colonial past from that of the metropolitan center. The history of the colonial master is not the history of the colony; yet the colony is perceived as having no history prior to its genesis in relation to the metropole of conquest and defeat, of the stasis of victor and victim.

In terms of Caribbean psychology, the absence in space is the lack of an identity other than the identity constituted by Caliban's relation to Prospero, which is the outgrowth of an interpretation of the history of the American region as defined by conquest and defeat. The absence in time, in terms of Caribbean psychology, is the resulting lack of ancestor, parent-origin, original homeland, as other than the colonial power.

Thus the novel of the absent center shows especially clearly why the novel of classical realism is inadequate in treating a situation such as that of *América mestiza*: The terms of such novels are the terms of centered structures, and *América mestiza* has only a shadow center and an identity as a double.

The kind of fiction that Harris is interested in writing might well be called a fiction of decentered structures. Because Harris's fiction is not organized around centered structures, he is able to write successfully about the creation of a work of art—very explicitly so, for instance, in *Ascent to Omai*. His premise is that the work of art is not an object but rather a system of relationships, and his emphasis is on the entire Real (in the Lacanian sense), including the Subject/I, as a system of relations in the field of the Symbolic, again in the Lacanian sense—that is, structured by language. The artist-novel of consolidation of character takes not only the work of art but also the protagonist as its object, and the relation between them is one of cause and effect—in other words an event, in the traditional sense. The artist-novel as Jameson describes it in the passage quoted above is written from a belief in the centered structure and purports to portray its creation. In this it is characteristic of the novel of classical realism. But in *Ascent to Omai,* work of art and Subject/I constitute each other mutually. Harris's novel is about the creation of art not as object or event but as an ongoing process in which subject and act are, within the system, interchangeable, with the plenitude of signification that Lévi-Strauss has described in considering such a linguistic system as Lacan's. One of the "characters" in Omai, the Judge, plays "card games" in an airplane flying to Omai, in the course of which by sleight of hand it becomes clear that the Judge "is" two other "characters," Adam and Victor, and that the airplane flight over Omai both follows and precedes a crash on Omai and Adam's trial, at which the Judge had presided forty years before. These transmutations constitute "decentering." In this way the meaning of an "event" is altered; so is the meaning of personality. Personality becomes a cut in a pattern that Harris calls a "ruined curve" of experience, and the Subject/I is an "organ of vacancy," where fortune and misfortune, time and event, individual identity as conventionally understood, are arbitrary sectionings of a curving continuum that has no beginning or end and is perceived as "wholeness" or "ruin," depending upon perspective.

Harris does not assert new, American, centers and origins but rather dissolves centers and origins in his fictional structures by dissolving individual entity, event, and object as understood in terms of traditional causality—so that they too become not centers and origins but in Harris's words, "watershed or escarpment, depending upon one's perspective." Harris's originality, and the difficulty a reader may experience in understanding his work, come from his conception of the Psychological/Literary Subject rather than from esotericism of vocabulary or syntactic convolution. But his choices of words and of syntactical structure are illuminated in their full value only in the light of this understanding of the Psychological/ Literary Subject—the nexus, in Lacanian terms, of the Symbolic realm, on the other hand, structured by language and by definition social, and on the other hand of the Imaginary. This conceptualization assists in understanding the relation between Harris's ideas of language and literature, of psyche, and of history, which is my main focus in this study.

The artist novel as a form of the novel of classical realism offers an especially clear example of the characteristics of what Harris calls the novel of consolidation of character, or the novel of persuasion. He describes linear plot line and development of character in the traditional novel as resting upon "elements of 'persuasion'. . . rather than 'dialogue' or 'dialectic' in the profound and unpredictable sense of person which Martin Buber, for example, evokes."[18] This concept of the "person," and therefore of the "Subject/I" of the novel, distinguishes

Harris from realist novelists. He draws an important distinction between the "self-sufficient individual" and the "human person." The "self-sufficient individual" is the typical character of the traditional novel of persuasion (or novel of consolidation of character), product of the emergent, victorious, and self-satisfied bourgeois and imperialist society of Europe. This style is imitated by most writers of the post-colonialist British colonies, which are societies trying belatedly to emulate this once-triumphant European bourgeoisie, although this act does not necessarily mean that the writers intend or desire such an emulation.

The "human person" differs from the "self-sufficient individual" in that the former is not constrained by the "persuasive limits" of character. Being unconstrained, he or she can be the ground of open possibility of perception and experience. Personality is understood, then, as a changeable locus of patterns of possibility.

The slave in Western society constituted a crucial case of the ancient riddle the Sphinx set Oedipus, the answer to which was, "A human being." Starting from this quintessentially Caribbean question and expanding far beyond it, Harris's art is a riddling, open-ended response (rather than answer) to the ancient riddle-question. Because the philosophy justifying slavery denied human status to human beings, this riddle-question is acutely relevant to the Caribbean.

In an era of deep distress and alienation in Western culture, Harris suggests that profoundly distressed and alienated figure, the Caribbean slave, as an appropriate symbol for "the grassroots of Western individuality." Radical dehumanization of the Black slave in political, theological, and philosophical theory accompanied and justified the radical dehumanization whereby the slave's labor was alienated from him and commodified, and the slave became not just a prize of war but also a thing—a commodity.

Hierarchy, subjugation, and domination all reached their acme in the introduction of Africans—Blacks—into the Caribbean as plantation slaves. Referring to this crucial population element, Harris notes in one of his essays that

[the problematic slave] found himself spiritually alone since he worked side by side with others who spoke different dialects. The creative human consolation . . . lies in the search for a kind of inward dialogue and space when one is deprived of a ready conversational tongue and hackneyed comfortable speech.

In the contemporary world, the West Indian is a member of a tiny minority. Yet just as the status of the "problematic slave" afforded a particular opportunity, so does the status of the modern West Indian: "What in my view is remarkable about the West Indian is a sense of subtle links, the series of subtle and nebulous links which are latent within him. . . ." These links incline to a view that "seeks to visualize a fulfillment of character . . . and [it is] this possible revolution in the novel —fulfillment rather than consolidation—[I would like first of all to look at . . . because I feel it] . . . is profoundly consistent with the native tradition. . . ."[19]

Some of Harris's work shares aspects of the philosophy and aesthetic principles of the Negritude movement in treating African culture as valuable. The Martiniquan poet Aimé Césaire and the Senegalese poet Léopold Sédar Senghor, as young students in France in the 1930s, launched the Negritude movement and proclaimed the positive values of African aesthetics, epistemology, and social ethics.

It is significant that the Negritude movement was at first associated with a European Modernist movement, Surrealism, principally through Aimé Césaire's close relationship with André Breton. Soon, however, Negritude assumed unique characteristics, reflecting its roots in a particular segment of a larger population responding to the political and economic situation of the time that affected all.

Negritude became the most significant literary and cultural movement among Africans south of the Sahara and Blacks in the Caribbean. Yet its critique of traditional European culture and of the Modernist movement is ultimately less radical than Harris's; it remains caught in the terms of European-centered structures. For by simply going into opposition—asserting the worth of that which the West has devalued—the Negritude movement fails to break out of the Nature-Culture dichotomy that constituted the ideological framework of the Black/White opposition that rationalized and justified the subjugation and devaluation of Blacks. The stasis of victor and victim is not transcended.

To understand Harris's idea of the relationship between what he calls the native tradition and the modern West, it is necessary to consider the relation between metropole and colony and the relevance of centered and decentered structures to Modernism, especially in connection with

América mestiza. It is necessary to consider the profound shift of which World War I is emblematic and to keep in mind Derrida's statement that the "moment" of such cultural shifts is first economic and technical.

The following passage indicates why the "war to make the world safe for democracy" failed so conspicuously to do so; basically, it had little to do with democracy at all.

Before American entry into the war [World War I] on April 6, 1917, President Wilson told Walter Hines Page, according to this pro-war ambassador to Britain, that there was little to choose between the belligerents, that the cause of the war was that "England owned the earth and Germany wanted it." President Wilson, considered the conflict as a "war of commercial powers over the spoils of the empire."[20]

Historians write of the agreements at Versailles that ended World War I as setting the stage for World War II and for the United States' emergence after the second war as Western culture's most powerful representative. As such, it has attempted ever since to exercise hegemony in many areas formerly under European colonial rule.

Less often do historians direct their attention to Third World nationalisms that emerged at Versailles and that were to become so important to the course of world history in succeeding decades—sometimes through movements organized by the same people who had sought without success to make a legal case for an end to colonialism before Europe at Versailles. Yet these nationalisms, no less than Euro-American events, signaled the advent of Modernism. And the efforts of the United States have not availed to reverse the disintegration of Western domination, political—cultural, and psychological—over the formerly colonized peoples.

The Third World appears to have burst irreparably asunder the Great Chain of Being. Increasingly, we see the flowering of the "seeds that corroded conviction,"[21] which refers to the ideas that emerged in the period just preceding the decline of the European bourgeoisie and European imperialism and also to the corrosive impact on the West itself of that imperialism, an impact finally revealed in the "irreducibility" and "undeniability" of the Third World.

To paraphrase Yeats, the European "center" could not hold. Its dichotomy and hierarchy of cultures and values, its positing of the Third

World as a "shadow-anima" of the West, of the projection of the West's own unacceptable double or other self that I have discussed in detail in Chapter 1, is threatened when the Third World emerges in its own right. The European Great Chain of Being cannot accommodate such a development. The impossibility of such an accommodation goes far to explain the West's attitude to the Third World, so often a bewildering composite of rational economic and political considerations, understandable in view of economic markets and political spheres of influence, and an irrational attitude speaking both from and to the West's own fears. This attitude is a modern version of the rational fear, during an earlier period, of slave and Amerindian uprisings, which went hand in hand with an irrational fear of Blacks, natives, and miscegenation.

The development of anthropology in the nineteenth and early twentieth centuries, singled out by Derrida and Todorov as a particularly significant discipline in modern Western thought, demonstrates the complexity of the situation.[22] The emergence of anthropology coincided with the consolidation of the European empires in Africa and Asia and with the definitive union of the two coasts of the North American continent under the Euro-American government—made possible by the defeat of the native peoples. (The Ghost Dance, the final major attempt at resistance by Indians in the U.S., occurred in 1891.) Anthropology developed in part from the practical necessities of imperialist expansion; however, the destabilization of the Western hierarchy of values was potentially implicit in the discipline's theory of cultural relativism.

Western Modernism represents a response on the part of European artists and intellectuals to an incipient realignment of material world forces. Painters, sculptors, and choreographers found the anthropologists' cultural relativism easier to accept than did those middle-class sectors of Western society whose churches were sending missionaries to Africa, the Caribbean, Oceania, and parts of Asia and whose governments, there and in *América mestiza*, professed to be carrying "the white man's burden," bearing responsibility for peoples described by European imperialism's apologist, Rudyard Kipling, as "lesser breeds without the law . . . half-devil and half child."

Ever since the sixteenth century, Africa posed a special problem for Europeans aware of a discordance between their behavior and their professed humanitarian values; the problem was imported into the Americas and remains unresolved to the present day. Africa was a procuring ground for black bodies, transported to the Americas to serve as slaves; at the Conference of Berlin in 1884, Africa was partitioned as colonial property among seven European powers, and racist White settler communities were established in several places. Out of the guilt-laden contact, Blacks (the ultimate "natives") were perceived in the Western system not only as "deformed" but also, more important, as "deforming." Their inclusion in this system required their firm location in an inferior position in the Great Chain of Being, a location that could not change without upheaval of Western values. Aesthetic and ethical values developed in such a way that the inclusion of Black people and Black culture—whether its customs or its artifacts—within Western sociocultural systems required the bursting of the West's traditional structure at the points of inclusion, an actual "deformation" of the systems. ("Deformation" is not used here pejoratively but descriptively.) The system included values of sexual and emotional expression structuring the ideal Western personality, aesthetic, and indeed its entire cultural configuration. The confrontation between the European Prospero and Caliban on his native Caribbean island stands as the central metaphor for this process; among other things, Modernism signaled the coming end of Caliban's subjugation. Thus, opponents who decried African cultural influences present in jazz and avant-garde painting as manifestations of "degeneration" and "decay" were, from the perspective of the present analysis, quite correct. The old Western system of hierarchy was indeed in decay; the disintegration of the European cosmology in terms of which the subjugation of the Caribbean Americas had occurred was well underway.

The aesthetic manifestation of these Black values appeared in the Western perception of what opponents called a "deformation" of musical and visual harmonies, "deformation" being used here pejoratively. Significantly though, Modernist trends in European painting included a fascination with African art, especially prominent in such seminal modern artists as Picasso and Modigliani. Museums began to display African artifacts as objects of aesthetic value and not merely as primitive curiosities.

The aesthetic values of Western culture were threatened by "grotesquerie," by an "imbalance of proportion" perfectly symbolized by the unfamiliar styles of African art and the rhythms of African and African-derived music. The artistic "imbalance of proportions" is the cultural manifestation of the changing of the world's political and economic system.

European Modernists might grasp the hope of rejuvenating their seriously ailing culture by adopting non-Western values but as heirs of Western culture, their attitude was almost inevitably tinged with melancholy. The position of Third World artists is, at least potentially, quite different. This is the context within which the critic must situate Harris's valuation and artistic use of grotesquerie, of what he calls alteration of proportions. His irony and his peculiar comedy, like the humor and irony of Caribbean carnival, have roots in a perspective on the world that is not European, where non-European cultural elements interact with European values with a possible benefit to both.[23]

Harris values cross-cultural resemblances and syncretisms. Much that is now tolerated in Europe as superstition or classified as folklore was once an integral part of ancient religion. Masks and dances, now a part of carnivals and spring and harvest festivals, were not dismissed as "fetish" in pre-Christian or even in Medieval Europe, although recognition of this fact is not always overt. In Latin America and the Caribbean, however, Afro-Catholic and Amerindian-Catholic syncretisms give open recognition to some elements of folk tradition that Harris insists must be retrieved without apology if the stasis of victor and victim is to disappear. In the Caribbean, a reexamination of the society as it was after the coming of the Europeans is essential, as is a reconsideration of pre-Columbian society and knowledge of its cultural elements that have survived in customs, art, and memory. Not Negritude alone but all premodern cultures—including those submerged in European societies—must interact with modern Western technological culture in order to develop the "cross-cultural imagination" within the "womb of space" that Harris emphasizes in his most recent critical work bearing that title. Experiencing the alteration of proportions is an essential step in the development of this cross-cultural imagination.

Most of the main "characters" in the novels I examined in the present study are "self-sufficient individuals" who undergo a crisis that is profoundly personal, yet also inseparable from cultural and historical calamity, as they go wholly or partially through the process of becoming "persons." Indeed, a crucial aspect of *Tumatumari*, the novel I discuss in chapters 5 and 6, is how in colonial society, especially in that colonial class represented by the tragic figure of Henry Tenby, people like him do what Harris describes elsewhere as consolidating "every advance by conditioning himself to function solely within his contemporary situation:—denying the ground of possibility represented by the 'human person.'"[24]

Yet *Tumatumari* is equally a novel of the death and rebirth of the ancient Amerindian societies that are also frozen in their half of the post-Columbian cultural stasis and before that were not immune to rigidification. The Amerindian myth of the Sleeping Rocks symbolizes this world that is reborn through Prudence, the representative of the "victorious" half of the "stasis of victor and victim," that alien and limiting colonial and conventional society; Prudence herself is reborn as a child of the defeated aboriginal Americas.

All of Harris's "characters" in the novels I discuss are in flight from their past but trying to reconstruct it so that they can accept it without pain, anxiety, and loss of hope. For some the remote past is especially painful, the past they know only as it has been handed down to them by tradition or through such fragments of its culture as they still possess. In coming to terms with themselves (as in *Tumatumari*), the Black people and mulattoes in the novels, descendants of African slaves, reflect the pain of self-discovery. The slaves among their ancestors reflected confusion in slave society. This confusion arose when a human being had to be defined both as an object and a commodity. It was also a confusion of values. The slave was an abstraction made flesh, provoking profound anxiety by making the Nature–Culture dichotomy "scandalous," in Lévi-Strauss's sense. By becoming incarnate in one's own relations, those mixed-blood people who came increasingly to populate *América mestiza* were an Unthinkable, a corrosion of the Western system of thought and values. After slavery had been abolished, the "corroding contradiction" still remained, in racial, ethnic, and class divisions.

The colonial Caribbean's struggle for a Caribo-centric sense of identity has been a central concern of Caribbean literature; as noted, González Echevarría calls it an obsession. Colonizer–colonial, victor-victim, have been the conventionally defining terms of Caribbean self-knowledge. Yet in accepting them in order to invalidate them, and

while taking them seriously and even passionately in recognizing the
suffering they have caused, Harris does not take them as having
absolute value. They are "watershed or escarpment," depending upon
one's perspective, and he accepts the premises in order to lay bare their
nonnecessity; in Harris's system, the very question of origins and
centers, in every dimension of human experience, becomes problematic.

An essential part of breaking the stasis of victor and victim is to
reconceive history through the imagination. The cultivation of this
creative imagination is essential to the regeneration of what the narrator
of *Tumatumari*, speaking of Henry Tenby, refers to as the political
conscience. Only a change in this political conscience will allow the
breaking of the stasis of victor and victim and of the cycles of conquest
and domination. The writer may play an important part, through
imaginative reconceptions of the history that is usually presented as a
"series of adventures"; Harris takes these as the surface-level plots of his
novels in order to undermine their conventionally accepted status as
ultimate truth.

We clearly see the principle of decentering in *Palace of the Peacock*.
The apparent resurrection of the crew shows how both event and
character are made fluid and boundaries are dissolved in such a way that
they are not really entities that can be delineated but rather are patterned
structures of relation. Some of the principal categories of pattern are:

> Time
> History
> Kinship
> Sex
> Racial and ethnic identity
> Settlement and fabrication (culture)

Elements are conceptually paired:

> Coast-Hinterland
> Civilizing venture-Primitivity
> Male-Female
> Parent-Child (generational relationships)
> Science-Nature
> Substance-Spirit
> Structure-Fluidity

They can be further arranged into parallel dichotomies, thus:

Organic-Inorganic   Human-Nonhuman

The human-nonhuman dichotomy involves two dimensions:

Human-Other animal
Human-Suprahuman (divine or demonic)

Such a static enumeration, although helpful, can be misleading. Emphasis is best placed not on the opposition of the categories but upon their fundamental inseparability. They exist only in relation to each other.

With *Palace of the Peacock* as an example, the diagrams on p. 46 illustrate the manner in which some of the paired opposites in the previous lists find expression in dynamic interaction. The circle (A), on the left, presents a model; the circle (B), applies it to *Palace.*

The model of a decentered structure analogous to a linguistic system is fruitful for thinking about certain questions of concern to Harris in his fiction. These questions pertain to the formulations of desire and seeking, conquest and subjugation, as communal *ways of organizing experience* on a national, cultural, or regional scale.

In concluding this chapter, I return to the questions implicit in the quotations by Todorov, Harris, and González Echevarría with which I began it. Why should Caribbean literature be so concerned with its own foundations?

Caribbean literature is origin-obsessed because the very definition of the Caribbean is as a region that has its beginning in a defeat by a culture that denied the validity and at times the existence of Caribbean experience prior to the Conquest. It is identity-obsessed because it enters history—that is, the version of reality created by and serving its conquerors—as a negation. At worst, it goes the way of the Chaguanes Naipaul describes. At best, it enters into the conceptual constructs of the West as a screen for projected fantasies or as a threatening and despised double.

I have identified Modernism as the response to the gradual dissolution of that world bequeathed by the Voyages of European Conquest, a world understood in terms of and justified by centered conceptual structures. Todorov, like Derrida and other Western thinkers, is uneasy with the

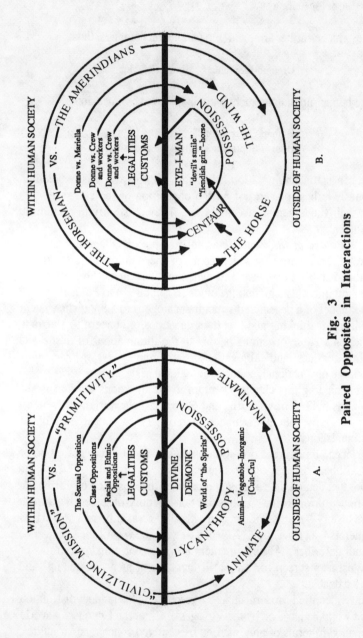

Fig. 3
Paired Opposites in Interactions

idea of beginnings and origins, recognizing in them an element of arbitrariness. They seem to recognize, too, that the centered world-view that mutilates the identity of the Third World may result in damage to the Western psyche as well; their observations about the role of relativism in anthropology, and Todorov's long discussion of different forms alterity takes, suggest such an awareness. But Todorov's surprising assertion that the West conquered because it knew those it defeated better than they knew the West casts the strength of his awareness into doubt.[25] It is ironic that Harris, writing from a perspective of Third World Modernism, seems better able to perceive the damage to the West as well as to the Third World than most Western writers; it is nowhere better portrayed than in the character of his "self-devouring" conquistador figure Donne in *Palace of the Peacock*, for the maintenance of a double on whom one projects inevitably means a severing of the projected qualities from the acknowledged self-identity.[26] I suggest that the position of being a Third World writer may permit a clearer recognition of this damage because it is less threatening to consider what may result from the dissolution of the Western-dominated world.

Let us now turn to a consideration of Harris's first novel, the first volume of the "Guiana Quartet", *Palace of the Peacock*. This tale of the second voyage of Donne and his crew is Harris's version of the basic Caribbean myth, the Search for El Dorado.

3
The Search for El Dorado:
Conquest in *Palace of the Peacock*

Conquest is the greatest evil of soul humanity inflicts on itself and on nature.

Wilson Harris, *Explorations*, p. 136

Palace of the Peacock, Harris's first novel, develops a version of the Caribbean Ur-myth that I discussed in Chapter 1. Harris explores how the attempt to find love and self-fulfillment, when misconstrued as desire and conquest, becomes the source of both personal and social disaster. Conquest, which he has called "the greatest evil," is the attempt to possess the object of desire or to attain a desired objective. Such possession is possible only if one assumes separation between subject and object. Thus the whole psychological and epistemological basis of the idea of conquest depends on the maintenance of identity and differentiation. *Palace of the Peacock* calls into question the conventionally assumed differentiation of subject and object and the possibility of satisfying desire through any conventionally purposive activity based on such a conventional differentiation. From this point of view the entire plot of the novel, as it is presented on the surface to the readers and as the characters themselves at first understand it, is fundamentally a delusion deriving from confusion about the nature and location of identity and of desired objects or objectives.

The theme of conquest is elaborated primarily through the figure of Donne, who embodies the principle of the conquistador. In this chapter

I focus on the theme of conquest and its relation to the doubling and multiplying of identity in the presentation of Donne, his brother-narrator, and Donne's mistress Mariella. In the next chapter I focus on the members of Donne's crew as they come slowly to an understanding of the sense in which they reciprocally create one another's "individual personalities." This creation is maintained by a kind of social conspiracy that allows the perpetuation of a conventional but illusory interpretation of reality. The interpretation permits them to confer meaning on their lives and actions through pursuit of desired objects and objectives.

The story *of Palace of the Peacock* is recounted largely by an unnamed first-person narrator who at times becomes omniscient, although, as the examination of the text will illustrate, such conventional categories are of only limited usefulness in understanding the book. When the novel opens, the narrator has come into the interior from the coast to join his brother Donne, who is already a legend in the region. Expelled from school and coastal society for his wild behavior, Donne has set himself up in the interior of Guyana, like Conrad's Kurtz, as ruler over a vast area of land that he works by impressing the Amerindians into forced labor. Yet curiously, when the narrator arrives, no one is to be found except Donne and Mariella, Donne's much-abused mistress, presumably Amerindian.

Shortly after the narrator's arrival, Donne learns that his labor force has vanished into the forest, carrying out a rite that must be undertaken every seven years to ward off drought. He flies into a rage, assembles a boat crew, and he, his brother-narrator, and the crew set off along a turbulent Guyanese river in search of the "labouring folk."

Their first stop is at the Mission of Mariella; but the Mission is deserted except for an old Arawak Indian woman. She warns them that although they can overtake the "folk" in seven days, the journey on the river is extremely dangerous. Donne nevertheless insists on going ahead, and after spending the night camped at Mariella, the expedition sets out in the morning, forcing the old woman to accompany them as a guide.

Like the Creation in Christian mythology, the journey proceeds through seven days. The crew is torn by internal strife, and its ranks are thinned by accidents and the escalation of dissension to murder. In the rapids at the foot of an enormous waterfall, the members of the crew who have survived thus far apparently perish; the novel seems to end in disaster. Yet the lost crew members reappear, in a strange vision of a strange paradise that concludes the book. The pursuit of the fleeing Amerindian "labouring folk" by the conquistador figure Donne, his brother-narrator, and their crew is significant on several levels.

First is the literal historical level, including psychological (emotional, attitudinal) overtones, as even a brief quotation from Naipaul's *The Loss of El Dorado* serves to illustrate. Naipaul's text refers to a group of early explorers:

The adventure wasn't over. They still had Baltasar, the Spanish-speaking Indian captive; and they had picked up another Indian. They asked Baltasar about El Dorado. He didn't want to talk. He was threatened with death; he talked. He said he would take them to El Dorado. . . . The man chosen to lead the party . . . wasn't happy about it. Wyatt heard him say that "in his dream the night before he did senciblie perceave himselfe drowninge. . . ."

The rivers of Guiana, so "faire, spatious and broade" when first seen . . . now became a setting for nightmare labour, "both in rowinge, towinge and caryinge the bote. . . ." In their stupefied state—they [the explorers] had had no water for three days—they began to row in the wrong direction[1]

Second is the psychological-historical level, in that the relationship Donne and the conquistador-crew bear to Mariella and the "folk" parallels the relationships between Europe and "America," with "America" understood as a screen for the projection of fantasies.

Next is the economic-historical level. The "folk"—referred to as "the labouring folk" by Donne—represent precisely that basic source of wealth that is labor and that first the indigenes and then the Africans and East Indians provided to the dominant stratum in the Caribbean. Also, socially designated groups like the "folk" are often considered less than human because of the close relationship to nature their social role imposes upon them. Consequently, they mediate between the "human" and the "natural" worlds.

The last significant level is that labor and wealth stand for spiritual-emotional labor, as exemplified in the use of alchemical analogies explored so thoroughly by Michael Gilkes in *Wilson Harris and the Caribbean Novel*.[2]

All these dimensions are summed up in the idea and the implications of *conquest* and *desire;* these organize the novel. Conquest and desire figure in the pursuit of the "folk" by the crew, in Donne's abuse of Mariella, in his near-hysterical injunction to his brother-narrator early in the novel to rule the land, and in the turnabout during the trip, when it seems probable that the "folk" may start pursuing the crew.

The sequential plot is only one line of movement in this complex book, and not the most important one. The plot line is contradicted from the opening paragraph, when Donne is shot off his horse under the narrator's eyes—killed by Mariella, we are soon told. But the narration is deliberately constructed so that it is impossible to determine whether the narrator is awake or asleep, alive or dead. Soon after, the plot is undermined again when the reader learns that this same crew has taken the same voyage before and been drowned.

Much of the power and artistic coherence of the work derives from the consistency and success with which Harris weaves his tissue of cross-associations, thus illustrating on the stylistic plane the presentation he is conceptually making of the nature of reality. At all levels, the underlying technique is to establish opposition in repetition and then to undermine the status of relations of opposition as a fundamental attribute of reality. The vision of paradise with which the book concludes constitutes a resolution of this opposition.

The repetition that is established first and most obviously is that of Donne and his brother-narrator. This doubling has itself a double aspect: Repetition of identity insofar as Donne/Narrator represent one consciousness, and opposition in repetition of identity insofar as they represent opposing and even antagonistic qualities. The opposition immediately moves, however, from the strictly dyadic (the double) to the multiple, with the introduction of the Watcher in the first paragraph and, most importantly, with the central triadic relationship of Donne/Narrator/Mariella. This central repetition in the text is elaborated in the two versions of the dream of Donne's death. Each of the two versions of Donne's death is fraught with menace. Yet they are crucially different and represent, as do the two trips of the crew, those "parallel possibilities" that, as I discuss in detail in the final chapter, form the basis for Harris's philosophy of hope in human psychological and historical affairs. What changes in the two versions is the point of view, or the nature of the identification the narrator makes, and therefore (insofar as Donne/Narrator/Mariella can be viewed as a single psyche) what has changed is the relationship of psyche to event.

In the first version, the paragraphs that open the novel present the narrator as an external observer who watches Mariella kill Donne but does not see her and does not participate in either Mariella's or Donne's experience of the event. And in the surface recounting of the event, conventional delineations are observed. There appear to be three distinguishable images, a horse that one of them is riding, a gunshot, and a landscape where the action occurs:

A horseman appeared on the road coming at a breakneck stride. A shot rang out suddenly, near and yet far as if the wind had been stretched and torn and had started coiling and running in an instant. The horseman stiffened with a devil's smile, and the horse reared, grinning fiendishly and snapping at the reins. The horseman gave a bow to heaven like a hanging man to his executioner, and rolled from his saddle on to the ground.

The shot had pulled me up and stifled my own heart in heaven. I started walking suddenly and approached the man on the ground. His hair lay on his forehead. Someone was watching us from the trees and bushes that clustered the side of the road. Watching me as I bent down and looked at the man whose open eyes stared at the sky through his long hanging hair. The sun blinded and ruled my living sight but the dead man's eye remained open and obstinate and clear.

I dreamt I awoke with one dead seeing eye and one living closed eye.

(pp. 13-14)

The horseman is likened to a hanging man, and the executioner is paralleled with heaven. Thus an implicit equation is made on the one hand between the horseman and humanity and on the other between heaven and his killer, implying less some divine retribution than an inevitable rebalancing deriving inherently from a transgression against the nature of things. "The horseman stiffened with a devil's smile, and the horse reared, grinning fiendishly and snapping at the reins": Here we have an association between human and devil and also an association of horseman-devil and devil-horse. The horseman has the devil's smile, but it is the horse that is grinning fiendishly. Not only the man but also the mount become eerie. The word "snapping" has disturbing, almost carnivorous, and certainly aggressive connotations. With the assimilation to each other of horseman and horse, the horseman easily becomes transformed into an infernal centaur figure. The historical associations also suggest the ominously looming figure of that man on horseback seen by certain of the Amerindian civilizations, unfamiliar with the horse, as a single unnatural form, and announcing the arrival of the conquistadors and the imminent downfall of traditional Amerindian civiliztions. (See chart on p. 46.)

There are two observers of this event: The narrator and an unseen watcher in the bush, presumably the assassin, experienced by the reader almost as the spirit of the bush or the bush itself rather than as a person. Although Harris does not invoke Kanaima explicitly, familiarity with the lore of the region brings to mind this Amerindian spirit of the bush, who always brings death. This association reinforces the suggestion that there is only one psyche here, for according to tradition Kanaima is always met alone.

The allusion to nonhuman agencies implicated in the murder is strengthened by the immediate assimilation of the "shot" to natural forces: "as if the wind had been stretched and torn and had started coiling and running in an instant." The next sentence, at first reading, could be a straightforward description of the reaction of an observer to such an event. We may say when shocked by something, "I was pulled up short," and we may describe our feeling as having our heart squeezed or stifled. Only the words "in heaven" strike that deliberately incongruous note that so often in the novel constitutes the area of overlap with a less obvious association at variance with conventions of the realistic novel.

A warning chord draws the reader back to the first part of the sentence. In this context there is a close association with the horseman, for a startled or fatally struck horseman may literally perform the act the startled observer describes himself as experiencing metaphorically—that is, "pull up" the reins. The "in heaven" then reverberates against the evocation of hell in the preceding paragraph, drawing together around the idea of death and an ambivalent hereafter. In this one sentence, narrator, horseman, and horse are at the same time identified with each other by the words "horseman" and "pulled me up," yet opposed by the divine-demoniac contrast of the phrases "grinning fiendishly" and "my own heart in heaven." They are also opposed by their presumably starkly opposed states in conventional reality of life and death, separated by an act and a result—the firing of a shot and a death. This last, life and death, has also split the association between horse and rider: "rolled from the saddle" (position of dominance, cultural artifact facilitating dominance, especially in the historical context of the European invasions) and "to the ground" (returned to earth, to Nature; passive, overcome, dead).

"I started walking suddenly." This action of the narrator plays off against the description a few sentences earlier of the shot-wind "coiling and running in an instant." Wind, gunshot, and narrator all move in the direction of the horseman. The narrator watches the horseman and is himself watched. The dead man's eyes are open and clear; the narrator is "blinded and ruled" by the sun in his living sight. Three spaces separate this imagery from that of the next sentence. "I dreamt I awoke with one dead seeing eye and one living closed eye." This sentence intensifies the merging, established in the preceding sentence, of narrator and horseman into one identity and one vision as apprehended by two separate persons. It calls still further into question the apparent stark realism and clear-cut action of the first paragraph (a waking realism and action already undercut, as we have seen, for the attentive reader by a subtly woven fabric of contradictory associations).

Finally, in the first paragraph there is on the one hand the suggestion of a grotesque kind of respect or recognition of defeat shown by the horseman to his assassin (hanged man to his executioner); his gesture is a "bow to heaven," suggesting an identification of heaven with the executioner and, by implication, of the executed with hell. Yet there is also the hint of the horseman's complicity in his own death—for he is riding suicidally, pounding away at the earth, the reader is told, "at a breakneck stride." Such complicity challenges again the clear-cut, temporal, causal, linear sequentiality of actor (murderer), act (murder), recipient of action (murder victim). On another level, it calls into question such clear-cut delineations of person, temporality, linearity, and causality and suggests the danger of delusion in the grammatical structure of English, which purports to describe this reality unambiguously, and of the "grammatical structure" of the realist novel—plot, character, event—which claims to do the same.

The repetition, the second version of Donne's death, occurs in a dream the narrator has during "the first night on the soil of Mariella," after the crew has set out in pursuit of the "folk." In the dream an animal stands over him,

neighing and barking in one breath, its terrible half-hooves raised over me to trample its premature rider. I grew conscious of its closeness as a shadow and as death. I made a frightful gesture to mount, and it shrank a little into half-woman, half-log greying into the dawn. . . . I sat bolt upright in my hammock, shouting aloud that the devil himself must fondle and mount this muse of hell and this hag, sinking back instantly, a dead man in his bed come to an involuntary climax. The grey wet dream of dawn had restored to me Mariella's terrible stripes and anguish of soul. The vaguest fire and warmth came like a bullet, flooding me, over aeons of time it seemed, with penitence and sorrow.

This musing re-enactment and reconstruction of the death of Donne ushered in the early dawn. . . . (p. 46)

As is the way with dreams or semiconscious fantasies, elements of the first version are present but rearranged and differently charged in this second version, which is a commingling of dream and hallucination. The experience is strikingly characterized by the fluidity and transformation of forms and states: animate–inanimate, human–animal. It is the narrator's experience, not that of another person observed by the narrator as in the first version. Its evocation of the same issues of life and death is cast in unmistakably sexual terms. The "aeons of time" are especially characteristic of certain agonizing and haunting dreams. The tone is much farther from classical novelistic realism than that of the first version. And its conclusion, unlike that of the first version, is not death but a kind of resurgence to life through an "involuntary climax" of a "dead man," characterized by the narrator's emotional participation in the experience both of the murderer and the murdered, an experience that is active and passive in both the grammatical and the behavioral sense. This symbolism of regeneration through sexuality in death appears also in *Ascent to Omai*, which draws on the Egyptian myth of Osiris, who is said to have begotten Horus after his death, the mourning Isis being the mother.

In this second version of Donne's death, the narrator has not merely attained a sympathy for Mariella or an understanding of her position and motivation. The text reads: "The grey wet dream of dawn had *restored to me* Mariella's terrible stripes and anguish of soul" (p. 46; my emphasis). In other words, Mariella's experience is an alienated experience of the narrator's, and therefore, because of the *association* of Donne/Narrator, of Donne's as well. Since the reader soon learns from the narrator that Mariella killed Donne, the relationship with Mariella is in fact introduced as early as that of Donne and the narrator and is inseparable from it. The title of Book 1, "Horseman, Pass By," is taken from the poet's desired epitaph in Yeats's "Under Ben Bulben." It conveys some of the same ambiguity as the first version of Donne's death: "Cast a cold eye on life, on death. Horseman, pass by." ("Horseman, Pass By" was a title Harris considered for the novel.) But in Harris's novel the horseman does not pass by, indifferent. He is ambushed by life and death, brought down, enmeshed in them, with a suggestion of an equivalence of the two states that is not foreign to Yeats's lines, with their even-handed emphasis "on life, on death." The horseman's bow is an acknowledgment of the impossibility of outriding either life or death.

The central organizing principle of doubling and multiple repetition occurs on several levels, including that of two kinds of movement: The linear and the circular.

Linear movement figures in the consecutive days of the journey along the river and in the lives of the crew members insofar as they are presented conventionally as having a beginning and an end. Yet the linear trajectory is not (as we are inclined to think of it) a unique trajectory, for both the river voyage and the individual lives of the crew members are repeated at least once. Donne and his crew have taken this journey before, and it has ended before in disaster; the men lie buried at the foot of Sorrow Hill.

The repetitive nature of the circular movement is symbolized by the most important organizing motif, the wheel. The wheel is a very ancient symbol for a spiritual journey. Asoka's wheel occupies the center of the Indian flag. The wheel-mandala as a symbol in Eastern faiths has many well-known variants. In the European tradition, Jung is probably the scholar who has most thoroughly explored the psychological significance of the mandala; it is extensively used in Tibetan Buddhism.[3] The Buddha is implored, "Come Blessed One [i.e., the Buddha] we pray Thee, roll the wheel of the dew-sweet Law—which is excellent in the beginning, excellent in the middle, and excellent in the end!"[4]

Thus the wheel's association with Eastern religions is especially strong, stronger than with Christianity. For although the cross may be interpreted as a quadripartite division of the circle, it is not generally so viewed in the West.

Another possible intriguing connection with Christian symbolism is the swastika as the "crooked cross." The Nazis' use of the swastika has given it a highly negative charge in the West in our time; but this ancient symbol of life was known long ago not only in India (the word derives from the Sanskrit root "to be") but also in Persia and Greece.[5] Probably, too, it was known in Northern Asia, for with the arms of the cross bent in the opposite direction from the Nazi symbol, it is an important motif among certain Indian peoples of the Americas, whose ancestors came from Northern Asia. Anthropologists generally believe this is an instance of diffusion. The figure itself is not so hard to come upon independently, but the similarity of the complex associations suggests a common origin. In Jungian terms, the common origin would lie in the collective unconscious. This Amerindian use of variants of the circle-wheel and broken wheel bestows a special appropriateness on its use in *Palace of the Peacock*, with its tale of the pursuit of the Amerindian folk.

Harris's use of the wheel image thus resonates against a rich mythological and psychological background from numerous traditions. It is certainly this, in part, that accounts for the almost archetypically haunting quality of the novel. His most explicit and detailed adaptations, however, draw on a tradition little known in the West—one that Harris also invokes explicitly in other fiction and in his essays. This is the West African mythological tradition, brought to the Caribbean by the slaves and subsequently given a Caribbean development by their descendants. The figure of this mythological pantheon relevant to the present discussion is Anancy, the spider, the trickster figure of several West African peoples. Anancy has certain qualities in common with the god Loki of Norse mythology.[6] As trickster, Anancy stands in a somewhat similar antagonistic relation to the other supernatural beings of the pantheon to which he belongs, but he does not have Loki's real malice. That Harris is evoking the associations with Anancy is clear in *Palace of the Peacock* from his use of Anancy's name and his frequent associations of characters in the novel with the spider through an association between the spider and the wheel; he accomplishes the association both through the wheel shape of the spider's body, with its legs as spokes, and through the wheel shape of the web. For example, when the crew member Wishrop hurtles to his death, he is described as cleaving the air "like a man riding a wheel." And the motor, "Jennings's machine," at this point "sent a hideous strangled roar out of the water. It. . . was dwindling into an indefatigable revolving spider" (p.101). Wishrop is assimilated to the machine, the wheel, and the spider; he, too, "dwindles," his hands aloft "for all the world like fingers clinging to the spokes and spider of a wheel"; the fingers are "webbed," yet another Harrisian play on associations, making him like a water animal and also associating the watery death he meets with web and spider.

The water "wheels," and Wishrop disappears again. He is broken on the wheel of death; his death is described in terms that recall the allusion to a dead man's ejaculation in the second version of Donne's death: "They [the crew] shuddered and spat their own—and his—blood and death-wish. It had been forcibly and rudely ejected. And this taste and forfeiture of self-annihilation bore them into the future on the wheel of life" (p. 102). Here, as in the second version of the death of Donne, life rises out of death; the wheel of death is also the wheel of life.

In the Amazon basin, various species of spiders are very prevalent. They may grow to great size; one kind is large enough to kill birds. (In The *Voyage of the Beagle,* Darwin commented upon the much greater importance of spiders in the catalogue of fauna in South America than in England.)[7] This fact no doubt made more likely the survival of the African Anancy theme in the Americas. The spider must be understood in this book in the context of its literal and cultural availability in the Caribbean, which differs from that of Europe and North America. Similarly, Harris accords a particular value to the sun not only as a life force, a common convention in fiction from temperate regions, but also as a tropical dealer of death blows. In the same way, he uses "the fever"—malaria, the great killer of tropical regions—not as an exotic disease but as having symbolic value exactly because it is a common fact of Caribbean life. Such uses are subtle but important indications of Harris's identity as a Caribbean writer.

The dense weave of *Palace of the Peacock* gives it its highly distinctive verbal texture. In addition to complex linguistic crossweaving, Harris makes a powerful use of metaphor to imply what R. D. Laing calls the "co-inherence" of states conventionally conceived as opposites.[8] This use is evident in the opening to Chapter 2. The first paragraph, quoted below, builds on the cross-associational technique that in the first chapter linked narrator, Donne, devil-horse, Mariella, and the natural forces such as wind, sun, and land to construct

a further merging of the "self" of the body and the "other" of the land
and to refute these two human conceptualizations of relationship:

> The map of the savannahs was a dream. The names Brazil and Guiana were
> colonial conventions I had known from childhood. I clung to them now as to a
> curious necessary stone and footing, even in my dream, the ground I knew I
> must not relinquish. They were an actual stage, a presence, however mythical
> they seemed to the universal and the spiritual eye. They were as close to me as
> my ribs, the rivers and the flatland, the mountains and heartland I intimately
> saw. I could not help cherishing my symbolic map, and my bodily prejudice
> like a well-known room and house of superstition within which I dwelt. I saw
> this kingdom of man turned into a colony and battleground of spirit, a priceless
> tempting jewel I dreamed I possessed. (p. 20)

Identifying names, Brazil and Guiana, are "colonial conventions."
They aren't real. Yet they are also described as "stone," "footing,"
"ground"—all words that convey solidity, substance. This "map,"
"ground," "actual stage"—an expression connoting "real," or "locus of
action"—refers to the physical topography of the earth. This
topography is identified with the flesh and bone terrain of the body, the
"symbolic map" that is a dream, yet one with a "body"—a "room and
house of superstition" within which the narrator dwells. (In the Judaeo-
Christian tradition, this identification is literally true, for the first
human beings were made of earth.)

The narrator must not relinquish that map of the savannahs; he
cannot help cherishing his symbolic map and his "bodily prejudice."
As the names are an actual stage, so does the body become the actual
stage for the individual journey. This body is "a well-known room and
house of superstition within which I dwelt," suggesting both an
identification with and a differentiation and distancing from the body,
which becomes the immediate and most intimate locale of the action of
the "I," but still conceptually separate from the "I" by being a locale at
all. There are intriguing similarities here, couched in far different
language, to the issues raised by Lacan and Fanon and discussed in
Chapter 1 about how we form these earliest bodily prejudgments and
how they may relate, psychologically, socially, and historically, to the
worlds we build. The world becomes one with the physical body, and
the human being incorporates the earth.

By the same kind of linguistic equation already examined in the opening passages of the novel, the substance of the body here becomes a "house," a "room." Earlier the narrator felt himself to be in a room that might be an operating theater where his physical existence is put at risk (whether saved, lost, or altered), or a maternity ward where he awaits birth (or giving birth), or a prison cell where he awaits execution. The body may also be understood as a vessel of life, a vessel of God, equated with the boat in which the crew journeys, and a room wherein we are all prisoners under death sentence, awaiting execution, like the horseman who bows to heaven in the first paragraph of the book.

The map of the physical world is declared to be symbolic. The physical world and the body, which are assimilated to each other, are designated "the kingdom of man," a phrase that acquires its full significance only when compared with the conventional Christian opposition expressed most succinctly and forcefully in Christ's assertion, "My Kingdom is not of this world." Yet the tight textual interweaving of allusion and association serves to undercut this dichotomy, to assert their absolute inseparability.

The essential repetitions and oppositions of the novel are presented in the eleven short, straightforward sentences with which Harris opens the novel. There is the opposition of the states of dream and waking, of life and death. There is the opposition between the horseman and the narrator. There is the opposition between the ambusher and the Watcher in the bush, almost a spirit or emanation of the bush itself, on the one side and the narrator and horseman on the other. And finally there is the opposition between the horseman and Mariella.

In the opening passage, Harris has laid out the set of structural conflicts and resolutions whose interplay is both subject and style, form and content, of the novel. He is engaged in that interplay of opposition, separation, and identification and, as dramatically as one could wish, opens a good frontier plot with a mystery (who killed the horseman?) that is very soon resolved, only to give way to more puzzling mysteries—of life and death, dreaming and waking, identity and event—already suggested in the nuances of the first page. His writing is difficult, not because of the difficulty of his language or the sequence of his plot (he is quite straightforward when he undercuts that sequence) but because of the context he creates by his techniques of cross-referential association and plurisignation. As the poet Derek Walcott has rightly said, the novel is "short and memorable as a dream, and troubles us with the evocativeness of a dream."⁹

The second version of Donne's death similarly adumbrates the resolution on the novel's final page. It also represents the conclusion of the first principal set of repetitions, Donne/brother-narrator/Mariella. The voyage itself represents the working out of the second set of repetitions, that is, the ways in which the members of the crew reflect and misreflect each other.

A woman first appears in the novel when Donne calls the narrator from "an inner contemplation and slumber" by rapping on the ground with his leg and reintroduces the theme of sleep (for the narrator, since the opening of the novel, has been sleeping and waking in patterns that deliberately defy a clear-cut delineation) with the words, "The woman still sleeping." Donne is speaking of Mariella, who responds to his rude shouts by emerging from a shack and feeding some chickens: "Donne looked at her as at a larger and equally senseless creature whom he governed and ruled like a fowl" (p. 15).

This first appearance of the woman is accompanied by the information that she, too, has been sleeping. She is the anima, and as I show shortly, the sleeping narrator shares certain qualities with her that Donne has rejected in himself, has as it were deliberately put to sleep. This anima figure is assimilated to the animal/natural member of what is for Donne the primal relation, that between the alternatives of "govern or be governed, rule or be ruled."

For the "second or third time," the narrator "half-awakes," this time to a rapping on his door. Mariella enters, sobbing and disheveled, displaying the whip marks from Donne's beating. The narrator soothes and caresses her. Apparently awake, the two of them descend the steps from the house, taking yet another advance on an earlier scene in which he and Donne watched from the window. The "hanging house," like many in Guyana, stands on stilts; this one possesses "the tallest stilts in the world," which recall the opening paragraph by bringing the house closer to both heaven and gestures are several times described as "wooden."

After the horseman is shot, the dreamer apparently awakes, his and the horseman's vision conjoined in one "dead seeing" and one "living closed" eye:

I put my dreaming feet on the ground in a room that oppressed me as though I stood in an operating theater, or a maternity ward, or, I felt suddenly, the glaring cell of a prisoner who had been sentenced to die. I arose with a violent giddiness and leaned on a huge rocking chair . . . the house stood high and alone in the flat brooding countryside. (p. 14)

In this paragraph a set of equivalences is introduced: Operating theater/maternity ward/prisoner's cell. All these are arenas of civilization, understood as referring to those early societies that became urban and developed complex polities generating such institutions as prisons. The first two are even more specific—they are the institutions of modern civilization. But all three also represent a conjoining of opposites; they are highly civilized arenas for the performance of the most basic biological functions that occupy the Nature half of the dichotomy: Birth, maintenance of threatened life, and death. And these arenas oppress the narrator, afflict him with giddiness, that is, with a dizziness and nausea born of spatial disorientation and generally arising from a disruption of visual processes, which is significant given the suggested visual or perceptual disorientation of a "dead seeing material eye" and a "living closed spiritual eye". In this context, giddiness also evokes the nausea of illness and of pregnancy. The connotation of oscillation implicit in giddiness is taken up in the rocking chair and the wind rocking the narrator—in context, also evoking the rocking of a cradle. The narrator's body stands inside a house, looking out at an external physical landscape and asserting a primal dichotomy of the human spirit: "the desire to govern or be governed, rule or be ruled, forever" (p. 14). This dichotomy can be imagined only by assuming the separation and opposition of subject and object, here and there, inside and outside:

Someone rapped on the door of my cell and room. I started on seeing the dream-horseman, tall and spare and hard-looking as ever. . . . I greeted him as one greeting one's gaoler and ruler. And we looked through the window of the room together, as though through his dead seeing material eye, rather than through my living closed spiritual eye.

(p. 14)

The paragraph consolidates the equivalences of the preceding paragraph discussed above. The enclosing space is now cell and room (with the underlying implication or resonance of "womb"). Here is the dream-horseman—is he alive or dead? The reader cannot determine, since the narrator has told us on the previous page that this sequence is his dream, even though he seems to awaken. But here the relationship already established in the first paragraph between narrator and horseman is made more precise: They are united by "the oldest uncertainty and desire in the world, the desire to govern or be governed, rule or be ruled forever." Thus united, they stand side by side and look out, each an eye, a window of a single soul, at "the primitive road and the savannahs . . ."—that is, at Nature and at the first human attempts to impose Culture, "civilization," a path through nature.

The next—narrative—paragraphs identify the horseman. "His name was Donne," the narrator tells us, "and it had always possessed a cruel glory for me." Again the notion of governing arises, for the narrator continues: "His wild exploits had governed my imagination since childhood." But the wild boy was expelled from school and left the coast for the hinterland, the "border country" with Brazil; he "turned into a ghost."

We also see the power attributed to the principle represented by Mariella in this passage:

"Donne cruel and mad, " Mariella cried. She was staring hard at me. I turned away from her black hypnotic eyes as if I had been blinded by the sun, and saw inwardly in the haze of my blind eye a watching muse and phantom whose breath was on my lips. She remained close to me and the fury of her voice was in the wind. I turned away and leaned heavily against the frail brilliant gallows-gate of the sky, looking down upon the very road where I had seen the wild horse, and the equally wild demon and horseman fall. Mariella had killed him. (p. 16)

This passage returns the reader to the opening paragraph of the novel. Mariella is the assassin, already in these few words herself portrayed doubly: As the battered, submissive woman under Donne's whip hand, literally, and also as his self-avenging assassin. She is furthermore assimilated to the sun, which smites the narrator as she smote Donne (thereby linking narrator and horseman again and also introducing into the novel the power of the Guyanese landscape). It is the dead, blind eye of the horseman that sees, and Mariella's blinding gaze that opens the narrator's inner eye to the "watching muse and phantom," thus bringing back the Watcher in the bush of the first paragraph. This mythical benevolent female personification is opposed to the assassin; Muse and Fates, Sita and Kali are present here. Mariella's breath is on the narrator's lips; in the next sentence the fury of her voice (voice is articulated breath) is in the wind, returning the reader to the shot that killed the horseman in the first paragraph, ringing out "suddenly, near and yet far *as if the wind had been stretched* and torn" (p. 13; my emphasis).

The narrator continues, "Mariella had killed him. I awoke in full and in earnest with the sun's blinding light and muse in my eye. My brother had just entered the room" (pp. 16-17).

For the first time in the novel, the reader is told that the world in question is unequivocally the waking world; and in that waking world, the psychological or spiritual link already firmly established between Donne and the narrator is given a material, physical basis with the information that they are brothers. The narrator tells his brother of his dream, admits his unfamiliarity with the local situation, and warns him nevertheless that his brutality is driving Mariella mad. "You are a devil with that woman," he tells him. Donne's reply is vehement and revealing:

"Dreamer," he warned, giving me a light wooden tap on the shoulder, "life here is tough. One has to be a devil to survive. I'm the last landlord. I tell you I fight everything in nature, flood, drought . . . beast and woman. I'm everything. Midwife, yes, doctor, yes, gaoler, judge, hangman, every blasted thing to the labouring people. Look man, look outside again. Primitive. Every boundary line is a myth. No-man's land, understand?" (p. 17)

"No-man's land" has a double meaning. Because it belongs to no one, it is the possession of anyone able to take and to hold it. And, because it intrinsically belongs to no one (that is, to anyone at all or to any single person), Donne is deluded in his belief that he can possess and hold it.

The narrator goes on to confess to Donne that the dream he has just had is a recurrent one that dates from Donne's departure for the interior. When he sees Donne mocking him, he offers the information that he is himself going blind in the left eye, although in the dream it is his sound right eye that goes blind. He concludes, "And your vision becomes . . . the only remaining window on the world for me" (p. 18).

He finishes with the remark that never before had he seen Mariella in his dreams. This remark constitutes yet another of the incongruities that alert the reader to the levels of the novel below the surface plot and dialogue, for how could the narrator have dreamed of Mariella before when he has only just met her—except, of course, insofar as he is one with Donne or is another aspect of Donne's psyche?

Donne offers additional information about himself in a rumination that establishes an additional link with the narrator. As the narrator has said that Donne became "a ghost" for him, Donne now acknowledges, "I had almost forgotten I had a brother like you. . . . It had passed from my mind . . . this dreaming twin responsibility" (p. 19). The passage continues, bringing out a submerged component of Donne's psyche in the recollection of his nurturing qualities and behavior toward the narrator:

His [Donne's] voice expanded and a sinister under-current ran through his remarks—"We belong to a short-lived family and people. It's so easy to succumb and die. It's the usual thing in this country as you well know. . . . our parents died early. They had a hard life. Tried to fight their way up out of an economic nightmare: farmers and hand-to-mouth business folk they were. . . . I looked after you, son." He gave me one of his ruthless taps. "Father and mother rolled into one for awhile. I was a boy then. I had almost forgotten. Now I'm a man. I've learnt," he waved his hands at the savannahs, "to rule this." (p. 19)

Donne here recalls an almost-forgotten androgyny. He immediately rejects it as part of childhood, that is, of a state prior to sexual differentiation. He reasserts his absolute masculinity and the nature of masculinity as the governing and ruling half of that "oldest uncertainty and desire in the world" (p. 14). He perceives the world as externality and surface. Although he recognizes his perception as superficial opposition, in a rare moment of reciprocity or doubt Donne asks for confirmation from the narrator that no need exists to penetrate either inward into his own psyche or backward into the past of his androgynous childhood: "One doesn't have to see deeper than that, does one?" (p. 19). Yet the conclusion of the paragraph and the chapter conveys a need to confront that femaleness.

On the obvious level, the "Mission of Mariella" refers simply to one of the numerous Christian missions that dot the banks of Guyanese rivers. But its other grammatically possible meaning is "Mariella's Mission;" a mission is a special task for which one is destined.

Harris's Mariella represents an "aspect of Mary" unique to him, powerful and both new in the Christian tradition and akin to elements in the much older tradition that gave birth to Christianity; I discuss this in detail later. The suffix "ella," Spanish for "she," seems to reinforce the importance of her function as a female principle. Wishrop, the only crew member involved with a woman identified explicitly as Amerindian—a young Arawak woman who nurses him after he is wounded and hides him from the law—conceals the truth about his past with the pretense that he speaks Spanish much better than English because of the long years he worked in Venezuela. In other words, truth and fiction function as a double for each other in the webbed "fiction" may be a "translation" of truth.

The grammatical structure of the phrase "the Mission of Mariella" is thus significant, and this kind of linguistic play is one of Harris's characteristic literary techniques. Mariella's Mission, which is its other meaning, emphasizes the importance of Mariella in the many forms she assumes in the novel. Mariella symbolizes Nature, the Americas, the Amerindians, the land itself. The parallel with the rapaciousness of Donne the conquistador figure assaulting the American earth is clear, with Mariella and Donne as Female opposed to Male, the Euro-American to the American, the Coastal-European society to the interior. These represent archetypical oppositions, with special significance for the Caribbean in its relation to Europe as a double discussed in Chapter 1. The metamorphoses of these "aspects of Mary" constitute a commentary on the relations of Euro-America and the Caribbean and, more fundamentally still, a commentary on the philosophical discourse in terms of which those relations are ideologically conceived.

Clearly, Harris intends references to the Christian mythological tradition in *Palace of the Peacock*. The number seven has mystical significance in the Judaeo-Christian tradition. The voyage of Donne and his crew lasts seven days, paralleling the seven days' creation of the universe, and the rite to ward off drought must be performed by the "folk" every seven years. Mariella's name suggests the name Mary, the female principle in Christianity. The figure of the carpenter near the end of the novel, the vision of the house of many mansions recalling the promise attributed to Jesus in John 3:14, and the madonna figure with the child are other suggestive images. And the idea of a journey toward salvation is certainly consistent with Christian belief.

Yet on a more fundamental level, the Christian framework does not seem as relevant to the novel as this enumeration of images might suggest. The Christian system of meaning is based on not only linearity but also uniqueness. The world moves from Creation to Judgment Day. A clearly distinguishable individual soul moves in human body from birth in original sin, through the chance of a single lifetime at redemption, to a final and irreversible judgment based on that single and unrepeatable life. Both this pattern and this conception of individuality are seriously at variance with the novel.

Most important is that despite the arduous journey and the final vision at the end, this is not really a tale of either salvation or redemption. Nowhere in the book does one find the peculiarly Judaeo-Christian idea of sin. The meaning of Christianity depends on linearity of time and singularity and uniqueness: There must be a single indestructible soul with a single unrepeatable chance for salvation or damnation. This crew, though, is on its second journey along the same route, and there is no suggestion that any limits exist to the number of times the journey can or even must be taken. Not sin, in the sense of transgression against some divine ordinance, but rather blindness, sometimes willful, keeps the crew repeating its journey despite a suggestion of a kind of fall from grace—Donne's earlier voyage is described as "innocent," and, once, Mariella had felt a genuine affection for him, which he cannot hope to regain in his present course. In many respects, this psychological or spiritual journey has more characteristics of Eastern religions than of Christianity, specifically the idea of reincarnation and the sense of a truth that, although it can be willfully denied and involves the play of *karma* (deeds) that carry consequences, is devoid of the idea of sin as a violation of laws promulgated by some external divine authority.[10]

Mariella in one aspect is presented as a submissive and downtrodden woman, not the only role for women in a rough frontier society (Magda, in Harris's fourth novel, *The Whole Armour,* is a powerful and dominant personality) but certainly a believable one. However, the multileveled presentation of Mariella is considerably more complex, so I do not wholly agree with Hena Maes-Jelinek when she says that Mariella is a traditionally subservient figure.[11]   The novel's opening scene, Donne's murder, has little enough in it of the worm turning and much that is suggestive of Kali the Destroyer in the Hindu pantheon. Mariella's killing of Donne is of such scale and significance that it transcends mere vengeance. Its mythic, cosmic overtones suggest that the killing is inevitable, that it is in the nature of things, given the behavior of Donne, which violates that nature. Donne's maltreatment of Mariella is also a maltreatment of himself. The novel's reference to the "self-devouring" character of Donne's behavior is apt. To borrow Jungian terminology, Donne is denying the anima or female aspect of himself, and, as in the Hindu image of Shakti, the female without which the male has no strength, his maltreatment of her leads to his own demise. But other "aspects of Mary," more important in the context of the novel, do not accord with Christian associations. The Mariella of the opening passage, as we have seen, is not an intercessor for mercy with a God who states "Vengeance is mine." Insofar as it is appropriate to describe Donne's murder as vengeance, she takes her own. She is not an intercessor at all. Neither is her maternal role much stressed. And the importance of the vigorous sexual dimension of the book, which in the end is not denied but resolved, is foreign to the Christian, especially the Catholic, emphasis on Mary as Virgin.

The aspect of Mariella that is finally strongest is that of Creator. Mariella is not the Mother of God; she is God, as we see in the role accorded the anima figure at the end:

One was what I am in the music—buoyed and supported above dreams by the undivided soul and *anima in the universe from whom the word of dance and creation first came, the command to the starred peacock* who was instantly transported to know and to hug to himself his true invisible otherness and opposition, his true alien spiritual love without cruelty and confusion in the blindness and frustration of desire. (p. 152; my emphasis)

This anima is not a passive matrix or cosmic womb-locus wherein creation occurs. She is a force that "commands," and she commands that aspect of existence that is clearly identified as the male complement to her femaleness.

The union of anima and peacock is suggested when the narrator, on the seventh day from Mariella, has a vision of the complex peacock symbol:

The living eyes in the crested head were free to observe the twinkling stars and
eyes and windows on the rest of the body and wings. Every cruel mark and
stripe and ladder had vanished. (pp. 146-47)

The reference to the "marks and stripes" recalls the description of
Mariella's beating by Donne early in the book. In the second version of
Donne's death, the precursor and prerequisite to reconciliation is the
restoration to the narrator of "Mariella's terrible anguish and stripes of
soul." Here, reconciliation means becoming one flesh, not only in the
union of male and female but also of all the universe. At a moment of
crisis during the journey, a crew member named da Silva, protesting a
stone thrown at a parrot that he considers an omen from the Mission, a
bird that is an object of his love and perhaps an incarnation of Mariella,
cries out, "I tell you when you pelt she you pelt me. Is one flesh, me
flesh, you flesh, one flesh" (p. 115).

The concept of the female as a powerful divine presence in her own
right has been a persistent if minority tradition throughout Judaeo-
Christian history. It was present in the Gnostic syncretisms, and the
elaboration of the role of Shekhina in Kabbalistic Judaism is the more
recent development of an extremely ancient set of beliefs, widespread in
the world and well represented in the Middle East.[12]

In very few areas of the world did the female aspect of divinity lose as
much power as in those where the Judaeo-Christian-Islamic tradition
holds sway. The ancient prominence of the female divinity is amply
attested throughout the Middle East by varied personifications of
Astarte, Isis, and others whose worship persisted until very late among
the Hebrews as part of their religion; certain explicit passages in the
Old Testament bear witness to this. It is to these deities, and not to the
more recent dominant traditions of Christianity, that the figure of
Mariella, without deriving directly from any of them, is akin.

Mariella in her various manifestations represents an aspect of the triad
Donne/Narrator/Mariella, on which I have concentrated in this chapter.
In the next chapter, I am primarily concerned with the crew's
experiences. For its members, too, represent part of a single psyche, as
the narrator indicates when he speaks of the "crew every man mans and
lives in his inmost ship and theatre and mind" (p. 48). Harris presents
their disaster as the result of the failure or refusal to realize that the
desire to conquer is a twisting of the "immortal chase of love on the
brittle earth" (p. 31).

4

The Search for El Dorado:
Desire in *Palace of the Peacock*

> I had felt the wind rocking me with the oldest uncertainty and desire in the
> world, the desire to govern or be governed, rule orbe ruled, forever.
> *Palace of the Peacock,* p. 14

The entire seven-day journey above Mariella, as the crew understands it
when they first set out, is fundamentally a delusion deriving from a
confusion about the nature and the location of their own identity and
that of the object of their desire.

The whole psychological basis of the idea of conquest, of dominance
and subjugation, depends on the maintenance of identity and
differentiation. In the last chapter we saw how these are maintained on
the intrapsychic level; we examined the complex relationship of
Donne/brother-narrator/Mariella, the psychological aspects of repetition
in doubling, and the further multiplication of identity. Doubling and
multiple repetition also operate in relations between the individual and
the natural/inanimate world, with regard to both identity and power
relations.

In terms of identity, the following passage is illustrative. The
narrator depicts the event early in the voyage beyond Mariella, in which
symbols previously discussed appear again:

I stopped for an instant overwhelmed by a renewed force of consciousness of the
hot spirit and moving spell in the tropical undergrowth. Spider's web dangled in

a shaft of sun, clothing my arms with subtle threads as I brushed upon it. The whispering trees spun their leaves to a sudden fall wherein the ground seemed to grow lighter in my mind and to move to meet them in the air. The carpet on which I stood had an uncertain place within splintered and timeless roots whose fibre was stone in the tremulous ground . . . I stopped dead where I was, frightened for no reason whatever. The step near me stopped and stood still. I stared around me wildly, in surprise and terror . . . I gave a loud ambushed cry which was no more than an echo of myself—a breaking and grotesque voice, man and boy, age and youth, speaking together. I recovered myself from my dead faint supported by old Schomburgh, on one hand, and Carroll, the young Negro boy, on the other. (pp. 27-28)

The narrator is succored by the oldest and the youngest members of the crew who, it turns out, are uncle and nephew or perhaps father and son through the intimated boundary-blurring union of Schomburgh and his sister. Here age and youth are separate in a field of terror: The Arawak woman captive, who starts out old and grows young, later unites them in a field beyond terror. We are told Schomburgh breaks his usual taciturnity with the uncharacteristically long observation about what has happened to the narrator: "Is a risk everyman tekking in this bush" (p. 28). The risk is the threatened blurring of conventional boundaries between animate and inanimate, human and nonhuman.

The acting out of event and relationship between the separate personae of Donne, brother-narrator, and Mariella demonstrates the illusory nature of their separateness; an understanding of what is going on depends, in Harris's words, on whether it is viewed as "watershed" or "escarpment"—in other words, on point of view. The crew's seven-day journey above Mariella constitutes a similar demonstration. We are given an ironic, almost humorous—if grimly humorous—indication of the importance of point of view on the surface level of plot when at the very beginning of the journey, all machismo and derring-do and furious at the assault on his authority that the disappearance of the "folk" represents, Donne insists on setting out at great danger to his own life to catch and capture them—and "kidnaps" the old Arawak woman to "guide" him. This Arawak woman (assimilated to Mariella as a female figure) is the only Amerindian member of the "folk" with whom the crew ever comes in contact. She undergoes a series of transformations (which are examined later in more detail), but because of this "kidnap" she is in their midst and exerts a potent influence on Donne and the crew all along, even while they are desperately pursuing her. The significance of her presence among them from the start, which renders their journey unnecessary, absurd, illusory, criminal in its brutality, and—in the sense in which they understand it at the outset—impossible, is made clear at the end of the novel: "The change and variation I thought I detected in the harmony [of the peacock's and Carroll's] song were outward and unreal and illusory: they were induced by the limits and apprehensions in the listening mind of men" (pp. 148-149).

The narrator comes to understand the "events" of the novel as a "unique frame" to

construct the events of all appearance and tragedy into the vain prison they were, a child's game of a besieged and a besieging race who felt themselves driven to seek themselves—first, outcast and miserable twins of fate—second, heroic and warlike brothers—third, conquerors and invaders of all mankind. In reality the territory they overwhelmed and abandoned had always been theirs to rule and take. (p. 149)

A little later, in the last sentence of the book, this understanding has proceeded still farther, beyond these remaining vestiges of the imagery of conquest that has given way to the imagery of love: "Each of us now held at last in his arms what he had been for ever seeking and what he had eternally possessed" (p. 152). More important than plot or character, then, is a movement of relationship, a shift of point of view, "watershed or escarpment." The novel begins with a rigid opposition, an antagonism that is not merely the opposite of love but an attack on love. We see this in Donne's contempt for Mariella as a woman, in his abuse of her, and in her murder of him. There is Donne's contempt for and abuse of the Amerindians as "labouring folk" and their withdrawal from him of his absolutely necessary sustenance, their labor.

As we have seen, the Amerindians, who are the "labouring folk"; Mariella, as woman; and the bush country, the "non-civilized" American earth that, Donne cries out, must be conquered, crushed, and ruled now that he has grown up and become a man, are all equated here.

This point of view, this striving to dominate and conquer, results in egotism, a kind of ravening hunger and sense of loss, lack, absence, that at one point, as noted, is described as "self- devouring" on the part of Donne. The reader is reminded of the demonic horse Donne rides in the opening paragraph, with its "snapping" jaws. Furthermore, Donne the "macho" conquistador experiences the departure of the Amerindians as an attack on himself; the "labouring folk" are both depriving him and challenging him, and his emotional response is rage. He will pursue them, force them to do his will; he will obtain his necessary sustenance and punish them. The clearly infantile nature of his behavior is consonant with the overall movement of the novel, which depicts the progression of both the individual and the human psyche from a state of psychic or spiritual infancy to psychic or spiritual fulfillment. This progression is not a straightforward path or an inevitable development but a possibility.

These assimilations mean that the "love" in question is not simply the individual love between a man and a woman. It is also the love between "male" and "female" in the psyche; between humans and other life forms (the imagery of the "huntsman and the hunt," the ancient and basic relation between human beings and animals, in which humans kill and consume other creatures in order to live); between human beings and the webbed interconnections of the animal, the vegetable, and the mineral earth, together with sunshine and water; and among human beings in specific historical contexts, in this case the American archetypical myth of the pursuit of El Dorado. That relation between indigene and conquistador is modeled around greed for and pursuit of wealth, the congealed wealth of gold and the abstract wealth of human labor—"the labouring folk"—which is also the crucial mediation and transformation of human energy to economic value. These assimilations, and the assimilation of Mariella, American bush country-woman, are significant in terms of the Nature-Culture dichotomy discussed earlier.

The Arawak woman who is in the crew members' midst all along while they risk her neck, each individual's neck, and one another's necks in her pursuit becomes an important figure. Her fantastic transformations represent transformations in one locus—her person—among all the elements mentioned in the previous paragraph. The transformations also occur in the categories of "entity" and "event," with the evocation of the wanderings that first brought the Amerindians to the Americas and of her "earlier dream" of "distant centuries and a returning to the Siberian unconscious pilgrimage" (p. 72).

The introduction of the Siberian pilgrimage thus makes the disaster brought to the Amerindian by the European Voyages of Conquest not an absolute end, as it seemed to the exulting Europeans and is interpreted in the history they subsequently wrote, but simply the most recent period of Amerindia's long succession of important events, most of which lie outside the scope of the "colonial convention" of that European history—once again it is a question of watershed or escarpment.

The Arawak woman is both young and old. The crew members, who have kidnapped her and abused her, then decide that she is a witch—that the misfortunes their actions have brought upon them are her fault, while at the same time they crazily recognize their fault:

Everyone blamed everyone else for being the Jonah and for having had an evil intercourse with fate. Donne had arrested the witch of a woman and we had aided and abetted him. A murderous rape and fury filled our heart . . . we saw only the spirit that had raped the old woman and invoked upon us our own answering doom in her daeomonic-flowing presence. (p. 74)

She merges with the physical world around the crew, thus manifesting the associative merging in the split-psyche world of the conquistador of "nature-woman-indigene-America" opposed to "them." Some of Harris's finest writing develops this theme:

Tiny embroideries resembling the handwork on the Arawak woman's kerchief and the wrinkles on her brow turned to incredible and fast soundless breakers of foam. Her crumpled bosom and river grew agitated with desire, bottling and shaking every fear and inhibition and outcry. The ruffles in the water were her dress rolling and rising to embrace the crew." (p. 73)

She also has an avatar, besides Mariella: The unnamed Arawak woman who once helped the ill-fated Wishrop escape in the life he is fleeing as a crewman here on the river, a life in which he shot his wife and her lover, the catechist who had performed their marriage ceremony. Wishrop had crawled into the bush, and there "met the inevitable Arawak woman (this was the crew's ancestral embroidery and obsession) who nursed him to life. In the mortal hullabaloo that followed the muse reported that she had seen Wishrop crawling like a spider into the river where he had been tangled in the falls" (p. 67).

This passage confirms an association made earlier in the book identifying the "obsession" the narrator tells Donne he hopes to overcome by this trip to the interior as the recurrent dream of Donne's murder by Mariella. The "embroidery," of course, associates this passage with the passage in which the woman's embroidered kerchief flows into the embroidery of the river and the wrinkles of her skin. Anancy, the spider, is also there.

Like the woman who saved Wishrop, the Arawak captive is also a guide on this psychic as well as literal journey. Vigilance, the only Amerindian crew member and the one who completes the psychic voyage first, does so in part because he pays better attention to the Arawak woman than the others. (Incidentally, the clear historical delineations of the opposition of conquistador-Amerindian are not equated with racial differences. Not only is Vigilance an Amerindian; Donne, the principal conquistador figure, is once referred to as having "a dark racial skin," and other crew members are racially mixed.)

Both this passage and the following come quite late in the book and in the psychic development, or journey, of the crew. The Arawak woman awakens and points at the bluffs and cliffs towering on either side of the river chasm. Vigilance follows her indication and sees "a spidery skeleton crawling to the sky . . . clutching the vertical floor that seemed to change in a shaft of cloudy sun into a protean stream . . . where every mechanical revolution and image was the inscrutable irony of a spiritual fate" (p. 103).

At this point, only Vigilance and the Arawak woman are described as alive. "Donne's boat had righted itself, he [Vigilance] dreamed . . . and the crew were all there save Wishrop's spider and transubstantiation: wheel and web, sunlight, starlight, all wishful substance violating and altering and annihilating shape and matter" (p. 105). A subsequent sentence refers to the "spider and wheel" of baptism. A few pages later the ethereal mood is evoked in a striking passage: "The Arawak woman pointed, and Vigilance, straining his mind . . . saw the blue ring of pentecostal fire in God's eye as it wheeled around him above the dreaming memory and prison of life" (p. 116).

As the crew members' actions in the days beyond Mariella indicate, the psychological experience of overcoming the conventional distinction between subject and object, self and other, is not to be taken lightly. Nor is its challenge easily accepted, either by an individual—that is, intrapsychically— or among individuals. This is evident in the repeated reluctance of the crew members, who have glimmering intimations of the limitations and biases of their psychological structurings, to credit these intimations. It is also evident in their reaction when one of their fellows attempts to communicate such an intimation. When Schomburgh, fairly early in the voyage, is "half-ashamed, resenting the uneasy foundation of knowledge he possessed," he is immediately teased by his fellows about his intuition; it makes them nervous. Thus one of the da Silva twins says, "Uncle thinking of his epitaph . . . 'pon Sorrow Hill." Other crew members join in rallying this wanderer from conventional reality. One, Cameron, roars, "Come, come Uncle. . . . You must try some of this ripe nice fish" (pp. 51-52). The meal of fish (with a kind of reversal of conventional Christian overtones) clearly stands as a lure away from insight; on the only occasion in the book on which Donne briefly acknowledges his failings in his relation with the "folk," he dismisses the idea of changing it when he comes to eat the fish.

Such relatively mild social pressure as Cameron exerts upon Schomburgh in this scene can escalate if the warnings go unheeded to the point of violence, as in the quarrel much later in the book between Cameron and da Silva that ends with da Silva murdering his crewmate. The roots of these "colonial conventions," these "necessary structurings" of personality, go deep; they are mentioned in the previously quoted passage that opens Chapter 2, in which the narrator speaks of geographical colonial conventions as a "curious necessary stone and footing, even in my dream, the ground I knew I must not relinquish" (p. 20). The deep roots are intimately bound up with the psychological experience of one's bodily boundaries. Laing, expresses a similar idea:

A set of primitive distinctions are formed. Rules govern the formation of this set and the operations performed on this set:

1. Inside and outside
2. Pleasure and pain
3. Real and not-real
4. Good and bad
5. Me and not-me
6. Here and there
7. Then and now.[1]

As indicated by the interiorized and exteriorized reluctances of the travelers, the pressures for conformity come from both within and without, from self and society. Certain rules are established for "reading the map" of relationships, certain expectations established that are not to be violated. All traditions concerned with mental or spiritual development emphasize that the process is frightening because it involves a radically changed relationship with the self. Christianity phrases it by saying one must "die to the world" to be reborn in Christ; the corollary is that in "living to the world" (its illusions) we are truly dead. Buddhism teaches that one does not know Nirvana until one has seen through the illusory self, or ego. Psychoanalysis and other psychologies recognize the tremendously strong pull, sometimes called compulsion, to repeat over and over again even destructive patterns of behavior, to invest them with value, to refuse to leave them for the unknown. This is a "neurotic pattern" of personality. Freud thought that the constraints placed on the impulses, constraints that alone made civilization possible, also increased the likelihood of neurotic adaptations by individuals. Some types of societies, by analogy, might be characterized as neurotic. Much as he valued civilization over what he believed to be the unsatisfactory alternative, Freud had no illusions about the damage inflicted on many individuals in conserving and extending it. Denial and repression were the ineluctable concomitants of the guilt and fear required to establish and maintain civilization.

Harris's voyagers, too, fear the process leading to insight and repeatedly reject the dawning psychological understanding they gain as the voyage proceeds. Cameron starts out with but little insight; suddenly, during a quarrel between Donne and the mechanic Jennings, he gains a profound understanding:

"Who want to fool you?" Cameron cried again. He listened closely to his own voice. It was the voice of dread: the voice of dread at the thought that nothing existed to fool and terrorize anybody unless one chose to imagine one was bewitched and a fool all one's life. . . . The ground felt that it opened bringing to ruin years of his pride and conceit.

Cameron momentarily gains a profound realization of the deeper significance of their voyage but almost immediately reacts against it:

He wished desperately the oracular grave under his feet would close forever and disappear and he could cherish once again his old pagan desire and ambition. It struck him like an acute dismemberment and loss and injustice. (pp. 96-97)

The physically arduous and dangerous journey is even more difficult because of this constant pull toward the familiar, the known, the pull to fall back into the sleeping dream that is conventional life. The crew eventually sinks into a stupor under the assault of the voyage's hardships. Their tongues are turning black; perhaps they are dead. Cameron and da Silva get into a fight, and da Silva begins to tell what has been going on within him in his stuporous state. If we examine the text and the conversation carefully, it is clear that it is not the original quarrel but da Silva's recounted inner experiences that threaten and enrage Cameron. Da Silva says:

"Ah been dreaming far back before anybody know he born. Is how a man can dream so far back before he know he born?" . . . "Because you is a big fool," Cameron cried. . . . "Ah telling you Ah dream the boat sink with all of we," da Silva said speaking to himself. . . . "Ah drowned dead and Ah float . . . Ah dream Ah get another chance to live me life over from the very start. . . . The impossible start to happen. Ah lose me own image and time like if I forget where me sex really start. . . ." "Fool, stop it," Cameron hissed.

"Don't pick at me," da Silva said. "The impossible start happen I tell you. Water start dream, rock and stone start dream, tree trunk and tree root dreaming, bird and beast dreaming. . . . Everything Ah tell you dreaming long before the creation I know of begin. Everything turning different, changing into everything else Ah tell you." (pp. 109-11)

Da Silva experiences the perception that, as Donne shouted at the narrator in the first chapter before the voyage, "Every boundary-line is a myth"—a "colonial convention" of sorts. Especially the perception that sexual boundary lines are myths upsets Cameron in this passage. Da Silva asserts that his memory extends to a time before his own life: Had he the terminology, he would perhaps speak of having an experience of reincarnation, confirmed by his dreaming that he will have a chance to live his life over again. But a still more remarkable perception has come to him: "'Is a funny-funny dream,' da Silva said slowly . . . 'To dream all this . . .' he pointed at the wall of cliff behind

him—'deh pon you back like nothing, like air-standing up. . . .' And,
quite simply, nothing at all really was there" (p. 111).

Harris presents a character trying to describe an experience conveyed
by Buddhist statements such as, "From the first, not a thing is"; "All
dharmas [things] are intrinsically empty."[2]

And at the end of Book 3, without da Silvas's bemusement,
Vigilance, the least psychologically conflicted of the crew, "rested
against the wall and cliff of heaven as against an indestructible mirror
and soul in which he saw the blind dream of creation crumble as it was
re-enacted" (p. 124).

Significantly, Cameron's order to da Silva to stop talking does not
constitute a denial of the truth of what da Silva says but rather a
threatening command that he cease breaking the taboo forbidding such
perceptions to come to conscious awareness or to be socially
communicated and publicly remarked upon. In Gregory Bateson's
terms, Cameron is forbidding da Silva to break a metarule.[3] A metarule
is a rule *about* a rule of thought and behavior. In this case, the rule
would be, "Don't lose your own image and time and forget where your
sex really starts." The metarule would be, "Don't consciously know
that there is a rule about this"; or, to put it another way, "Don't even
let yourself know it is possible to lose your own image and time and
forget where your sex really starts." Clearly, this formulation has
affinities with Bateson's hypothesis of the "double-bind" in those
disorders often classified as schizophrenic. He argues that such disorders
occur when a person is given two mutually exclusive rules and a
metarule forbidding acknowledgment of the contradiction. In ordinary
establishment of "mythic boundaries" by social, or "colonial,"
conventions, the metarule will facilitate acceptance of the idea that any
given conventions are natural and unalterable, because any alteration has
become literally unthinkable if the metarule is obeyed.

Describing his perceptions, da Silva says:

"Water start dream, rock and stone start dream, tree trunk and tree root
dreaming, bird and beast . . . "
"'You is a menagerie and a jungle of a fool,' Cameron's black tongue
laughed and twisted. . . ." (p. 111)

Cameron's odd description—"a menagerie and a jungle"—emphasizes
his understanding, which he violently rejects in attacking da Silva's

experience, of the coinherence in humans of the nonhuman animal and of the vegetable and inanimate world. Later, as tragedy seems to impend:

A groan rose from their lips to silence their half-hopeful half-treacherous thoughts that oscillated over their predicament. . . . The vessel had struck a rock. And they saw it was the bizarre rock and vessel of their second death. The life they had clung to and known before was turning into a backward incoherent dream of the first insensible death they had experienced. Even so a groan rose to their lips and a longing to reestablish that first empty living hollowness and brutal habitation. Surely ignorance was better than their present unendurable self-knowledge and discomfort. (pp. 100-101)

They do not want to know they are afraid. The basis of society—theirs and by implication society in general—is, it is suggested, a mutual complicity in deception and self-deception: "After awhile this . . . identification of themselves with each other brought them a partial return and renewal of confidence, a neighbourly wishful fulfillment and a basking in each other's degradation and misery that they had always loved and respected" (p. 100).[4] The crew members have struck the rock of their own self or soul, and their illusions about themselves are being shattered upon it. It is both death—of those illusions—and life.

It is actually because they have understood more than they know consciously, and more than they wish to understand, that the crew sinks into dejection. The rock does not destroy the boat: "They had forgotten the miraculous escape they had had and recalled only fear and anxiety and horror and peril. . . . There was no simple bargain and treaty possible save unconditional surrender to what they knew not" (p. 106).

One central image of movement in *Palace* is that of the pursuer pursuing the pursued. Initially, this means the pursuit of the "folk" by Donne and the crew. But in the course of the voyage, the situation becomes ambiguous, at times perhaps reversed. The "folk" may be pursuing the crew; the hunters may have become the hunted. Given the analysis in the previous chapter and in this one, the terms of conquest and desire in which the crew understood their activities in the world have been undermined by a developing insight into a profounder set of relationships.

This formulation is important in terms of the relation of style and content. The apparently unceasing action, given substance or "incarnated" in the verb "pursuing," constitutes the locus and the energy of both subject and object. Subject and object become aspects of a unity that is reconciled temporally and spatially in a kind of motion that, at the conclusion of the novel, annuls both time and space. Time, then, becomes reversible, as indicated in the quotation from Hopkins's "The Wreck of the Deutschland," opening Book 2: "The widow-making unchilding unfathering deeps" (p. 35). If time is reversible, then cause and effect do not function in the usual way, and the nature of both character and event is fundamentally altered. This permits, among other things, the repetition of the trip taken by the crew.

From the perspective of psychology, one can say we are dealing with the development of the conscious and unconscious in infancy and with their impact on adult functionings. I have called attention to the infantile aspects of Donne's character. The psychoanalyst Lacan suggests that, in a profound sense, desire can only be a function of the Real—that is, what is structured as real through the Symbolic order, which is entered through and constructed by, language. Desire, then, is a function of the Real and not of "reality" (that is, external, objective reality). It derives from the nature of language as a system that does not function like a system of integers. In a system of integers, there is a one-to-one correspondence: One chair, one person. But the signifiers of language can have multiple referents within the linguistic system, a property that allows for language's plenitude.

The distinction made here is that between the "countable unity" and the "unity of language." The trait of unitariness is a characteristic of countable unity, of one-to-one equation. To incorporate the desired thing psychologically, to incorporate it in the Symbolic order, its thingness has to be changed in such a way that it can function in a system such as the linguistic one, where one signifier can signify more than one signified. In other words, it has to be modified so that it can become interchangeable. In Lacan's words, "if the 'thing' exists in this symbolic structure, if this unitary trait is decisive, the trait of the sameness is here. In order that the 'thing' which is sought be here in you, it is necessary that the first trait [the unitary trait] be rubbed out because the trait itself is a modification."

But the taking away of the trait is the taking away of difference. It is the difference that makes the trait what it is, and with the removal of difference it is simply lost. The attempt to reproduce in the symbolic order of language something whose fundamental characteristics are incompatible with that order is doomed to failure; and the human being making the attempt, for whom "reality" *is* that symbolic order, is therefore doomed to frustration: "The key to this insistence in repetition is that in its essence repetition as repetition of the symbolical sameness is impossible."

In the very structure of repetition, the samenesss—which derives from countable unity, unifying unity, and therefore precludes its appearance in the linguistic system of signifiers— cannot be repeated. The subject is therefore a double: "In any case, the subject is the effect of this repetition in as much as it necessitates the 'fading, the obliteration, of the first foundation of the subject, which is why *the subject, by status, is always presented as a divided essence'.*"[5] (my emphasis).

The subject comes into being through the attempted repetition of something that is inherently unrepeatable and, were the repetition accomplished, it would entail the obliteration of that which is sought.

By definition the universe cannot be lacking in anything: "The subject is the introduction of a loss in reality, yet nothing can introduce that, since by status reality is as full as possible."[5] But the possibility, indeed the inevitability, of the notion of loss or lack is inscribed in the very structure of language. In other words, it is impossible to use the system of language without generating the notion of lack or loss. Such an approach has important implications for fiction, whose artistic medium is language. As we shall see in a later chapter, in Harris's theory the great importance of language lies in this fact too, for language is capable of generating the possibility of alternatives, of indicating the existing plenitude of reality, which preoccupation with our Real obscures. We perceive the universe as lacking, and the motivation of human repetition is the erasure of trauma or the repetition of pleasure, both of which, as understood in this context, are impossible and illusory because they imply that something is missing. Nothing can be missing. It is language that permits the human being to experience, as such, loss, lack, and desire—desire for the reparation of the loss and lack. Without language, certain states may be experienced, such as discomfort and ease. They undoubtedly are experienced by prelinguistic humans and other animals. But the positing of subject-object that introduces the possibility—indeed, inevitability—of lack, loss, and desire cannot be experienced without language.

Lacan believes that the root of all neurotic structure is linguistic twisting. It is in the order of the Symbolic, constituted by language, that all human self-definition and relationship as we know them occur. Language, that defining human property, is a particular kind of system whose characteristics require a particular disjunction and alienation from reality as opposed to the Real.

In *Palace of the Peacock*, linguistic association and plurisignation in the novel's narrative portions conspire to undermine the conventional subject-object delineations by which we linguistically divide and emotionally experience our world and that we allow to determine the framing of our objectives (a word that connotes an external object and a linear time frame within which cause and effect operate) and our desires. This undermining, as the textual analysis in this chapter shows, finds verbal expression in the increasingly disjointed, confused, and inappropriate attributions of the subject and object and of conventional delineations as the journey beyond Mariella progresses. One might describe the Harrisian subject as sliding its locus along a chain of signifiers in a linguistic system of the universe, which for the characters becomes *at the same time* a "countable unity where each object" is itself and no other and adequate to itself, and a "linguistic unity" in which the signifiers of the universe become interchangeable within the system. Much of the frustration and fear the characters experience in the novel arise from their attempt to arrest this sliding and to locate and limit the subject and object within conventional boundaries—to avoid the truth of Donne's cry early in the novel, "Look! . . . Every boundary line is a myth!" They fight for the centered unit that we are taught constitutes the human personality and for a relationship between that personality and the world, a relationship habitually defined by the exertion of power to gain objects of desire for the subject, a relationship that, so our societies teach us, constitutes reality and identity and must be maintained because our very existence depends on it.

Until the end of the novel, the crew members do not understand what the author wishes to show the reader: That the true object of their desire is the experience that breaks the obsessive-compulsive repetitions of perpetually frustrated desire, the chain of psychological and historical disasters arising from the repeatedly failed pursuit. This failed pursuit, as we have seen, is both personally and socially repetitive. After Cameron's death, the exhausted crew spends the night huddled in a cave beside his body; they are too tired to bury him. The next morning "they hurriedly abandoned him in the cliff, turning the room in which they had slept into his grave again" (p. 118).

Here we have again the room the narrator describes at the beginning: Maternity ward/operating theater/cell were all associated with it; now this arena becomes a grave as well. The assimilation of the cave to the body is reinforced in the next passage, which characterizes Jennings: "His face was no longer the same as before . . . the cheeks were hollow as the caves in the wall" (p. 118). This image is reminiscent of Laing's comment in *Politics of the Family* about his patient Paul. Five generations of twisted relationships had affected the boy's mind, and this was expressed in peculiarities of bodily movement. Laing writes, "His body was a walking mausoleum; his family had buried their dead in each other."[6] The members of the crew have come to understand the ways in which, through their complicity in one another's delusions, they created one another psychologically; here, with the assimilation of Jennings's body to the cave in which they have just left Cameron's corpse, they are buried in one another physically.

Jennings, who in the passage quoted above is still seeking a way to avoid insight, is presented in his relation to the "rock" (the natural world). Only a little earlier, attending to the Arawak woman's indications, Vigilance has a related yet radically different experience of these rocky walls: He feels himself becoming a webbed climber. The geological aeons are alive in the walls of the river cliffs. Fossils fly in the rock.

Near the end of the novel, Donne dips his hand in the river and, like da Silva before him, perceives that nothing is there. This is the man who cried at the beginning of the book, "Rule the land and you rule it all!" Images of the early stages of the voyage reappear, but their tone has changed, much as the tone changes in the altered proportion of similar elements in the two versions of Donne's death. Whereas earlier the river is described thus: "A white fury and foam churned and raced on the black tide that grew golden every now and then like the crystal memory of sugar" (p. 21), it is now seen in this way: "The sun rose into the blinding wall and river before him [Donne] filling the stream and water with melting gold. . . . The boat ran smoothly, until the stream seemed to froth and bubble a little against it. . . . The vessel seemed to hasten and the river grew black, painted with streaks of a foaming white" (pp. 127-28). The first passage evokes turbulence and rage, the history of the ravaging of the Caribbean for wealth, with its white pillagers in search of gold, a black tide of slaves, and the attainable wealth of sugar crystals instead of the fabled gold. The second passage conveys tranquility and clarity, an "alternative version," without the historical disaster that Donne in his rage has been repeating. Soon the voyagers arrive at the highest waterfall they have ever seen (Kaieteur comes to mind). On the cliff walls, they see that:

Steps and balconies had been nailed with abandon . . . making hazardous ladders against the universal walls. Donne looked at the engine and felt its work was finished. . . . Jennings and da Silva assisted him also in hauling the boat out of the water and upon a flat stone. In a couple of months it would start to rot in the sun like a drowned man's hulk in the abstraction of a day and an age. As he bade good-bye to it—as to another faithful companion—he knew there was some meaning in his farewell sadness . . . but it baffled him and slipped away from him. All he knew was the misty sense of devastating thoroughness, completion and endless compassion—so far-reaching and distant and all-embracing and still remote, it amounted to nothingness again. (p. 129)

This passage is reminiscent of the saying attributed to Buddha: That his teaching is a raft for crossing the bitter sea of birth and death. When one has crossed and understanding is attained, even the Buddha's teaching must be relinquished. [7]

As Donne starts the ascent of the ladder and scaffolding in the cliff, he remembers the house in the savannahs, understanding it as a "horror and hell he had himself elaborately constructed from which to rule his earth" (p. 130). He tries to shake this "obsession," climbing higher. He slips and falls with a noose around his neck. After he has regained his purchase and continues, "the shock made him dizzy—the mad thought he had been supported by death and nothingness. It flashed on him . . . that this dreaming return to a ruling function of nothingness and to a false sense of home was the meaning of hell" (p. 130). In other words, if one perceives nothingness and then tries to make of that a ruling function and a home (permanent locus), it is that, not the content of the ruling function, which creates hell.

Donne is seized by a desire to see "the atom, the very nail of moment in the universe" (p. 130). He keeps climbing the ladder through the falls "as a workman in the heart and on the face of construction" (p. 131). The "hammer of the fall shook the earth" (p. 131). He finds himself on a house, looks through a window, and sees a young carpenter. "He hammered again loud to attract his attention, the kind of attention and appreciation dead habit had taught him to desire" (p. 133).

His efforts are to no avail; the carpenter does not turn from his work. "Every movement and glance and expression was a chiselling touch, the divine alienation and translation of flesh and blood into everything and anything on earth" (p. 132). This statement echoes Donne's desire a moment before to see "the atom . . . of the Universe," even if in seeing it there was "frustration in that the distance between himself and It strengthened rather than weakened" (pp. 130-31).

Here, Donne and the young carpenter are doubled implicitly; the doubling becomes explicit later when Donne feels "it was he stood within the room and it was the carpenter who stood reflected without" (p. 133). Both passages imply a necessary contradiction at the very heart of being and creation, a contradiction akin to Meister Eckhart's "little moment" when entity stands Janus-faced to godhead and earth. But this alienation, like the two trips on the river described above, is far different from the raging, discordant alienation of the savannah kingdom and the river journey. It is an alienation necessary to differentiation, but it does not imply opposition and enmity.

Through another window Donne views a remarkable ageless woman with a child, and so looking melts into his own death with this understanding:

it was the unflinching clarity with which he looked into himself and saw that all his life he had loved no one but himself. He focused his blind eye with all penitent might on this pinpoint star and reflection as one looking into the void of oneself upon the far greater love and self-protection that have made the universe. (p. 140)

The angle of narration shifts. Chapter 11 opens on the seventh day from Mariella. The point of view is that of the first-person narrator, who stands with Vigilance "at the top of the sky" that Vigilance had "gained at last following the muse of love." Being is emerging from the Void, yet it is not different from it. The empty savannahs of the beginning of the book are taking on form: "A metaphysical outline dwelt everywhere filling in blocks where spaces stood and without this one would never have perceived the curious statement of completion and perfection" (p. 144).

The pursued "folk" in this novel represent the experience of the self in harmony with the universe. This is evident on the level of plot, and it is evident from the intuitions of various members of the crew in the course of the journey. Thus: "They saw the naked unequivocal flowing peril and beauty and soul of the pursuer and the pursued all together, and they knew they would perish if they dreamed to turn back" (p. 73). And it is evident in the tale of Wishrop. After being saved by the Arawak woman, for no discernible reason he turns on her and kills her: "The curtain vanished upon this last act removing the web of death within himself. An eternity dawned. His victims had never perished, constantly moving before him, living and never dying in the eternal folk" (pp. 67-68).

The end of the novel constitutes a possibility of experience, on an individual and on a social and historical level, that will break the obsessive-compulsive repetitions of perpetually frustrated desire. Before the members of the crew end their second journey, they experience the world in a way similar to the kind of experience Lacan describes thus:

The question of desire is that the fading subject yearns to find itself again by means of some sort of encounter with this miraculous thing defined by the phantasm. In its endeavour it is sustained by that which I call the lost object that I evoked in the beginning—which is such a terrible thing for the imagination. That which is produced and maintained here, and which . . . I call the object, lower-case, a, is well known by all psychoanalysts as all psychoanalysis is founded on the existence of this peculiar object. But the relation between this barred subject with this object (a) is the structure which is always found in the phantasm which supports desire, in as much as desire is only that which I have called the metonomy of all signification.[8]

The final paragraph of the novel reads:

It was the dance of all fulfillment that I now held and knew deeply, cancelling my forgotten fear of strangeness and catastrophe in a destitute world. . . . I felt the faces before me begin to fade and part company from me and from themselves as if our need of one another was now fulfilled, and our distance from each other was the distance of a sacrament, the sacrament and embrace we knew in one muse and one undying soul. Each of us now held at last in his arms what he had been for ever seeking and what he had eternally possessed. (p. 152) [9]

As this beautiful passage indicates, the crew members have attained an understanding that bursts the bonds of the Lacanian torus.

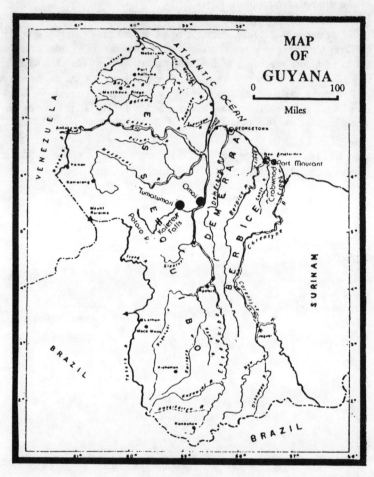

Fig. 4
Rivers and Localities in Guyana
Referred to in Harris' Fiction

5
Tumatumari: The Great Game

"We play the game of history, my child."
Henry Tenby,*Tumatumari*, p. 127

"History never repeats itself but it never outlasts itself either."
Comrade Block at Port Mourant,*Tumatumari*, p. 74

The consequences of centuries of failure to resolve social oppression in Guiana are explored in *Tumatumari*. The oppressive relations obtain among races and between the sexes; the exploration is organized around shifting patterns of identification and differentiation within the collective psyche of a family. The principal locus of this reorganization of collective familial and societal experience is the mind of Prudence Tenby Solman. The almost simultaneous deaths of her newborn child and her husband precipitate her mental breakdown; the reorganization occurs in the brief period between these events and her suicide, which has a paradoxical quality of finally triumphant and redemptive sacrifice and rebirth.

The great game, the game of history to which Henry Tenby, Prudence's father, refers, is played out in several arenas. The individual psyche of Prudence is a distinguishable locus. But it is not conceivable apart from its place in the structure of the family pattern, and the family pattern is not comprehensible without reference to the social patterns of Guyanese society.

The narration takes the form of a complex set of flashbacks during
Prudence's breakdown. The organization of the narration reveals
Harris's idea of the way in which collective trauma, and the individual
trauma to which it gives rise, may be translated into memory and into
art.

The daughter of a respected, highly conventional historian, Henry
Tenby, and his even more conventional wife, Diana, Prudence grew up
in Georgetown as a member of the urban, coastal bourgeoisie. Her
crisis occurs in the Guyanese interior at Tumatumari, where, about a
year before the novel opens, she has come to join her half-Amerindian
husband, Roi Solman. He is an engineer supervising a crew of local
Amerindians; he sees himself as involved in an important historic task,
"the electrification of the Amazon."

The Tumatumari site, overshadowed by Konawaruk Mountain, is
deep in the interior; the roaring waters of a rapids break on the
"Sleeping Rocks"—Tumatumari, in the local Amerindian tongue—near
the camp.[1] While exploring the area around the Tumatumari site,
Prudence discovers an abandoned well. The remaining ledge of stone
becomes her favorite spot to sit and reflect. Later, she learns that Roi
fell down here and injured his head. In the course of the novel the place
is called The Chair of the Well and The Chair of History (after the chair
on which her father sat when he held her as a child); Prudence identifies
it as the place where her psychological "conception" and "birth" occur.

But trouble comes. The Amerindian crew takes the appearance of a
mysterious file of Indians as an ill omen. Both the crew and Prudence
believe that Roi has impregnated Rakka, the Amerindian servant,
although Roi denies this. The appearance of the Lost Tribe of the Sun
confirms the Amerindians' feeling that the crossing of boundaries
indicated by this miscegenation is evil. The crew deserts. In a
desperate gamble to get them to return to work and save the engineering
project from failure, Roi resolves to exorcise the evil by playing the
sacrificial role of scapegoat in the Ceremony of the Rock, a role a half-
caste must fill. Prudence warns him of the danger in treating the
Amerindian beliefs in such an instrumental way.

Roi is away on an expedition when he hears of the birth and death of
Prudence's child. He rushes to return. Camped on the far bank of the
river from the house, unwilling to wait for morning, he tries the

crossing alone in the night. His boat crashes in the rapids, and he is decapitated on the Sleeping Rocks of Tumatumari.

The two basic components of Prudence's psychological reevaluation during her breakdown are confrontation with Guyana's African and Amerindian heritages. Her parents' lives were dominated by a veneration of the values and symbols of Euro-America. Diana, her mother, who grew up in Canada and could pass for White, is an ardent enthusiast of the British royal family. Henry, her father, who is visibly of mixed racial ancestry, was educated in the United States and Europe at the cost of great sacrifice by his father, a struggling rice farmer. For them, the good, the beautiful, and the true are to be found in Euro-America. The rejection of the Caribbean self, the fear of Caliban, is carried to its most sinister extreme in Diana's rejection and mistreatment of the darkest child, their only son, Hugh. Henry acquiesces in this rejection of son and self.

Their behavior indicates that the location of personal value lies in rejecting the truth of the physical self, and the location of social value lies in rejecting the truth of the Guyanese historical and cultural self. Henry's public and professional life has been as hypocritical and destructive as his private life. He remains passive during periods of political repression by Britain and tailors his historical writings and policy recommendations to avoid disturbing the status quo.

Henry Tenby has been dead for thirteen years when the novel opens. He has bequeathed his papers to Prudence, his favorite child and spiritual heir. His true legacy, however, is a confrontation with the profound cleavage of psyche that her father's self-imposed hypocrisy and repression inflicted on him. This cleavage or wound drives such a division into his life that he experiences each of his five children as having had two separate conceptions. The first conception occurred in the Brothel of Masks, a secret domain and a region of psyche where he chose—like masks—the faces he presented to the conventional world and according to which he lived his life. Paradoxically, the true meaning of his relation to his children and to his society lies in understanding these profoundly false self-conceptions.

His childrens' second conception is the normal biological one. To borrow Laing's terminology, the second conception belongs to the biological family; the first, in the Brothel of Masks, belongs to the introjected family. The disastrous incongruity between the two kinds of family does not constitute only a private tragedy peculiar to the Tenbys but it also derives from and represents the cleavages and incongruities bequeathed by Guyana's painful collective history.

From her father's papers Prudence has learned that he attributed the distortion of his life and work to

fear of the deepest confrontation with the shackles of humanity, fear of the total transplantation of himself, voyage of himself, expenditure of himself, expenditure of all he possessed. He was Eurasian (Amerindian on the wrong side of the blanket) and though he never directly confessed it, afraid of his African cargo, African momentum, African legacy. (p. 102)

Prudence does not truly grapple with her familial and cultural inheritance, revealed in her father's papers, until her own crisis at Tumatumari. To meet the African legacy, she must confront the family's treatment of Hugh. She must also confront her sister Pamela's decision to marry a White soldier from the United States, immigrate to New York, pass for White, and put her Black child up for adoption. To meet the Amerindian legacy, she must confront life at Tumatumari and her relationship with Roi and the equally disturbing and ambiguous relationship each has with Rakka.

Prudence's growth in the novel pivots on patterns of familial equations she makes during her breakdown. The central equation is the doubling of identity she senses between her husband and her father: "different as they were in poise or carriage they shared indeed one vehicle of the imagination. They both appeared to her . . . like outriders of remorse—closely guarded 'secret' . . ." (p. 46).

This doubling has two sources. One is the intersection of Nature and Culture in marriage, especially in the simultaneous joining and separating of Nature and Culture represented by the incest taboo. The other lies in the two men's meeting of the social tasks history bequeaths them—tasks each fails to resolve and that pass to Prudence. In Harris's words, the whole burden of conception falls on her. Prudence succeeds in meeting the challenge—paradoxically, in the course of suicide.

I discussed in chapters 3 and 4 Harris's unusual combination of traditional, almost mythic, presentations of women at the same time that he introduces powerful variations. In *Palace of the Peacock*, Mariella is a defeated, subjugated, oppressed woman; a muse; and the most powerful, vigorous, initiating creative principle in the universe. Donne the conquistador turns out to be an androgynous, nurturant figure, a "mother" as well as a conqueror and ruler.

In *Tumatumari*, Prudence appears first as daughter to a historian; then, as her father wished, as wife to a "cultural engineer." The mythic elements are traditional. Roi is the huntsman, set the manly task of slaying game. In a role recalling traditions common in Africa, he, as Roi Solman—"King Sun-Man"—must play the sacrificial victim for the good of the "folk."

Yet the "game" Roi pursues when he sets out to hunt as his "first task" is also the "game of history." And Roi, like Donne, becomes an androgynous figure. At book's end, it is not father (Henry), son (Hugh), or son-in-law/husband (Roi) who fulfills this task, a task that in its mythic form is always a male one and in its current form—the life of scholarship, engineering, public policy—is conventionally a male one. Remarkably, Harris uses the metaphors of conception, pregnancy, and birth not to apply to male creation but to stand for his *female* protagonist's successful accomplishment of cultural tasks that in both mythic and modern terms are conventionally allotted to males and that the male characters in the novel undertake and fail. Her success is not by dint of roles as daughter, wife, or sister but by dint of her own courage. She succeeds in her own right—and the symbolism of her success is female.

The passage describing Roi's decision to attempt the river crossing conveys his enigmatic personality, which troubles Prudence from the beginning of their life together in the hinterland. As he stands ready to cross the river, a foremost concern is a flare-up in the border quarrel between Guyana and neighboring Venezuela. Venezuela claims the land on which the campsite at Tumatumari stands, and Roi reacts passionately:

Why the very ground beneath him and the very house on the hill where his wife lay across the river were involved; territory he had lit however flickeringly: his own matchless wilderness. And no one would take it from him he cried: deep exacerbation, physical exhaustion, the long journey he had made, half-dreaming, half-waking bridges of sleep. The engineer within him like a subterranean spirit of desire drew close to the surface of his mind and he sprang to his feet. (p. 18)

It is the "engineer within him," which he identifies later as his "devil," that drove him to bring flickering light to the backlands. It is this devil that impels him to quit the borderland of sleep and try the night journey across the river, which ends in his death. There are echoes here of *Palace of the Peacock* and Donne's drive to acquire and possess. In a manner suited to his name, which means "king," Roi speaks in the passage quoted above with insistent possessiveness of "his" wife, "his" wilderness. There are echoes too of the horseman's breakneck ride across the land, which kills Donne just as the Sleeping Rocks kill Roi. A passage in *Tumatumari* that refers to Roi as "severed head of ruler/ruled," recalling "the oldest uncertainty and desire in the world . . . to rule or be ruled, forever" (*Palace*, p. 14), and a description of Roi as an "outrider" also link him with Donne the Horseman, who outrides neither life nor death. Indeed, Roi's death ultimately results from a failure to respect the land and the people and from his attempt to manipulate them for his own ends.

Yet Roi's relationship to the land, to the Amerindians, to women, to the interior, is more complex than Donne's. He is half-Amerindian himself and mentions this as significant to him. He sees his own intentions as being progressive and generally benevolent, and at the same time he becomes increasingly aware that they are inadequate, even wrong, in the context in which he works.

When Roi calls for his gun after the desertion of his huntsman, raving that he must once again play the role of half-caste and outcast in the Ceremony of the Rock, Prudence calls him mad. "'Call it what you like,' he was beside himself. 'The death of the old king . . . the birth of a new creation. . . .' He was looking at her from a great distance" (p. 52). Yet Roi is aware of the deficiencies in his relationship with the Amerindians. Thus, when Prudence demands to know who the "wretched Indians" are, he tells her "'They're the conscience of our age . . . in this part of the world anyway'" (p. 35).

The Lost Tribe of the Sun, the mysterious strangers whose appearance precipitates the desertion of the crew, comes as a warning to Roi, too:

Who were the lost Indians of the sun anyway? No one knew. And yet clearly one had seen them and would continue to make news of them until one was brought to book for the use one had made of credulity/incredulity in the name of science, emancipation, industry all rolled into one (self-interest). (p. 34)

The Amerindians reject the intrusion into their world that Roi's impregnation of Rakka represents; Roi implicitly rejects Amerindia in his intention of deliberately manipulating Amerindian belief in the Ceremony of the Rock. The Lost Tribe of the Sun will continue its periodic visitations until the cultural dilemmas are satisfactorily resolved.

Prudence's recollections during her breakdown are heavily concerned with her heated discussion with Roi at the time of the work crew's defection. It is then that Roi tells her of the serious head injury he sustained in the fall down the well five years earlier. The company funding that project had subsequently gone bankrupt, and the undertaking was abandoned. In words equally applicable to the injury he sustained, Roi calls the financial abandonment "the final blow" (p. 7). This failure is important in the context of his telling Prudence of the Amerindians' "kinship with the Rock of the Sun which they had once made in their own light" (p. 32) but that "with the extinction of an original myth of creation after Conquest had retired into what was virtually for them their 'death' or 'sleep' of fire. They saw the sun now as an archaeological ruin . . . at the end of an age within which they had lost a primal vision" (p. 32). But Roi's scientifically advanced, "civilized" company has gone bankrupt, too. It is not the Amerindian myth alone that is out of resources. The conquest signalled the ultimate defeat of both sides of the victor-victim stasis.

The Lost Tribe appears to Prudence, too. She and Roi encounter the mysterious folk separately. Prudence sees them from the Chair of the Well as they file silently through the forest and glide away down the river in a corial, an Amerindian canoe. The reader learns that Roi "runs into" them under the waterfall. The significant phrasing sends images through Prudence's mind of the "scene of arousal," of sparks and metallic waterfall, of *"headlong collision"* (p. 34). Because of the nonlinear narration, these phrasings, which come to Prudence before Roi's death, become in the retrospective narration after it prefigurations of the fatal shattering collision with the Sleeping Rocks of Tumatumari. They also express the novel's metaphors of sexuality and reproduction. Chair of the Well (Western history-mythology) and Sleeping Rocks (Amerindian mythology-history) both represent an encounter with the past. A reconception and rebirth of both cultures is needed by both and requires the participation of both. Prudence's stillborn child, Rakka's ambiguous pregnancy, and especially Prudence's successful sacrificial suicide and rebirth must be understood in this context, which involves Guyanese ideas of the relationship of coast and interior.

Roi's affinity for the interior deeply disturbs Prudence. At times she can no longer recognize in him the man who courted her in the genteel Georgetown setting where she was raised: "His [Roi's] capacity for singlemindedness . . . seemed to her there within the artifice of society—an enormous hidden fire. But now in the heart of the interior it turned almost menacing" (pp. 21-22).

The crisis at the work site requires Roi to perform tasks that on the level of plot are mundane and yet are narrated to the reader and experienced by Prudence in mythic terms that emphasize his rapport with the landscape of the interior and his increasing immersion in archaic myth. Because his huntsmen have fled, he goes after game himself for Rakka's semimagical stew pot, which is never empty. Significantly, too, he calls not for Prudence but for Rakka to bring him his gun. When he goes after game it is described as "the first task he must perform in the absence of his huntsman" (p. 53). The description of his return suggests something close to a merging with the very geology of the landscape. He is half-naked in the heat, bent almost double, and appears to be crowned with the grinning tusked head of the slain boar he carries on his back:

The line of the mountains appeared now like a lofty crest of the water breaking its own wave ceaselessly . . . the vast waving outline of the mountains and the transparent ocean of the sky within and beneath which fell away other exposures, shorelines, crests and seas like interior jungles of oceanic worlds. (p. 53)

By contrast, Prudence's sense of alienation at Tumatumari is strong. It is increased by her estrangement from the reaction Roi and Rakka share when Rakka's mother dies. The older woman had refused to join her daughter in settling at the Tumatumari site, continuing to wander with her husband and a remnant band of nomadic Amerindians. She comes to visit Rakka from the upper reaches of the Potaro River, above Tumatumari:

The day began when Rakka's mother fell on the hill and died almost instantly, vomiting blood. . . . Roi declared noncommittally that the symptoms she revealed were those of chronic malnutrition. . . . Prudence was horrified at his and Rakka's acceptance of the death. (p. 21)

Prudence's reaction reveals her attempt to forge a bearable relation with the inorganic world and with organic processes:

Sometimes when she stared into his [Roi's] eyes and the memory returned of the ancient Amerindian woman lying dead on the hill covered in filth it was as if the horror of immunity dawned upon her—Archangel of Sewers—and she wanted in an instant of revulsion to slam fast the lid of the well. Who would in her right senses drink at such a poisoned spring? One drop on her lips was instant plague, death. Yet the old woman had drunk and survived all her life and subsisted upon the scum of the elements. Rakka had been conceived by her when she was fifteen. At forty-five when she died her body looked old as the hills, old as Konawaruk, her face made of wood, her eyes of stone—chronic assimilation of environment . . . subsistent upon poisons. (pp. 81-82)

Prudence is horrified by "immunity" because she understands that it is a kind of contamination. Physiologically, immunization is a process whereby one organism learns to live with another life-form by incorporating it. Paradoxically, one becomes safe from danger by accepting it within oneself.

Immunity and many other biological processes are significant metaphors in *Tumatumari*. One of the most important is pregnancy, which like immunity is seen as a kind of contamination. The basic analogy, on the individual level, is to the ways in which people see themselves in other individuals. Thus at one point Roi sees Prudence for what he was "—a pregnant vessel bearing within the treacherous soil of another" (p. 37). On the societal level, the analogy is to both cultural and to physical cross-fertilization in a society like Guyana's, with many ethnic groups and a history of miscegenation. Thus as Prudence's understanding of Roi's and Rakka's ambiguous relationship matures she begins to see that the significance of a fruitful union between him and Rakka lies in Roi's attainment of a psychic integration of his Amerindian ancestry and a cultural integration of two sources of power, Western science (electrification of the Amazon) and the resources of the Sleeping Rocks ("frozen sun"). At one point, in a half-dreaming state, Prudence identifies Rakkas as "the cradle of the

sun." At the same time she intuits the future birth and death of her
own child and thinks, "That Rakka could be Roi's mistress and play the
part of newfound child (lost tribe of the sun) seemed, at this moment,
to possess a primitive foundation of of rightness" (p. 43). This idea
differs from the patronizing attitude toward the "native" as "child."
Rather, the context here implies the Amerindian as "oldest ancestor"
who must be born again—reincarnated—as flesh and as cultural
continuity, before Guyanese society can have any true descendants.
This is the significance of the word play on the "barren" Sleeping
Rocks and Roi's insistence on a "barren Rakka," unable to conceive
because of a fall—as he fell, down the well.

Prudence's dawning comprehension of the relationship between
herself and Rakka is as important as her growing understanding of how
Roi relates to Rakka. In a fundamental sense, Prudence and Rakka
"impregnate" each other as much as they are (or are not) impregnated by
Roi. At one point when Rakka bends over her, she meets Prudence's
mouth with her "dreaming lips."

Adding to the complexity of relations with the Amerindians and the
interior is a paradox: At the crucial point when the work crew deserts,
Prudence, who feels estranged from the Amerindians, nevertheless
understands better than Roi both the deficiencies and the dangers
inherent in his treatment of the crew's beliefs. She warns him: "You
still don't see the rapids—how deep and swift are the emotions on
which you gamble for control" (p. 37).

This retort to her husband illustrates the double level—familial and
societal, psychological and sociological—on which the novel functions,
a complexity that Prudence comes to understand still more fully in the
course of her breakdown:

What had started as an adventure into the hinterland of ancestors (an explorer's
game, marriage to an explorer) suddenly turned into the night of the womb . . .
to put one's "history" together again was to begin for the first time to face the
dangerous game one had been playing all along (one's ancestors, one's family)
with nature. (p. 152)

Prudence's words of warning also become prophecy, for the power of
the Tumatumari Falls will shortly kill Roi. In the equation between
the rapids, the feelings of the Amerindians, and the feelings Prudence
discovers when she becomes an explorer not only into the Guyanese

interior, to Tumatumari, but also into the psychological interior of the
Guyanese mind as represented by her family, Prudence is also
prophesying her own death in those same rapids.

The warning, however, is not a warning to eschew the gamble. In
fact, the whole book conveys the idea that the gamble is the only hope
of awakening the "frozen sun" of Tumatumari, that guiding conception
that died for the Amerindians with the European conquest.
Electrification, associated with the person of Roi, represents science,
the set of concepts most distinctively characteristic of modern Western
culture. In the name of science, and by means of material results
obtained from applying the concepts to the physical world, *nuestra
América's* subjugation was accomplished.

The question of Rakka's pregnancy becomes a stimulus for the
understanding of the relations obtaining at Tumatumari as a doubling of
those obtaining years before in the Tenby family. Thus, Roi tells
Prudence that the Amerindian work crew, who walked away because
they thought the Lost Tribe of the Sun disapproved of miscegenation
between Roi and Rakka, saw "the incestuous barricade of families in the
name of virtue as FEAR . . . Fear of the stranger creeping in" (p. 71).
They are like Prudence's family, he continues; they want Rakka to
"pass" as "a barren woman," to which Prudence rejoins, "'This isn't true
at all—about me—my family. You have no right to say such
things . . . '" (p. 71).

Prudence's indignant rejection of Roi's remarks is belied by her own
recollections of her family. "Hugh Skelton knew from the beginning
he was born black," the reader is told (p. 119); and Prudence remembers
how, at their mother's insistence, he was

given the hardest chores . . . to perform. Sometimes when there were
distinguished visitors from overseas . . . he was told to go to his room. Play
skeleton in the cupboard. Cruel and absurd. Her father always protested but his
wife and daughters knew how forbearing he was and ignored him with impunity.
(p. 45)

Prudence's father, Henry Tenby, has thought of his son Hugh as the
"brick in his fist" (to which Prudence alludes in her musings). There is
also an "element of fear" in his longing for a son: "The black warlord
which might spring from his head, fully equipped. With a fist like a
hammer" (p. 130). This son is born like Minerva and personified as

Mars. To Henry, Hugh represents both the suppressed part of his personality, which is celebrated as being a gentle one, and the wisdom he has failed to show in many important ways. Hugh in fact dies as a "warrior." He is killed in the course of his political activity, attempting to affect the country's direction during a crisis that had long been building and that Henry Tenby, succumbing to his paralyzing fear, had never sought to avert in its incipient stages.

Prudence's recollections of her family are related primarily in two episodes. The first is a conversation she overhears at age fifteen between her parents and her older sister Pamela, who has just informed them that she is pregnant by a White disc jockey from the United States who is now in military service. She intends to marry him, move to New York, and pass for White. She does not understand her father's violent reaction, given his own toleration of the mother's attitude toward Hugh. But at last Henry Tenby starts to speak out, telling Diana and Pamela that he was "done for" years ago, "echoing" Roi's words to Prudence much later at Tumatumari that what he is doing (being an engineer) is capable of "doing him" in the end. Henry Tenby says: "'I must put up a front for you and for society. Propped myself up to serve your interests. . . . Wouldn't it have been healthier if I had *struck*?'" (p. 62). But Diana is having none of it, intent only on calming him down and calling for the doctor. She says "'My dear. . . . How could you hit me? . . . You're not a violent man. . . . Lie back . . .'" (p. 63).

Henry calls for an article he once published, "'In that bookcase over there. That's where I lie . . .'" (p. 64). His advice at the time of writing the article, he remembers bitterly, had been:

"Stick to what you know. . . . Bow to institutions. . . . The conservancies had emerged at great cost—capital and labour. They represented a necessary non-reciprocal historical nucleus, sugar above all, which must remain dear to us. Their design went back two centuries if one contemplated the earliest of polders and dams to withstand the floodplain of coastal rivers. . . . Hold it at bay."

p. (64)

Apparently Henry Tenby is talking about a joint project he engaged in with an engineer years before, a project whose title he now says ironically should have been "Sarcophagus of Industry." He goes on, in the same scene, to admit that he was wrong—"Christ forgive me"—in trying to impose common sense on the findings he wrote up, when "comprehensive spirit-level investigation (uncommon sense) showed the lie of the land rising and falling significantly, however gradually, however secretly" (p. 64). Henry Tenby believes that the revolution for which he hopes, the attainment of the "psyche of the new world," will not soon occur, for Prudence reads in his papers after his death:

Man lives in history and it will take centuries—whatever mask of emancipation he wears—it will take perhaps another thousand years of flight through space for him to emerge from the psychology of fear. . . . Decent people (so-called)—good people (so-called) are all trapped by Fear. Fear of race for one thing. Fear of sex for another. (pp. 103-10)

Henry Tenby knows that to overcome these fears will be both difficult and painful. Where these two fears are deeply interwoven—as they are in the saga of Guyana that Harris relates in *Tumatumari* and as Frantz Fanon suggests they are throughout the European-colonized areas—the psychological knots are compounded. This difficulty is especially evident in *Tumatumari* in Henry Tenby's relations with women in his life: Prudence, his favorite child; Pamela, whose racial and cultural defection through marriage precipitates his first open acknowledgment that he believes he has betrayed himself, his children, and his society; Isabella, the woman he met in Europe who is presumably White, his first love; and Diana, his wife. Prudence conflates her father, husband, and child who died at birth; Henry's images of the important women in his life shiver, shatter, and reappear fragmented and differently reflected and associated from their first appearances. Both processes constitute a form of doubling. Thus, only near the end of his life does he admit that Pamela is "the spitting image" of Diana. The resemblance extends beyond physical appearance. He is speaking of Pamela's rejection of all things Guyanese, and especially of Black Guyana. By implication Tenby thereby acknowledges that his wife, Diana, has in fact rejected both herself and him. The price she has exacted for being a loyal, loving, and supportive wife throughout their marriage has been Henry's consent to her denials and his acceptance of the "colonial conventions" to which she is devoted. The relationship is founded on a complicity in lies, evasions, and rejections concerning both race and sex.

The distortion of relations between men and women with regard to sex and race is central to the pathology of Henry Tenby's own marriage. He married Diana thinking her to be a sexually experienced woman of the world, an illusion that she deliberately fostered. On their wedding night he acted on this misconception and in effect raped her. Their relations were from then on insincere; neither understood the other:

He felt that she hated him but in fact just as he had misconceived her game before, he misconceived her sorrow now. This was clear to him at long last within the royal seal of death, marriage-bed of history. She did not hate him at all—she hated herself, shattering of an illusion. (p. 147)

Harris identifies the perversion of relations between men and women and the perversion of relations between races as being at the root of the psychological and social paralysis that he describes as arrested maturation. If the novel focuses most strongly on Prudence's consciousness and the equations she makes between her father and her husband, a strong secondary focus is on the relation between Henry and his daughters, Pamela and Prudence, and between Henry and his son, Hugh.

In Henry Tenby's uncommunicated grief over his son's death, conveyed only long after the tragedy, he makes an association between the lie of his life work (his historical writing), his relationship to his political community (shown in the phrase in the following quotation "to confirm his state or constitution, I + I = O"), and his relationship with Hugh. The last association is indicated when the title he suggests for an article, "Sarcophagus of Industry," is echoed in this passage:

Sarcophagus of industry in which he beheld the sum of all his hopes. Frozen capital.
    Sum and son of all his hopes—*Hugh Skelton lying upon his bier. Shot in the streets of Georgetown. Budget Riots 1962.* The shock of confrontation, of standing upon a frontier of frozen resources—frozen profits—broke him into two to confirm his state or constitution, I + I = O. . . . As if the score . . . had been fused long before Hugh was born in his own barren breath. . . . *Message for Hugh Skelton. This bullet fired by your father's rich kith and kin all races of endeavour—white + brown + black.* (p. 120)

In a brief passage immediately following, a passage whose quality as an almost bitter aside is emphasized by its italicization, the reader learns that Pamela goes to New York and there gives up for adoption the Black child born to her: "Pamela continued to pass for white: economically rewarding. But something in her she confessed died for good turning her into an ornament, lovely skin, lovely like the label on a box of soap" (p. 66).

Prudence, who becomes responsible for the necessary cultural reconception after her brother's death and her sister's defection, first undertakes the encounter with rejected ancestors. She does this by confronting her own reaction to the body of Rakka's dead mother and her own jealousy of Rakka and then through facing the unpleasant fact of her father's refusal to accept the "African cargo" in his ancestry and his collaboration with Diana in rejecting Hugh.

When Pamela tells her parents of her intention to leave Guyana forever, Harris writes that Henry Tenby "would have given his right arm to establish himself upon a watershed of time—one slope leading back into the abyss of slavery—the other moving forward towards a contour which invoked the past again but not upon a level of 'connivance,' rejection, 'conspiracy,' consent . . ." (p. 62). But it is Prudence who explores both slopes.

Henry and Roi are both described as owing a debt to their historical origins (p. 86). As the bourgeois economic system that arose in Europe amassed capital—congealed human energy—and turned it into potential economic power at devastating human cost, so did that social system exact a devastating psychological cost, both in Europe and in the colonies. This damage is revealed especially clearly in the personality of Henry Tenby. The enormous repression in the psyches of individuals in the society constitutes, however, an equally powerful latent energy for healing and growth as well as for destructiveness. In this respect it parallels the possibilities latent in the economic accumulation of the European society that colonized Guiana, becoming what Harris calls "spiritual capital." I discuss his development of this idea of latent psychological and cultural resources in Chapter 7; he casts it in a specifically African idiom in *Ascent to Omai*.

In portraying the inner voyage that Henry began but would not finish, into what is called "an immensity of origins," the novel invokes a litany of Guyanese place-names in a context of significant symbolism:

> ... lanterns which rose up here and there to greet one with a password—road to Mahaica, Mahaicony, Abary, Berbice, Canje, Crabwood Creek, Courantyne. Or a welcome signal of lamps which spelt a brilliant punctuation mark of industry upon the sugar estates domain. . . . These were, in short, the coastal defenses one expected to find which some three centuries (invasion and penetrative settlement) had erected against the inroads of Night—the womb of the Amazon.
>
> (p. 37)

Henry's journey through the night leads inland toward the "womb of the Amazon": "His destination was Tumatumari. But first he must turn into the ghetto of Canje—land of the runaway slave —in search of the footprints of Eve rechristened Pamela" (p. 37). Only thus can he come to terms with the "African cargo." But it is Prudence, not Henry, who arrives at the destination and who also makes the necessary detour through Canje, which was in fact the "land of the runaway slave." The journey must go through Canje on the way to the goal the conquistadors sought in El Dorado: Gold and precious stones, here the Rocks (stones) of Tumatumari, and "the buried lapis of unity" to which Henry Tenby refers in the scene dealing with Pamela's pregnancy and that is identified with the Sleeping Rocks of Tumatumari; *lapis* is Latin for stone, rock.

"Prudence" is the great bourgeois virtue and the central personality quality Henry Tenby has cultivated. "'Prudence is the watchword,'" he thinks at one point. Yet it is his daughter Prudence, of whom he says at a period of crisis, "'She'll find it [his article] . . . that girl has imagination'" (p. 63), who takes the enormous psychological risk that may awaken the Sleeping Rocks of Tumatumari for a new age. On one level, the generation to which Henry Tenby belongs and that of Prudence, Hugh, Pamela, Rakka, and Roi are "destroyed." No progeny survive in this novel. On another level, the very repression and distortion provide the power for the psychological breakthrough at Tumatumari.

This breakthrough is accomplished in the concluding book of the novel, a brief six pages, when Prudence's "translation," to use Harris's word, becomes as it were the true Ceremony of the Rock, as Roi is forced finally to recognize it, a game

which Roi had played with Rakka until it ceased to be a mere game and turned into a matter of life and death. His blood froze within the waterfall. . . . No longer a jealous idolatrous game, a business deal with the natives, a stilted house on a hill, a fertile or infertile illusion. But the trial and judgment of the soul of Prudence descending to meet him. (p. 154)

Conformity to external social convention destroys Henry Tenby inwardly. Roi goes through the motions of the Ceremony of the Rock, "playing" himself as half-caste outsider. He does this, like Henry Tenby, "for the good of the tribe/family," in the name of science, progress, the electrification of the Amazon. Roi's behavior is equivalent to that of Henry Tenby, who acts, he says, to "preserve the conservancies." But the price Roi pays is to play the game in earnest—as Prudence, instead of Henry, must as well. They play "the game of history," and it is a "dangerous game," as Prudence retorts to Roi when she learns that he intends to participate in the Ceremony of the Rock. History, society, and psyche will not be mocked, and they cannot be escaped: In the words of another character named Comrade Block, spoken at Port Mourant, "History never repeats itself but it never outlasts itself either."

6
Tumatumari: River of All Ages

> The great procession—river of all ages—paused in awe at the phenomenon it beheld.
>
> *Tumatumari*, p. 84

Tumatumari is constructed around the psychological equation Prudence makes between her husband and her father: "The ghost of resemblance stood between Roi and her father" (p. 46). A conflation of father and husband occurs in Prudence's memory and imagination when she sees an Outrider in the Well of the Sun: "It seemed at one moment to turn into a familiar shape [her father]—historian of the twentieth century: at another it appeared dense and unfamiliar, tribe or fore-head adopted-son, engineer of the twenty-first [her husband] . . . " (p. 79). Specifically, they are connected through her understanding of their relationship to Guyanese society. On one occasion:

> They both [her father and Roi] appeared to her at this instant of recall . . . like outriders of remorse. . . . Art of control. For the good of the tribe/family. Pass law. Virtue. Reins upon an underground imagination which they exercised over a lifetime of bitterness until from their own lips a heart-rending cry arose. . . . Was it the older man's senility or the younger man's madness, brain injury?
>
> (pp. 46-47)

The "art of control," for both Henry and Roi, involves a survival strategy that makes a virtue of accepting "reins" upon the psyche.

"Pass law" associates the self-imposed racism of Henry's decision to accept the colonial conventions of Guyanese society, with its "law" of "pass for white" if you can, with the externally imposed racism of such societies as South Africa, with its formal "pass laws" that reverse Guyanese meanings. Social mores are internalized to become psychic demons. The verbal association expands to signify barriers between consciousness and psychic depths, a recurrent Harris theme. For the phrase "reins upon an underground imagination." recalls the "shared vehicle of imagination" that links Henry and Roi together for Prudence. It recalls, too, the "subterranean spirit of desire" that impels Roi to take the fatal trip across the river.

Within the Tenby family pattern, Prudence had a special relationship with her father, which in turn makes her relationship with Roi, and his with her father, a complex one. One of Harris's techniques for working out the doubling and mirrorings of identity in the novel is to elaborate on Henry Tenby's seemingly bizarre idea that Hugh, Prudence, and Pamela each had two conceptions. Harris writes of this mental disjunction: "Where there existed such a spiritual gap—break in the metaphysics of succession—there was bound to be a material sale, lost contract, sacrificial grandchild, auction block of remorse" (p. 146).

The rich metaphor about the conceptions in the Brothel of Masks can be illuminated by the Laingian "introjected family" already described, that is, the complex of *ideas* that members of a biological family have about themselves and their relationships, as distinguished from the biological fact of their kinship; the metaphor applies to the family constituted by marriage as well as the one constituted by blood.[1] Roi is Prudence's husband and therefore stands in the symbolic relationship of "son" to Henry Tenby, her father. He therefore becomes associated with Henry's own son, Hugh, in a symbolic doubling and paralleling of a biological relationship. Our use of terminology such as "son-in-law" illustrates the complexities of this type of relationship that involves both Nature and Culture.

In this novel, Harris plays on a double meaning of the word "conception": As physical fact and as abstract idea. Both are important in the novel. The reciprocal meanings are suggested by the important insight of Henry Tenby's that "who" his children are in his mind has less to do with their physical conception than with his image of their conception in the Brothel of Masks. The disjunction between their physical existence and their symbolic significance to him results from the ethical choices he makes that set the course for his relations with his family, his society, and himself. Thus, Pamela, who carries self-rejection to its logical extreme, is conceived in the Brothel of Masks in the year that Henry "gives himself over to abstractions."[2] Henry eventually expresses his secret hope for a son who would be aggressive; Hugh is "conceived" in the Brothel of Masks in the year that Henry yields completely to the pressures of Guyanese "colonial conventions." These choices are made in a "brothel" because from the time of his relations with Isabella, the European woman who returns to haunt him in the form of another woman in Guyana (apparently East Indian), his relations with women are all determined by an attempt to purchase love and social acceptance by dishonesty, misrepresentation, and money.

Dishonesty in Tenby's public reactions to crucial events in Guyana, and in his relations with women, catches up with him on the road to Crabwood Creek on the Courantyne Coast of Guiana, years after he has returned home from the United States and Europe. Recollections surge up as he drives his family to a political rally. Many years will pass before Prudence understands the reason for her father's profound shock on this occasion.

Harris introduces the episode with a technique reminiscent of John Dos Passos and effective because it differs so strikingly from the style and tone already set in the novel:

> COMRADE BLOCK SPEAKS
> AT PORT MOURANT TO P.P.P.
> (Jagan and Burnham may attend)
> Prudence was eleven/twelve years old.
> The year 1952. (p. 72)

The place-name reverberates: "Mourant" is French for "dying." The election campaign in which Comrade Block is speaking is highly significant as the last before nationalist leader Cheddi Jagan, East Indian, and Forbes Burnham, Black, broke with each other. Both were then politically on the left and thought by the British colonial authorities to be "subversive." The following year Britain suspended Guiana's constitution, landed troops, and instructed the governor to rule by decree. The People's Progressive Party (P.P.P.) subsequently split along racial and ethnic lines, resulting in serious intercommunal rioting. Ten years after the Port Mourant episode, when limited self-government had been restored, riots broke out during the attempted imposition of an austerity program. In *Tumatumari*, Henry Tenby's son Hugh is killed during these Budget Riots. During all the years between Port Mourant and the riots, Henry had remained silent about public affairs, and his silence had begun long before.

On the way to the rally, Henry Tenby narrowly misses running down an emaciated peasant woman, presumably East Indian, adorned with bracelets and anklets of gold; Comrade Block seems to refer to this incident in his speech. Henry and Diana Tenby are outraged by his suggestion that an East Indian woman has been callously killed; the crowd is outraged by the assumed careless killing. Neither the Tenbys nor the crowd understand the metaphorical nature of Comrade Block's address. He is talking about relations between the sexes in Guiana specifically but is also using the episode as an example of more general social relations when he says:

You may not believe it but that woman with gold on her legs was the ghost of love telling us we are all grasping and selfish to the bone. . . . East Indian, Amerindian, African, Portuguese, Chinese, European—It's all bloodywell the same. In death she has acquired immunity from race. Zero. She has fled to eternity. But in life she had to pass. To work in the rice industry she had to pass. *Brownskin. Straight hair. Grass-skirt.* To work in a British or Canadian bank she had to pass. *White skin. Middling hair. Looks like straw.* To work in anybody's brothel she had to pass. *Clean skinned. Grease her palm.*

(pp. 75-76)

Harris thus presents observations about the effects of history on the human psyche in terms normally reserved for the impersonal fields of economics and history. This technique constitutes a reversal of an earlier presentation of Roi's understanding of the state of development of the human emotions and psyche. This first presentation is phrased in terms of the contemporary political situation of the South American continent, when Prudence sees him as "bound . . . at the heart of a continent" (p. 81).

Comrade Block's speech constitutes a resounding indictment of the position Henry Tenby had taken in a scholarly paper he wrote but never published. Because of the nonlinear chronology of the novel, the reader already knows during the scene with Pamela and Diana when the paper is discussed that Tenby will ultimately criticize his own apolitical stance. Chronologically, however, his indictment follows Comrade Block's speech by three years and, again because of the novel's nonlinear chronological structure, it "echoes" words Roi speaks to Prudence almost twenty years later concerning the management of labor in the interior.

Block's speech and its aftermath come when Henry Tenby is already far along the road of "spiritual demise." Harris lays out the "humiliation, frustration, and terror" (p. 131) of Tenby's generation and social class in a roll call of actual political events during this period, when England arbitrarily restricted Guianese liberties:

The year 1926. . . . He had not resisted measures by the Crown through its law officers to muffle and disqualify a Popular party—measures followed by the dispersal of the old Court of Policy and the assumption of undemocratic powers by the Governor of the Colony. The year 1953 (Year of the Battle of the Unions)—he was already a sick man, apathetic it seemed to the suspension of the Liberal Constitution. (p. 132)

The year 1953 is the year after the ambiguous accident on the Courantyne Coast on the way to Comrade Block's speech. Henry Tenby is deeply shocked by the near accident, but his reaction is intensely personal rather than specifically political. The woman he almost hits reminds him of Isabella, whom he met in post-World War I Europe. Recollections and evaluations that break the barrier of his repressions merge with reflections on the near accident: "Loved her. A near thing. An inch more . . . met her as a student in Marseilles. We traveled to London. . . . Put a smooth face on it. Keep the mask in place. Conceal the sickness, corruption. . . . *Reject*. Smooth operation. Slam the bloody brake . . . " (pp. 75-76).

Henry Tenby "falls in love" with Isabella, but he also "buys her love," for the war has left her impoverished and hungry. Henry's money, though little, looks like much. Furthermore, to keep her he does not tell her how little it really is, "muck and metal," scraped from his father's Guianese rice fields. Then, one night in London, Isabella steps out ahead of him on the Thames embankment and disappears forever.

Racial and economic exploitation, with their profound sexual ramifications, become symbolic in *Tumatumari* of relations between

men and women generally, mediated by images of gold and the wealth
of the soil—"muck and money": The gold bracelets and anklets on the
trembling arms of the East Indian peasant woman who is almost run
down on Crabtree Road and who becomes the subject of Comrade
Block's tirade and Henry Tenby's soul-searching, and the gold chains
(largely the product of Henry's guilty imagination) with which he
sought to bind Isabella to him, taking advantage of her hunger. These
gold chains failed to hold love.

When Henry returned to Guiana after World War I during the
Depression, he began "shopping in the womb of place for the mask of a
lifetime—the mask of virtue" (p. 93). He became known as a quiet,
thoughtful, and gentle man. But he had an inner life that was "peculiar
to himself—he kept to himself for conversation with devils—dark
corner—heresy—bargain counter of flesh" (p. 93).

From some of her father's writings, Prudence becomes aware that
Henry had perceived the historic oppression of women and, like other
men of his time and place, feared a reversal of roles:

"LOOK"—he pointed at the ROCK HEART of the well—"*there they go*"—the
fabled women of dream beneath all polished exteriors, Brothel of Masks. . . . No
longer devouring male upon scarce female but devouring female upon passive
male. (p. 104)

The "psyche of history," Henry had believed, although he never
shared that thought with anyone, dreams of a situation in which the
"renovation of premises" will "suspend or reverse the humiliating
circumstances of the past" (p. 104). These circumstances include the
oppression of women. He confesses to himself the necessity of making
the "full circle" of psyche; the only way out is *through*. These ideas are
developed with subtlety and sensitivity as a part of the description of
Prudence's attempt to understand the meaning of her father's masks.

Upon his return to Guiana from North America and Europe, Henry
Tenby's assumption of masks, as Harris puts it, has disastrous
repercussions in three areas of his life: The public or political sphere,
his relation to his work (inextricable from the first since he is a
historian), and his relations with his family. Prudence becomes aware
of the first and second while going through his papers after his death.
She not only finds a play and an article, both unpublished (abortive),
but she also learns of his ongoing private dialogue with his

imagination, conscience, or muse, which variously appears as "the muse of history," "psyche of the new world," and under Henry Tenby's personifications, "The Waif of the Streets" or—abusively—"the little bitch." He is "struck dumb" in his writing when he refuses to take the Waif's suggestion that he speak out against Guianese racism and colonialism. The Guianese situation, especially as concerns Black Guiana, is represented by a bawdy folktale, and Henry Tenby has the idea of blaming this embarrassing and scandalous "cultural rumor" on her. The Waif responds:

"I don't understand. Why don't you report the unvarnished truth that I saw? . . ." Henry Tenby paused. As if to contemplate a way of compromise—a postponement of confrontations. It was a fatal choice, fatal miscalculation. He opened his mouth to speak but his tongue was seized by the Waif of the Streets. (p. 107)[3]

Henry Tenby's mask slips for the first time in the episode with Pamela. It slips for the second and final time on his deathbed, soon after his sixtieth birthday. Prudence, then seventeen, is the only person at home when he stumbles and starts to fall. She holds him up and helps him to his bedroom. Disgusted with himself and partially delirious, he strikes out at his favorite daughter, catching her on the forehead:

His expression was so twisted he became a creature cloven in two, one face on top mask-like as before, the other face beneath emerging from the old. . . . "Anything I would give," he cried, "for a new start. . . . What have I done to deserve this . . . pain, clarity, remorse? My black . . . white . . . children . . . Divided. . . ." He lifted his hand to strike his own progeny, generations of inbuilt prejudice, histories, volumes under which he suffocated. . . . Her father was dead. (p. 45)

Years later, pregnant at Tumatumari, Prudence wonders: "Would her child be black or white? She herself was mixed and so was Roi. And in families of mixed race it was normal to find brown sisters and fair brothers or vice versa" (p. 44).

Henry's reference to his divided family suggests no reconciliation with Pamela. However, Pamela is also the "space" within which Prudence, as artist-creator, can follow the alternative route implied by her father's choices. By undoing "the lie of the land" (as he phrases it), she gives him the chance to live again that he cries out for on his deathbed. This reciprocity of art and life, of word and flesh, the word *made* flesh, finds powerful expression in such passages as the following, in which Prudence reacts to Henry Tenby's death:

Wake up She [Prudence] cried. Deathbed Scene. His heart lay by his side like his fist on the battlefield of a book. Torn play. As if he were truly exhausted . . . torn lines, ravages of flesh . . . pages he had forgotten to burn which were secretly therefore astir within their own right—waif of the streets blown hither and thither—Gorgon of love he had invoked—which would turn each and everyone into a sheaf of Remorse, rose and splintered bullet under its glance—rock page, eggshell. (p. 124)

As we have seen, the "Ghost of Resemblance" that links Henry and Roi so closely for Prudence also merges Roi as son-in-law, a sibling, with Henry's son, Hugh. The idea is developed through a complex series of associations; in averting his eyes from the African past, Henry

confessed to something upon which he, too, collided (metaphysical Rock). . . . The death of Roi: conception of Hugh Skelton (Who-you Skeleton). . . . SHIP OF THE WAIF. As its timbers crashed upon his bed he saw his own signature upon their death-warrant—nightmare death-warrant, son of the future, son-in-law of the future—ultimate treaty of sensibility to which he moved, as it were, by degrees of marriage to the muse of history . . . psyche of a new world. (p. 103)

The "who-you" is the cry of the bird in the bush that Prudence hears after her breakdown. The death of Roi becomes a rebirth of Henry's son Hugh, brought about by Roi's collision with the Rock of History. Mention of the Waif in this context, of course, serves to associate Roi with the Waif of the Streets, who had proposed to Henry Tenby that he "tell the unvarnished truth" about Guianese society. Henry had rebuffed her as a "little bitch," with the result that she "seized his tongue." He is silenced, as a man and as a writer, until Prudence frees him by facing, "translating," and rewriting the history he has created as "the lie of the land."

Both Henry Tenby and Roi Solman, though sensitive to the tensions of their situation, feel bound to uphold "colonial conventions" because of the specific historical conditions and place of their births: "he [Roi] dreamt his age was an age of marvel and transition. Copernican alienation of cultures. Yet it remained premature to look too far ahead through the cleavage of horizons." So, Roi asked, "What alternative had he therefore but to continue to prop up an ailing centre in the name of rules he knew to be obsolete?" (p. 81).

The following passage consolidates the imagery linking father and husband with the spiritual conception Prudence is undertaking in all their names, seated on the birthing chair of the Well:

The engineer of the well of science—husband of scarce resources—was equally part of it. They—the old and the young—were related like fabric which collided and broke and yet in falling acquired a new shape and command. Metamorphosis of the game—tongue of the rapids. . . . Rock Spirit. Father Spirit. Husband of Scarce Resources. Tribe of the Sun. (p. 124)

In a passage quite early in the novel, Harris introduces "in embryo" many of the principal images and ideas that he later develops:

The head of ruler or ruled severed in a flash. . . . One was tempted to erect a model of self-deception within which to harden oneself against the womb of time, against the decapitation of the ghetto . . . against a "secret" conception of nature and society overthrowing all things, a "secret" violation of incestuous premises reflecting the deepest alien unity of mankind. (p. 67)

Here we have Roi's death at Tumatumari; Pamela, the "model of self-deception," who is described as having "hardened" herself against "the face in the womb"; and Roi, raving of the "decapitation of the ghetto" at the end of an age. These, and the themes of violation and alienness, "conception" of Nature and Culture, all evoke overtones of the anonymous quotation that Harris uses to introduce the novel:

The half-world is the world of the shadow wherein the union of nature and society violates and kills the incestous image. An enormous mourning camouflage develops around the occasion, an occasion that is itself lost in deepest correspondence with what is lost and alien and dies to be reborn. (p. 8)

In *Tumatumari* we find most of the symbols that recur in Harris's early fiction. The clothing of conceptions and of souls with flesh, here equated with love in the human realm (or at least love expressed in the human realm through flesh), the Eye and the Scarecrow both (soul's straw, stuffed man); and the elusive and compelling intuition, so close

to Marx's in the first chapter of *Capital*, of the reciprocity, the
interchangeability, the conceptuality of money, economics, social
arrangements, and the fetishized ideas that freeze the movement of the
human heart.

Later in the novel, in a passage that unites many of the images,
Harris writes of Prudence and Henry Tenby:

Her father's mask grew tight across his brow like a shell—the shell of the sun in
the sky—an intercourse of elements. The father of history was an egg upon
which hands and feet were mothered by infinite tragic design. . . . Upon it—the
skin of the shell—Prudence breathed her inscriptions of tenderness—the curved
shell of her lips, a baby's mask of flesh—all the appurtenances of anatomy. In
addition she drew . . . the landscape in which he rested . . . hills and plains in
relief. An imperishable inheritance and vista. Total harmony of intention from
a grain of his hair to grass or leaf. (p. 112)

This act of mothering becomes a reversal of the act of fathering, of
the "inscription" made on the egg by the sperm. It evokes images of an
androgynous reproduction. We see here the interpenetration, mutuality,
and reciprocity of earth and flesh, of landscape and the human body, of
word made flesh.

In this novel, Harris does not employ to the same extent as he does
in *Palace of the Peacock* the dense interweave of verbal cross-
association. He relies more on image systems and metaphor than on
the paradigmatic aspects of language. The novel is divided into five
books, each subdivided into chapters whose numbering is continuous
throughout. The title of each book indicates one of the image systems
around which the novel is organized: Book 1, "The Mask of the Sun";
Book 2, "The Ceremony of the Rock"; Book 3, "The Chair of the
Well"; Book 4, "The Brothel of Masks"; and Book 5, "Conception of
the Game." None of these image systems is confined to the book that
bears its name. Indeed, one of the main principles of organization of
this dense and complex novel is the manner in which the image
systems are cross-associated throughout. The principal metaphors used
in developing these image systems are as follows:

1. Hairline fracture, appearing in the book as: Wound (for instance, Henry
Tenby's psychological cleavage represented by the double conceptions of his
children); Roi Solman's fall down the well, when he hit his head, leading

Prudence to suspect brain damage and insanity (yet she acknowledges that it is precisely because of this injury that she loves him); geological fault (earthwound); horizon (cleft of night and day); and (implicitly) genitalia, both male and female, which contain a potentially fruitful cleft, split, or space. Fracture, flaw, horizon are opposed to consistency, solidity, and are thus related, in the larger arena of Harris's thought, to the dialectic of victor-victim, stasis-movement, and the contrast between the "novel of consolidation or persuasion"—the classical nineteenth-century novel of bourgeois society—and the novel that meets the need for a new vision by using language to evoke mental images that will overturn old ways of thinking. "Hairline fracture" is one of these images.

2. Sun, mask, fetus/newborn.

3. Digestion, excretion, ingestion (both nourishment and poison), resorption, birth.

4. Marriage, the unifying metaphor.

During a conversation at Tumatumari, Roi asks Prudence if his "sceptical law" and her "sympathetic love" must not "restructure themselves through dislocation, poison, fissure, weakness . . . Prudence has already felt her unborn baby to be an "alien fountainhead" (p. 44). This imagery supports the central metaphor of marriage. Marriage is understood as that "union of nature and society" mentioned above and of which Harris writes: "Violence (no longer monolithic) became subordinate to 'life' (declaration of marriage between objects in space) . . . sheer undiluted movement and expression" (p. 242).

This definition of life as marriage and its description as process (movement and expression) show the opposition between the Rock of History, the Sleeping Rocks of Tumatumari, "dead blast furnace of the sun" on one hand and "life" on the other. Rock of History, Sleeping Rocks, and furnace, frozen by the Gorgon of "colonial conventions," must be quickened out of stasis into growth. Life, "no longer monolithic," free of the Rocks (liths; Greek lithos, stone), or "Gorgon of love" as Harris also calls it, can move again. The passage further reinforces the novel's emphasis on psyche as process rather than a static pattern of individual separate, personalities.

The ideas of hairline fracture (associated with the geography or geology of the Guyanese interior), mental breakdown, horizon of historical past and future (signposted significantly by Black and Amerindian Guyana), brain damage, sun (with its association to the idea of horizon, which may be conceived as the hairline fracture or fault out of which both night and day are born), and mask are all drawn together through complex associations within the mind of Prudence. They are furthermore given an ethical dimension, for a sense of choice is suggested:

There were two proportions of "post-natal" breakdown in which Prudence was involved. . . . *On one hand* she found herself searching for a concentration or location of loss to serve as a medium out of which a new illumination of feeling could emerge. . . .
   On the other hand she found herself divided upon a hairline of clarity so extreme it made her despair of the very foundations she wanted to find. (p. 17)

This passage near the beginning of the book finds its echo near the end when at last Prudence has completed her psychic journey through inner space: "She now knew herself to have been blind up to that moment. . . . A fantastic reciprocity of elements which in encircling her had no alternative but to release her since it subsisted on a hairline or crack within the Obsessional Mask of an Age" (pp. 151-52).

Uniformity is equated with ordinary vision; it is contrasted with another kind of vision that is necessary to break "absolute consistency," stasis of victor and victim, and to begin the movement of "structure and fluid participation":

As if . . . the quality of one's vision rested much more on an alien fracture or sun than on a uniform pattern of illumination, that is necessary to recapture a profound intuition of both loss and gain, reconstructive order. One's blindness to uniformity, in fact, was the beginning of one's vision of a particular creative/uncreative humanity immersed in the origin of the sun. . . . (p. 69)

Particularity, opposition, and the potential for alteration and creativity depend on a certain kind of blindness to consistency and a sensitivity to that hairline fracture and to the possibilities inherent in collision. For Harris, these qualities are equally necessary for creativity in literature, society and politics, and psychological activity.

Harris employs the biological imagery of birth and digestion, health and illness, as metaphor. The physical manifestation of nausea is common to pregnancy, to illness from eating an indigestible substance, and to illness from eating a poisonous (alien) substance. It is

significant, in this novel of profound dialectical interplay between
opposites as conventionally conceived, that the body's reaction is the
same to the most intimate physical human relations (pregnancy) as it is
to the rejection of what is perceived as foreign and highly threatening
(toxins). Illness through infection by foreign bodies (germs, viruses,
pollens) enters in the description of the death of Rakka's mother, in
connection with an object symbolic of rectum, mouth, and womb:

The ancient Amerindian woman lay asleep on the hill. Her haversack or
warashie stood now on the ground beside her: its open mouth was half-green
with mildew and the items slowly spilling from it were equally fluid as a flame,
heap as well as pool of refuse—refuse of fire/sun—refuse of river/water. . . . Ash
and mildew. Phoenix. Vegetation. Flesh. Faeces. Endless proliferation. . . ."
(p. 22)

In the death of Roi and her child, Prudence for the first time comes to
an understanding of Roi's relation to Amerindia as symbolized by
Rakka's mother lying dead on the ground:

It was this [her awareness of Roi's debt to "this influx from the pit of hell" [i.e.,
the Well] that drew Prudence—a wavelength or contour which seemed to invest
the Archangel of Sewers within Rakka's world with something akin to a
hierarchical electrical function—an uprush . . . from the bottom of the
pool—from the depths of history. . . . A structure of involvement whose every
grain or element had been forged by an all-inclusive act, total grind, digestion,
assimilation. . . . (p. 83)

This "total grind, digestion, assimilation" relates Rakka to Pamela,
Prudence's sister.
As a child Pamela, like Rakka, had a fall. It resulted in a neck
puncture that interfered with her swallowing normally. At great
expense she had to be "put right in the States" (p. 61). All of the
characters have distorted relations of one sort or another with their
environment, natural or social. Rakka's mother "subsists on poisons"
and becomes petrified. Other characters suffer from nausea of various
kinds. None is able to achieve that constructive digestion that would
result not in resorption or fossilization of psyche (to adapt the title
Harris gave to one of his essays, "Fossil and Psyche") but in
psychological growth; Pamela's case is most extreme. Pamela is not
poisoned by her environment, nor does she find it indigestible. She

literally "can't take it in." Not only can she not "stomach it" but she can't even swallow it. She rejects it absolutely. Pamela is the least able of all these characters to assimilate her own environment constructively and to grow from it. Her father ruminates on the importance of "waste" to creation, but in social rather than physiological terms. The valuable refuse, to him, consists of certain groups in society considered worthless. When Pamela announces her pregnancy and Henry speaks out for the first time, he stresses the necessity of utilizing "every discarded feature, every creative scrap, every dunghill, every true inch of the way" in order to "release the lie of the land" (p. 65).

The single long chapter called "The Chair of the Well" contains a central image of the book. It opens with a dramatic view of a transfigured Roi being slowly pushed down the Potaro River, which is moving like a flow of lava and giving off a lavalike sheen as it drops over the Kaieteur Escarpment:

All seemed lost save for the grimmest *loci* of community he grasped—negative and positive poles, whirlpools: . . . these were *Prudence* on stilts of fire above him in her balloon of labour, childbirth, and *Rakka* beneath him like a sack of refuse. He stood halfway between them suspended in the volume of the waterfall—riven by an arrow of pain—divided by a hairline of sensibility. The circumference of fire and water revolved around him until it seemed that Rakka had changed places and stood above—ballooning with child—whereas Prudence fell below sweating in the heat or grind of the waterfall.

The great procession—river of all ages—paused in awe at the phenomenon it beheld. The arrow of diameter which pinned him to the centre of a dying world pinned in turn—above and below—Rakka and Prudence upon its circumference.

(p. 84)

This vision, suggestive of an allegorical painting by Hieronymus Bosch, continues:

. . . as if it drew a mountain of souls upon its spinning wheel which Prudence discerned now ran in concert with other revolutions—black histories and wheels—whose outline seemed so black it possessed a fantastic purity of sheer darkness . . . as if the wheels of the mountain of souls served to intensify on different levels the convertible legacy of wealth and illusion in *Prudence* and *Rakka* revolving beneath and above the waterfall. . . .*Sun-centre. Sun-wheel*.

(p. 85)

In this immense "wheeling" Prudence catches sight of a centaur figure which she recognises as her father which she sees in connection with the "political anguish of soul" he underwent. Through the bars that caged him, "reins of the devil, prison house—shown clear at last the political conescience of the race. . . . The debt [her father] owed his historical origins was so immense it addressed her as capital (p. 86).

In *Tumatamari*, the unifying metaphor, marriage, transcends this value to represent the enormous fundamental movement of the universe. The definition of the novel's title is part of the front matter introduced in the book. The literal meaning, "sleeping rocks", is translated (as Harris speaks of Prudence's "translation" of conciousness) from Amerindian, to English; The meaning of "Sleeping Rocks" has been discussed.

The sound of the second part of the word has a meaning in English: "to marry." (The auditory linguistic association is, of course, confined to the one language.) This cosmic marriage is fundamentally involved in the movement of birth and rebirth. In their capacity as male and female, Roi and Prudence play archetypical roles, Prudence in conceiving and giving birth, Roi as sacrificial victim, King of the Sun. Yet Harris's insistence on the quality of coinherence makes Roi androgynous: He experiences himself as a pregnant woman, and Prudence, with her "translation," becomes a sacrificial "King/Queen" victim as was Roi.

The cosmic dimension that the novel accords to sexuality and reproduction becomes something more than the presence of each in the other, something more fundamental, more universal, and more vigorous than a conception. It is almost like the exchange and entwining not only of bodies in intercourse but also of chromosomes. This is a sexual exchange and also the transubstantiation, translation, transmutation, involved in digestion. (Digestion is, as I have shown, another important metaphor in the novel.) The vigor comes not only from the reciprocity and the exchange but also from the result.

The novel is one of enormous process: The waking of the Sleeping Rocks, the electrification of the Amazon, the death of Rakka's mother, the death and funeral procession of the King of the Sun, Roi's death in the rapids as corollary of his part in the Ceremony of the Rock, the death of Prudence's psyche in her breakdown and its resurrection in her mental healing, the death of her and Roi's child, and that child's psychological rebirth in the psychological rebirth Prudence gives to her family, especially to her father.

The marriage metaphor is central in this process. It operates in the sense in which marriage is said to make of two one flesh, and then, with the birth of children, those two make of their one flesh another flesh. But marriage in *Tumatumari* is not confined to the relationships of a couple or even to relations within a family. Nor is it a metaphor confined to relations among racial and ethnic groups. It also represents the movement and process along a "hairline crack" or "fissure" that appears related to what Harris called in *Palace of the Peacock* "the atom, the very nail of moment in the universe" (p. 130). This movement and process constitutes an altering of relations in time and space that suggests an alteration in the arrangement of matter. The entire process is recapitulative, set in motion by the decapitulative process that ends Roi Soloman's life. It ends his life in "reality" in the novel, but in psychological reality, in the mind of Prudence, the process continues that was set in motion by her marriage to Roi and her undertaking of a double "exploration of the interior" in coming to Tumatumari and in reading (understanding) her father's "forbidden papers"—the inner truth of his life.

In the damage of her breakdown, along this hairline horizon, the process of Prudence's psychic reconstruction occurs. Space is related to an outline of weakness. Yet it is precisely these borderline breaks, cracks, faults, flaws, failures, points of weakness that Harris prizes. For him they seem like the weak spots along the seams of plants, which break, rupture, and split in order for growth to occur. At these points matter gives way to space, and it is because of these "flaws" that all creation is possible. "Break in order to build, " Henry Tenby said (p. 41).

Harris elaborates the importance of absence and of space as vital loci of creativity that are often conventionally regarded negatively, as manifesting weakness and deficit without redemptive qualities.

In *Tumatumari*, space is furthermore clearly associated with the womb, carrying imagery of gestation from the image of marriage. Space is a womb: birth is the creation of something from nothing, going to nothing again with death. Similarities obtain between the process of gestation and the process of digestion. Symbolic associations are widespread in agricultural societies, for instance, in the equation between planting seeds and the phrase "fruit of the womb." In fact, in some animals if the conditions for gestation are unpropitious, a process called resorption occurs in which the fetus is broken down and reabsorbed by the maternal tissue. This reversal of the process of gestation, which involves a furthering and feeding of the fetus via the maternal tissues, is a striking example of the profound ambivalence and reciprocity of birth and death, creation and destruction, at the very root of mammalian physical existence. By analogy, the association of these processes is implied in *Tumatumari*, where space itself is both stomach and womb, evident in the opening passage of the novel:

The glazed anatomy of the sky appeared to her [Prudence] at the moment stricken of its true digestion of fire—of both native stars and sun—like a curious inner constellation of blindness at the pit of her stomach as well. Prudence scooped up, swallowed a mere thimbleful of water as if it were yeast and raindrop. She felt she had confirmed a hollow vessel of flesh in the opaque light void of the sky. (p. 13)

(There is a play on words in following the reference to "her stomach" with the word "well," given the symbolic importance of the unfinished well that Roi began digging at Tumatumari.)

Both Roi and Prudence die on the Sleeping Rocks below the falls of Tumatumari, but Prudence's psyche undergoes profound transformation before she joins her husband (and her father, too) in death. Throughout the novel, Harris employs the Gorgon's head as a symbol of hope as well as of horror. In classical mythology, to look upon the Gorgon's head—ugly and crowned with writhing snakes—was to be turned immediately into stone. Harris speaks of the "translation of the Gorgon into the Queen of necessity," with the implication that a courageous and unflinching look into the depths of one's own soul, and at the web of familial and societal relations, can result in the acquisition of enduring compassion. Thus, the Gorgon's head itself can be transmuted into love. The transformation, for society as well as for individuals, is not without pain:

Prudence stopped. There was nothing more she desired to say to the shadow of the waterfall. Nothing more to do save yield herself to its depths, let herself slip step by step, hand over hand from the nervous precipice of breakdown into the bottomless pool of memory. As Roi had been pushed until he descended towards his translation within the Rock of history—so she, too, began to yield, to let herself slide into the glass of river where she drifted secure and plunged. . . . The shadow of the Rock at the bottom of the waterfall (which had risen towards Roi on the night and morning of his death) now rose towards her—on the night and morning of hers—from the heart of whirlpool, community. (p. 153)

Tumatumari is grounded in specific historical events and specific characters in a social situation, as in a novel of classical realism. Exactly because the novel is firmly rooted in cultural conventions, which Lévi-Strauss suggests are the only tools we possess to construct a critique of our tradition, its exploration of their limitations acquires particular strength. Prudence's reconstruction of history—for the conception of that Great Game that ends the novel is the game of history—involves a revolutionized experience of space-time in terms of both history and personality. In *Tumatumari* this territory is explored as experienced subjectively by a clearly delineated human being in the process of the reevaluation that permits the transcendence of those delineations.

7
Ruin and Resurrection:
Ascent to Omai

"The rubbish of civilizations you mean. What a mess. . . ." "Yes, indeed. . . . But mess—rubbish—is invaluable. It is, in fact, a new experimental source of wealth. . . . Adam is trying to salvage or uncover . . . a sacramental vacancy within the flotsam and jetsam of a collective experience that has oppressed him. . . ."

From the trial in *Ascent to Omai*, pp. 72-73.

Of the four novels I discuss in this study, *Ascent to Omai* is organized most explicitly around Third World systems of meaning. In my consideration of the novel I focus on three principal uses Harris makes of these systems of meaning.[1] The first is his development of the meaning of "Omai," an Amerindian word. The second is his use of the West African figure of Anancy the Spider. This trickster figure of West African and Caribbean lore serves in his Caribbean embodiment of tarantula as what Harris calls a "robot of memory." His bite precipitates in the character Victor the freeing of the memory of a collective past. The third is Harris's use of African Osirian religion, which dates from dynastic Egypt and becomes the framework for Harris's exploration of the relations among life, death, and collective continuity. At bottom, Harris investigates the meaning of time and change; not incidentally, time is the subject of the "novel history" another character, the Judge, aspires to write as well as the conceptual framework of personality and communal identity. Using the ancient

Osirian religion also serves to express Harris's faith in the creative potential of the "rubble" of Caribbean history and its polyglot cultural amalgam. He makes a special development of the Third World particularities of belief. For instance, characteristics of the African resurrection that distinguish it from the Christian one are very important in *Omai*.

Harris's use of these Third World belief systems is unusual and especially significant for two reasons. First, he finds in the collective beliefs of Amerindian, African, and Afro-Caribbean cultures the terms to discuss cross-culturally relevant concerns such as the nature of time and of personality. Second, although much modern fiction by Third World writers reclaims Third World traditions, Harris goes beyond reclaiming tradition to reclaim values. He transmutes ancient beliefs into sophisticated modern terms.

Ascent to Omai has a plot, which can be identified as taking place in a particular Guyanese locale. Adam is a Black working man in the coastal urban setting of Albuoystown. His wife died at the birth of their son Victor. He had been warned of this danger, and guilt has driven him to alcoholism. The alcoholism in turn makes ever more unlikely his dream of leaving his job as welder in a factory and owning his own store.

Adam acquires the habit of bringing a woman to a single tenement room he and Victor share, after his long day of labor in the factory. The child cowers beneath a huge petticoat that had belonged to his mother, crying with fear and disorientation at the adult goings-on. Sometimes disturbed by his sobs, Adam reaches out and cuffs him through the petticoat, which thus becomes for the boy an only partially effective shelter but a powerful symbol of lost maternal security.

In school, Victor develops into a phenomenally gifted student. Then in his early adolescence, during a bitter strike at his father's workplace, the factory burns to the ground; their tenement home burns, too. Adam is arrested, charged with arson, and, on ambiguous evidence, convicted and sentenced to flogging and a long prison term. Victor, who has attended the trial, disappears on the day of his father's sentencing, and from that day forth the people who knew him never learn his fate; rumor has it he became a cabin boy on the ship *Osiris*.

The novel opens with Victor, now an adult, ascending a steep hill. Far above him an old Black pork-knocker climbs laboriously upward.

The reader eventually identifies him as—possibly—Adam. It seems that after his flogging and release Adam went into the hinterland and staked a mining claim at Omai, a small community in the interior. It is toward Omai at the top of the hill that both the wraithlike pork-knocker and Victor are now climbing.

Subsequently, we find that at the same time the two figures are toiling up the hill to Omai a plane is flying overhead. One of its passengers is the man who was the judge at Adam's trial, which, the reader learns from the Judge's extensive meditations, occurred in 1929, forty years before. The Judge is still disturbed about the event, first because there remained always some doubt about whether the culprit was Adam or his shadowy, doublelike friend Brimstone; and second because of the sudden disappearance of the child, Victor. Above all, he ponders the questions: "Why would Adam destroy the factory and tenement?" or, as he puts it, "Why would Adam 'burn bed and board?' " As his plane flies over Omai the Judge reviews "rapid gnomic scribbles" made at the first trial. They include a defense plea that he interprets as "a fantastic kind of pentecostal masculine feminine brooding light, charisma of motherhood (MAGDALENE), flux of fatherhood (CHRIST), voices within voices, lamentations and blues, Negro/Jewish/Toltec/ American/European, etc., etc. . . ." (p. 82). The Judge incorporates his reflections on these notes into his reassessment of the trial. The defense attempts to plead that the death of Adam's wife, the fire at the factory, and other diasters have unbalanced his mind but that under hypnosis Adam, the illiterate welder, has written a remarkable poem, "Fetish." Ideas from it become a part of the defense plan. As the Judge flies across Guyana and over Manoa, which is, according to legend, the location of El Dorado's Palace of the Peacock, he seems to have premonitory knowledge that the airplane soon will crash on Omai.

For Victor, the "ascent to Omai," where the plane bearing the Judge will crash, involves making the difficult climb in the footsteps of the pork-knocker figure who is possibly his own father. On the level of the plot, this opening scene represents that inner and outer quest for self and for community that Harris explores in *Palace of the Peacock* and *Tumatumari*. As in those novels, the psychological and historical "interiors" in *Ascent to Omai* are symbolized by the geographical interior of the South American continent. Omai is located inland. It is not part of the coastal, "civilized" enclave where Adam was tried and condemned. In this book, however, the emphasis on the hinterland shifts from its organic to its inorganic features: Geology is more important than river or rain forest. We see this, for instance, in a description of "fossilization" suggestive of an inorganic analogy of mummification. Some ancient Egyptian texts refer to Osiris, who is central to this novel, as the first mummy, so the association is striking. As Victor climbs, his eyes fill with "mineral tears, sandstone, earthstone, greenstone, rainbow, slate." He is experiencing "exquisite fossil. Magdalene of geology. It had taken ages of transference, evolution of fin, evolution of feather . . ." (p. 27).

The pork-knocker in front of Victor also takes on some of these inorganic characteristics. He is described in terms that establish interconnections between matter and mind, flesh and "inanimate" environment, already familiar from my discussion of *Palace of the Peacock* and *Tumatumari*. The bedraggled pork-knocker, dragging himself up the mountain, is called the "patron saint of the wasteland," a watershed "compounded of vague mists, vague solid: part moisture, vague sky . . . the diffuse character of the environment seemed to embody the figure of the scarecrow, ruined pork-knocker, ascending the hill. Rags of gold" (p. 15).

Ascent to Omai is divided into three books: "Omai Chasm," "Ascent," and "Omai." The first two tell the story in a relatively conventionally organized narrative line. The third book is a recapitulation, a key to the meaning of the first two. The recapitulation, or doubling, is at points an exact repetition of what has appeared earlier: what appears first as narration is presented later as the creation of the Judge (who may be Victor's double), in the same kind of movement as that which takes the reader outside text and beyond narrator to author by identifying Adam's poem, referred to at his trial as "Fetish," one of Harris's own early poetic works. This technique tends to identify author with character, erasing the gap between them. An earlier such erasure in the novel creates a deliberate ambiguity about who—Adam, Victor, Judge—was actor in which events. The ambiguity is achieved by shuffling and rearranging the same elements of event and character. This idea is symbolized by the Judge "shuffling cards"—a description of the way he handles his note cards on Adam's old case while reconstructing it mentally during the plane trip. As he reflects, speculates, and mentally rearranges past events, they collapse in on one another, thus collapsing spatiality, identity, and temporality. Harris further undermines linear time by such techniques as implying the piece of metal with which Adam staked his mining claim (after his flogging and his move to the interior) comes from an airplane—the airplane carrying the Judge—although the claim staking must have preceded the crash on Omai by close to forty years.

The central symbol of the psychological and historical interior is Omai itself. Omai is an "Amerindian word that has a number of meanings generally inclusive of mystical 'peak experiences.' "[2] The novel identifies Omai as a "mushroom" village in the bush, one of the frail, evanescent communities called into being and extinguished by the settlings and renewed wanderings of pork-knockers. Omai is also, by its sound—"oh my"—identified as the void and ground of the frail, evanescent, and creative human personality. Harris establishes the network of associations as follows: "Was it [Omai] a mirage of the senses, ruined faculty but therapeutic lighthouse?" (p. 20).

At the end of the first chapter, the lighthouse image returns in the term "illuminating conceptions." Much later in the novel the reader learns that the Judge hopes

to write a kind of novel or novel history in which the spectre of time was the main character, and the art of narrative the obsessed ground/lighthouse of security/insecurity. (p. 83)

By this kind of association, Harris suggests that Omai is a lighthouse and that the art of narrative is also a lighthouse. By the same association, the art of narrative is also "a mirage of the senses," a "ruined faculty." This concept of narrative is closely related to Harris's conceptions of personality and of history.

The "novel or novel history" (the play on "novel" as "new" and as a kind of fiction is characteristic of Harris) that the Judge wants to write is by implication the only fiction or history adequate to the "ruined faculty"; Victor, we are told, could "still discern . . . a frail multiform conception of unity, terrestrial and transcendental" (p. 22), a conception of unity akin to the "hairline fracture" of *Tumatumari*, along which rebirth occurs.

Harris establishes yet another set of associations when a sentence speaking of "a ruined instrument of unruined consciousness" continues:

"*persisting* through and within all ruined personality, like a salutary
lighthouse within and beyond desolation of claim, fortress or wall"
(p. 50).   These associations connect lighthouse/Omai with the
trial—for Adam's main defense was to be provided by a Dr. Wall. But,
the Judge recollects, for some reason Dr. Wall never actually testified or
even appeared in court.

The play on "claim" refers to Adam's mining claim on Omai, to the
claims of a defense and a prosecution in a trial, and beyond that to all
the claims that human beings make in defending their own and
persecuting other people's "personalities" (or prosecuting them, as in
Adam's trial), making personalities into fortresses.   The complex
significance of "personality" is clarified in this passage

. . . the light of grace, omen . . . this sacramental union of life and death . . .
pain and joy, opposite existences—exists fundamentally upon a curvature of
ruined personality within which we subsist by degrees, degrees of insulation
when we appear blessed with arbitrary fortune, degrees of annihilation when we
appear cursed by fortune. . . .

(pp. 76-77)

Personality is always "ruined" in that it is partial, a segment of a
curve, but it is not to be disdained for that.   Indeed, it is exactly in its
ruin that it is to be treasured: only there, in abyss or chasm (the chasm
of Omai, for instance), is it possible to find that which is not ruined.
This is so not simply because something whole is transmitted through
something partial but because the very wholeness consists in the
partiality, the completion in the ruin.

Memory—recreation of event and identity over time—becomes "a
delicate screen to sift a balance of natures" (p. 75) if restorative and
creative possibilities of the curvature of ruined personality are to find
expression. Otherwise one would have "psychosis, that is, impossible
self-rejection (total loss) or impossible self-fulfilment (total gain)"
(p. 75).   The disaster of total fulfillment can be equated with the
conventional idea of the victor: it is the ultimately suicidal goal of all
those bent on conquest, as is the case with the Donnes and other
conquistador figures of the world.   Harris has written that conquest is
the greatest evil man can inflict on himself or nature; we remember that
Donne, in *Palace,* is in Harris's words "self-devouring."   Total loss,
conversely, in the Caribbean context would consist of the complete

self-rejection inherent in identifying the Caribbean Self with the European Other. In *Tumatumari,* Henry Tenby manifests this kind of loss to a high degree.

Adam, Victor, and the Judge appear frequently in the first two books of *Ascent to Omai,* but the Judge (assimilated to Victor) emerges as the central figure in Book 3, reinterpreting and providing a recapitulation. The key to the recapitulation is in a symbolic statement of stages in Victor's psychological development: the seven movements of "the dance of the stone" as presented in the final chapter of Book 3. The stages are portrayed earlier in a diagram of concentric rings (prepared by the Judge) with the title "Factory of the Gilded Man" (see the figure on p. 134). "gilded Man" is a translation of "El Dorado." Movement from one stage to another—death and rebirth—is symbolized by animals and inanimate objects carved on a stone at Omai.

Meanwhile, the pork-knocker fascinates Victor. As he climbs he assimilates the known eccentricities of this Guyanese figure to another image, "saint and constable of the watershed." Elsewhere, an odd magical transformation is taking place among pork-knockers: "Sometimes they would appear quite naked in a village in the bush except for a constable's uniform they might whip from their haversack ... sometimes a cassock (of all things). . ." (p. 19). Pork-knockers embody and parody the officers who enforce spiritual and secular colonial conventions. Victor's relation to the wraithlike figure above him, and the importance of the ascent, is expressed thus:

As if one day he [Victor] would meet the ruined pork-knocker face to face, *doppelganger* of the heartland, and since their conversation would entail speculations about the death as well as life of history, immortal as well as mortal values—he must prepare himself by every means at his disposal for such a dialogue. (pp. 18-19)

The preparation for dialogue turns out to be a profound experience "thirty thousand feet up on the ridge of Omai; thirty thousand years down in the chasm of OH MY" (p. 49). Harris skillfully conveys the state of mind annihilating time and space that overwhelms Victor when he reaches the top, exhausted. In confronting these legacies, he is led to identify with his father. And when the dialogue comes, much of it is in

Fig. 5
Factory of the Gilded Man

("Heir of El Dorado, Black Welder" [p. 94])

1. Frontiers of conquest/death
2. Terrestrial/transcendental lighthouse
   [from *Ascent to Omai*, p. 90]

the course of the "(re)trial" of Adam in which, at times, Victor and the Judge appear as a single character, or contrasting aspects of one personality confronting one another. Harris's conception of the nature of personality involves a relationship to the nature of time (personality being, to borrow a Laingian conception, a kind of persisting pattern, a set of ratios or relationships that appears to persist). That memory that "becomes a delicate screen to sift a balance of natures" must attain its own balance, to avoid psychosis, "self-rejection (total loss) or impossible self-fulfilment (total gain)" (p.75).

As the dialogue proceeds within Victor's psyche and between Victor/Judge and other characters, "gain" and "loss" are associated with "fetish" and "omen," the subject of extensive discussion between Judge and counsel for the defense in Adam's (re)trial. "Fortune" is presented as an aspect of "the delicate screen of memory" that can

animate intuitions of splendour or intuitions of crisis and downfall—can, as it were, set up its own spectres *before* and *after* an event and thus from its inferior ground of rank superstition come into uneasy collaboration with *spirit* as fetish collaborates with *omen*. (p 77)

This passage establishes an equation: "fortune" is to "spirit" as "fetish" is to "omen." This equation leads to a consideration of "time, the spectre," the "main character," of the Judge's "novel history."

"Time," said Adam's defense counsel, "is the spectre of humanity" (p. 80). This quotation by the defense counsel at Adam's trial was applied specifically to the enigmatic Dr. Wall, who, like time, is "only a spectre." Harris calls him the "ruined vacant organ"—himself a kind of time—through or within which both personalities and events exist in past, present, and future.

As the plane flies over Omai and the Judge has a premonition of the crash (a premonition requires an annihilation of our subjugation to the seriality of events that is inherent in time), he thinks:

Had time—the Judge weighed the spectre in his mind—had the years since 1929 when the trial began, hung heavy and secure, padlock and prison; or light and insecure, feather of Manoa, stigmata of the void?

(p. 81)

Answering his own query, the Judge concludes that "the claim of OMAI/OH MY—my factory of Albuoystown, gold, oil, silver or base metal, soil of industry—lay within the vision of time" (p. 81).

The theme of doubling and multiple personality figures in *Omai*, then, in the doubling of the Judge, Adam, and Victor. It also occurs in connection with Harris's idea of the nature of personality and the possibility of its freedom from psychosis. This theme becomes clear in the following passage about the climb up the mountain:

The [pork-knocker] . . . dislodged a couple of stones; . . . they struck Victor a heavy blow on the brow before he could avert it. . . . When Victor regained consciousness . . . the ruined constable [the pork-knocker] had vanished. Was it a mirage of the senses, *doppelganger*, self-appointed ruin compounded of his own *losses and gains*? (p. 16; my emphasis)

The process of doubling is carried farther in Victor's musings:

It was a question of agencies. Agents—all of whom,however misguided, however perverse—were instruments beyond themselves, subconscious, involuntary perhaps, invoking a light of compassion within the abyss of history. . . . "Nonsense," Victor grumbled. "How can one begin to translate a fiend of a conqueror, an infernal conception into a mine of proportions—agency of compassion?" (p. 17)

The figure of the secret agent becomes at different times a double agent, *doppelganger*, twin, or shadow. *Ascent to Omai* has the same repetition through the doubling of character we encountered in *Palace of the Peacock* and *Tumatumari*.

The "fiend of a conqueror," the principle of Donne appearing once again, is also associated with such usually negative ideas as filth and waste. Harris's view of the use of filth and waste in the universal economy was explored in *Tumatumari*. A similar idea, which I address shortly, is important in Ascent to Omai, but the role of biological waste in *Tumatumari* is largely taken in *Omai* by cultural waste, expressed by the ideas of "ruin" and "rubble" and their relation to resurrection. Victor answers his own question of how "a fiend of a conqueror" may be translated into an "agency of compassion":

"One must view the conqueror from the rear" . . . a backhanded agent who
exposes himself and appears to confirm (even as he denies) his own grotesque
function. A kind of megalomaniac: child and sleepwalker who dreams of
subjective filth. Dreams of an obscure order in which he was involved from the
inception of conquest, the inception of contamination, the inception of gold. . . .
(p. 18)

The comment on Victor's response reveals a particular view of
history and society with the suggestion:

The landscape of history is constructed by a daemon of the heartland, a daemon
of internality, daemon of possession within nevertheless an ironic dislocating
factor. (p. 18)

Anancy, the spider, the supernatural trickster who became a central
figure in the Caribbean as in his homeland West Africa, first appears in
Palace of the Peacock. Anancy is a complex figure, going beyond
tricks to embody the concepts of chance and paradox, even irony. And
in Harris's hands he acquires additional dimensions. In *Omai*, Anancy
embodies that "daemon of the heartland, a daemon of internality,
daemon of possession" within nevertheless that "ironic dislocating
factor" that Victor credits with "constructing the landscape of
history" (p. 18).

When ascending Omai, Victor is "entangled in an ancient web . . .
dangerous adventure—psyche of history, stigmata of the void" (p. 23).
The web is time, for elsewhere the Judge calls time itself "stigmata of
the void" (p. 32). Immediately after the climb Victor is bitten by a
tarantula. In a later section of the novel, the "Sailor-Victor" who may
have gone away on the ship *Osiris* is stabbed ("bitten") by a street
fighter and limbo dancer named Tarantula. The episode constitutes a
parallel and further progression of the ascent to Omai. This second
tarantula manifestation of Anancy functions as the "dislocating factor"
that frees Victor to speak in "buried tongues" (a phrasing that recalls
how Henry Tenby's tongue was seized in *Tumatumari* following his
rejection of his "African cargo"). These buried tongues reappear as "the
buried tongues of consciousness, African, Manoan, ancestors, limbo
dancers of Albuoystown, the masked dead of several continents and
centuries who passed his door on holidays and holy days" (p. 91). The
tarantula is referred to as "the obsessive robot of memory." Ultimately

the robot must be killed to set us free. The killing constitutes the transmutation of memory—what Victor thinks of when the tarantula stings him as *"trickster transubstantiation"* (p. 26) into "a delicate screen to sift a balance of natures" that, if carried to their extremes, end in the psychosis of loss and gain. It is this transubstantiation that will break the stasis of victor/victim and free language for a new fiction. The introductory epigram to *Ascent to Omai* is from "Victor's Bible":

Since "adventure" and "science" have led over many centuries to . . . robot law, unfeeling yoke, there is no ground of alternatives but to recover the "dangerous" chasm, the "forbidden" ascent, and seek a new dimension of *feeling*—an oath of humanity. (p. 10)

The novel explores the resources and processes necessary for completing such an "ascent to Omai." Victor becomes a redemptive figure, the vessel capable of this transcendence of historical and cultural trauma (stigmata, psyche of history, time itself), which can be brought about only by the release of the "buried tongues" of cultural forms, precipitated by Anancy's bite. This transcendence is fundamentally communal, expressed in *Omai* through Harris's development of the literary possibilities of *grotesquerie* in Caribbean Carnival.

The last movement of the "dance of the stone" is repeated at the end of the novel. The subject concerns the incident that has persisted throughout the years as the Judge's central question about the case: "Why did Adam burn bed and board?" The meaning of Adam's action becomes clear when Victor has fulfilled his vow to follow the pork-knocker-father to the ends of the universe, to find again the chasm and the ascent, searching for a novel arena of feeling. At the end of the psychological climb to the top of Omai:

Victor turned and saw him, amazed to find his father had been engaged in fighting the blaze, the very blaze he had started. Originator of the fire . . . Victor stared. He was dressed in rags, trousers in cloud, but most astonishing of all was the ragged petticoat he had unwittingly acquired going back and forth into the blaze of the sun. (pp. 124, 128)

Just as Adam has become both initiator and extinguisher of the fire that burned bed and board, he has also come to embody the male and the female principles in Victor's life and psyche: his father's trousers and

his dead mother's petticoat, within which he had sought shelter as a
child. The novel ends with this passage:

It [the petticoat] lay there now across his father's breast like a shield and an omen
of godhead: the godhead in the man: the man in the godhead: ultimate
sacrifice: ultimate sentence: ultimate forgiveness.

Victor blew—breath of wind—upon it. It crumbled, very slowly, across the
pavement, very majestically. His faint breath lifted it, expunged it of fear of
loss, of degradation, of extinction of species, so that—in conformity with the
very ruin of catastrophe—it retained a living spark, a frail star, star of the
Madonna. (p. 128)

The Christian symbolism is evident in the reference to the Madonna.
Yet, as with Harris's treatment of Mariella in *Palace of the Peacock*, the
symbolism is metamorphosed by Harris's highly individual imagination
much as, on a collective level, Caribbean religion (in the forms of
Vaudoun, Santería, and Macumba) represents a distinctive cultural
syncretism. For *Omai,* as for the other three novels I examine, an
understanding of the non-European sources of Caribbean culture is
essential. The reference to Amerindia is clear in the symbolism of the
Factory of the Gilded Man. The Guyanese pork-knocker should also be
considered within the context of cultural syncretism: his odd behavior
constitutes an ironic commentary on colonial conventions.

Two principal forms this irony takes are Harris's use of the Anancy
figure and the significance of Caribbean carnival.[3] Carnival's official
roots in the Americas are Catholic and European. It became a major
festival first for the slaves, then for the freed Blacks, and subsequently,
in varying ways and degrees, for other Caribbean populations. It was
approved by the ruling stratum because it was a Christian celebration,
but no one can observe it without remarking both characteristically
African features and a characteristically African festival spirit. It was an
occasion tolerated by the powerful and on which the latter could be
mocked. As such, it was especially important for populations barred
from all civic participation.

Carnival's use of altered proportions—mockery often assumed the
form of various kinds of caricature—becomes both inspiration and
metaphor for Harris's work as a whole. In *Omai,* this function shows
clearly in the passage concerning limbo dancing, often a part of the
Caribbean carnival. This specifically Caribbean custom keeps alive, in

the form of a social folk art, the community's experience of the Middle Passage, their nightmare journey from Africa on the slave ships. For Harris, the dance is a transubstantiation of a collectively experienced trauma that is reclaimed by the "victim" and triumphantly metamorphosed into art. It is collective memory: and memory, we remember, is the sieve that must establish a balance if psychosis is to be averted.

It is the value of *grotesquerie* as an alteration of proportions that makes the word so frequent and the concept so fertile in Harris's fiction. His scarecrows, his limbo dancers, his pork-knockers, his clowns and eccentric mad personages have both a symbolic and surrealistic value that, although idiosyncratic, does not obscure the set of significations that recur in his novels. These characters also have an important frame of reference with regard to which they can create their own spaces of meaning. These new spaces of meaning derive from roots in the constituent cultures of the Caribbean. Thus, Harris's scarecrow is particular to his fiction and also finds meaning in reference both to its practical function and to associations in literary traditions out of which Harris writes. Furthermore, as is especially well exemplified in *Ascent to Omai,* Harris draws importantly on the folk culture of the Caribbean—although that might not be immediately apparent, because he is little concerned with the realistic presentation of such vivid events as carnival. Nonetheless, through "altered proportions" in their representation, his fiction is very much concerned with the *meaning* of such events and with exploring the social and psychological possibilities inherent in those cultural meanings. By altering the reality of the external representation of limbo dancing, for example, he remains truer to its internal reality than a more conventional realism might. This is so exactly because carnival's true reality is an alteration of proportions that constitutes a commentary on colonial conventions. Consider, for instance, Harris's use of the limbo dance in a passage referring to the "robot of memory":

His [Victor's] head almost touched the ground like a limbo dancer—one of those fantastic performers he remembered seeing as a child in Albuoystown on holidays dancing under a horizontal pole through what seemed the keyhole of space. . . . the dance of the soul expressed itself through latent formations of appetite and memory, expression and mood, agility and rigidity, vertical pole, horizontal couch, wheel and spin, limbo aircraft. (p. 48)

The possibilities of the alteration of proportions and reversals of roles
in carnival are expressed in the following passage, a recollection from
Victor's childhood:

His father was drunk. Boxing Day. [The day after Christmas, an English
holiday.] The room was a shambles. Victor remained hidden there [within the
petticoat] until it was safe to emerge: crawled on the floor towards a window.
Twentieth-century window. It was raining outside. Raining blood. Global civil
war. Insurrection Day. He could hear the drums on the road—lightning and
thunder—the rowdy band of Albuoystown. He pulled himself up—*There
they were*—rowdy elements, descendants of "free" men and "slaves." Apochrypha
of the living and the dead. Insurrection womb and race. Dance of ironical victor
and victim. Strong ageless women dancing on stilts in waistcoat and trousers
(high up—off the ground—in the sky); and great limbo men in striped drawers
and dresses sliding under a bar. Limbo bar. Inverse location of sex. Door of
rebirth. Sanctification of otherness. (p. 118)

Earlier, the intrinsic psychologically revolutionary possibilities of
this economic lower-working-class population, which embodies the
folk history of the people, are expressed:

Victor felt as if he studied the legend of his father, fresh from slavery, fresh from
the factory, rum-soaked labour (Boxing Day overtime) that here was the masked
creator of Insurrection Day long before the Russian Revolution, Lenin or
Trotsky, Stalin or Devil. . . . His father was the yoke shared by all of the sacred
and profane (Christmas Day/Boxing Day/Insurrection Day) and he (Victor) felt
his eyes being welded too, soldered too by frustrated divinities (copulation of
idols—Africa, Asia, Europe) so that as the dancers swept by on the holiday
street—shape-changing, shape-shifting in a dream—he perceived them through a
veil of profanity, a veil of sanctity, man/woman, holiday/holy day,
father/mother. (p. 31)

Carnival and Anancy are of African inspiration. In this novel, so are
the other important organizing motifs of alchemy (which is a
widespread belief) and the nature of ruin and resurrection. Adam's job as
a welder, in a factory where there is a fiery furnace, evokes the image of
Hell. As a child, Victor fears the foundry he glimpses through the open
factory door.

Forge and foundry are fundamental to the alchemical tradition. Mircea Eliade's *The Forge and the Crucible* discusses them and also, at some length, the common assimilation of alchemical procedures to agricultural ones.[4] In fact, the alchemist really conceived of his activity as accelerating the embryonic growth and maturation of metals. This maturation was thought to occur in the womb of the earth in a progression from poorer metals to the ultimate valuable metal, gold. In effect, metals, like plants and animals, "grew." In *Ascent to Omai*, this progression is indicated in the personifications "Alias Copper" and "Alias Tin," steps in the alchemical process identified with heavenly bodies with which the petticoat under which Victor takes shelter is starred. The process becomes symbolic here of psychological or spiritual progression.

We have encountered the connections among alchemy, the alchemist, metallurgy, and warrior before. In *Tumatumari*, Hugh Skelton Tenby exists in Henry Tenby's consciousness as a "black helmeted warrior" sprung from a brick, clearly evocative of Mars, the god of war, who is associated with iron in the alchemical tradition. The figure of the metallurgist and the role of metalworking in the novel form a link with the African alchemical and metallurgical tradition.

Metallurgy is a very old art in Africa, and the metalworker commonly has a special, even religous, status in African societies, including the society of ancient Egypt. Although less exclusively than is the case with the Anancy figure and carnival, alchemy, then, is also connected to the African tradition. It came directly from West Africa, where it takes special forms such as the rites connected with divination and sowing, planting, and reaping. These areas of Africa are the seedbed of old traditions and customs that were elaborated and refined by the Nile Valley civilizations and then through diffusion and migration reacted back upon the areas that brought them forth.

Characteristically, African cultures combine fertility rites and the cult of the dead in a manner described by Egyptologist R. T. Rundle-Clark:

The ancestors, the custodians of the source of life, were the reservoir of power and vitality, the source whence flowed all the forces of vigour, sustenance and growth. Hence they were not only departed souls but still active, the keepers of life and fortune. . . . the place where the ancestors dwelt was the most holy spot in the world. From it flowed the well-being of the group.

He further states: "The living did not worship their ancestors, but hoped that some of the power which resided among the ancestors could be transmitted for their own needs. . . ."[5]

The Nile Valley cult of Osiris-Isis that eventually spread throughout the Roman Empire was a precursor of important symbolism in early Christianity. Isis—sister, wife, and protector of Osiris—was the patroness of alchemy. Concepts related to Osirian myth appear implicitly and explicitly in other Harris novels, but they are especially clear in *Ascent to Omai*. The novel's specifically Osirian reference, as opposed to its more general reference to the theme of death and resurrection, is twofold. The first lies in Harris's great emphasis on "family" and "community" as interacting with the dead. The second lies in the importance Harris attaches to the concept of waste—whether organic, as was discussed in *Tumatumari,* or more specifically cultural, as in *Ascent to Omai*. Waste, rubble, is in fertilizing contact with its conventional opposite, that which is whole and valuable. In the same way, death is a plowing under in relation to life. Thus, whether it is strongly or weakly emphasized explicitly in a given text, the Osirian legend offers a fruitful background against which to read some of Harris's most basic ideas. The Osirian version of the idea of death and resurrection places a strong emphasis on this reciprocity of waste and wealth, "muck and metal" (gold), as Harris phrases the connection in *Tumatumari*. Such an association is not found in the Christian version. The importance of the idea in Osirian religion is probably attributable to the central importance to Egyptian society of the annual "death" and "rebirth" of the Nile. Each rebirth was accompanied by the depositing of the life-giving "waste," "muck," "organic rubble" that would grow the crops and feed the land.

The essence of the Osirian myth is given by E. A. Wallis Budge:

The central figure of the ancient Egyptian religion was Osiris, and the chief fundamentals of his cult were the belief in his divinity, death, resurrection, and absolute control of the destinies of the bodies and souls of men. The central point of each Osirian's religion was his hope of resurrection in a transformed body and of immortality, which could only be realized by him through the death and resurrection of Osiris.

Budge goes on to make the central point of his book, that the culture of Egypt, including its basic religious expression, was indigenously and characteristically African and that the evidence for this can be found in an examination of the cultures of African peoples all over the continent.

> Osiris became incarnate in a mortal body, which possessed the nature of ordinary man. Other dogmas made Osiris to suffer death at the hands of Set, to beget a son by Isis after his death, to rise from the dead in a transformed body, and to dwell in heaven as the lord of righteous souls. This information is derived from texts which are as old as the VIth dynasty, and thus we see that as early as 3500 B.C. the Egyptians believed that gods became incarnate in man.... if we examine the religions of modern African peoples, we find that the beliefs underlying them are almost identical with those described above.[6]

In both traditional African and Christian cosmology and religious doctrine, communion between the living and the dead is not only possible but also ritualized—in Africa with the ancestors through prayer, sacrifice and libation; according to the beliefs of the Catholic Church through Christ, the Virgin, and the saints on behalf of self, friends, and kin in Purgatory. The ceremony of the Mass unites the believers in a reenactment of the Passion in which the god-man is killed by wicked men inspired by Satanic forces but rises from the dead triumphant to become, as St. Paul phrased it, "the first fruit of them that slept."

The rites associated with the myth of Osiris and Isis were a more ancient, African passion, highly stylized in Egypt and Ethiopia. That both religions spread far beyond the geographical area where they first arose suggests that they embody some fundamental sociopsychological truth. This truth appears to be repeatedly rediscovered by psychoanalysts as well as mystics, poets as well as prophets, and by many writers of fiction and drama. In *Ascent to Omai*, Harris achieves something that in other times was attained by participation in drama either as spectator or active participant, and he places death and resurrection in a Caribbean context.

That the African idiom provides a clue to the deeper—and perhaps even esoteric—meaning that Harris intends to convey in this novel is indicated by a portion of the quotation from Gerald Moore's *The Chosen Tongue* with which Harris introduces Book 2 of *Ascent to Omai*. It pertains to a basic belief widespread in African societies and in the African-derived religious communities of the Caribbean and Latin America. Moore writes: "Since the dead are concerned with the living, the initiative . . . comes as often from them as from their descendants. This is no inert debris of vanished cultures but a dynamic source of energy seeking for release."

Moore's observation is elaborated by the Ugandan scholar Dr. John Mbiti.[7] The African attitude seems compatible with Harris's ideas concerning the relation between the living and dead and between different members of single communities, or among communities when the human species is viewed as a whole. It is not too much to say that Harris's entire style is intended to constitute a means of exploring his ideas about these relationships, ideas that are unconventional from traditional Western perspectives. Moore concludes the passage quoted above with the further observation that African societies believed that if creative channels for the energy of dead ancestors were blocked, catastrophic ones would be found. This belief is an expression in mythological terms of Harris's conception of the underlying source of social and psychological disaster.

The quotation from Moore indicates, too, that given such a view of reality death does not exist in the sense of an end to communication with, and influence in, the ongoing human community. I now consider the victor-victim dichotomy in *Ascent to Omai*. The name given the principal character, Adam's son Victor, is the clearest symbolic expression of this as a central theme. The novel examines the process by which Adam's son ceases to consider himself victim after he has completed the ascent of Omai. It is a gradual transformation, as revealed in discussions between the Judge and Dr. Wall ("field-marshal, judge, hypnotist, and gynecologist" who had delivered Victor by a Caesarian operation), by the reflections of each of these characters, and by remarks of individuals who represent persons Victor had known. The circles in the diagram of "The Factory of the Gilded Man" are used to explain Victor's movement from a fear-stricken, resentful childhood (circle of the Petticoat) to his maturity when he becomes aware of "an omen of godhead; the godhead in the man; the man in the godhead; ultimate sacrifice; ultimate sentence; ultimate forgiveness (circle of the Madonna)." The circles of the Whale, the Rose, and the Iron Mask symbolize an imaginative recreation of changes in Victor's psyche during adolescence and young adulthood, a part of which was spent as a sailor. An ambiguous character named Sailor is introduced without specifically identifying him as Victor. But the Judge remarks that "the first vessel Sailor found was called *Osiris*." Thus the ancient African myth of the Osirian resurrection provides a point of view on the victor-victim dichotomy. (*See* Figure 2, p. 134)

The question of victor and victim is fundamental to the Osirian myth, even more than to the Christian one for Osiris is more thoroughly a victim than is Christ, and his resurrection follows an even more prolonged and absolute passion, in that word's original sense of passivity and of suffering. The Osirian myth conveys the inseparability of activity and passivity, of victor and victim, of male and female power, of past and present. Out of Osiris's seemingly fundamental stasis comes new movement. Egyptologist Rundle-Clark emphasizes the duality of the Osirian character: "Osiris was always helpless. He is never represented in movement, but as a swathed figure with black or green face—for he is both a mummy and the life-spirit."[8]

Osiris was murdered by his younger brother Set, and his body was dismembered and scattered throughout Egypt. Isis, his sister/wife, and her sister Nephthys went in search of his parts, reassembled the body, and from it made the first mummy. Dr. Wall in *Omai* admits that some people will see only "fetish" in the myth of the reassembling of Osiris's body, but suggests that

it could reflect through the illumination of the body—a density and transparency that brings into focus the torment of divided power, evil and good, the fortress of the soul, the terrifying genius of man to see though blind, hear though deaf, feel though unfelt. (p. 104)

One traditional representation of Osiris portrays him as supported between his sisters, Isis and Nephthys, from whom he is deriving movement and life.

[Set] remained a potential danger to Osiris until the latter was redeemed. Hence, in the rites Osiris had to be protected by Isis and her sister Nephthys until the coming of Horus [the son of Isis and Osiris, begotten after Osiris's death]. . . . They had to watch over him during the difficult time of his helplessness which was symbolized by the night watches.[9]

In *Ascent to Omai*, Harris insists on the profundity of this ancient faith, transforming Osiris into "an omen of indestructibility, omen of continuity, rather than monument of absurdity" (p. 104). It is possible, suggests Dr. Wall, to view as mere *grotesquerie* the action of the "mummy with the long member" who was reported to have "impregnated a living woman." For some, it is simply an account of "an excessive mythological ornament" that gave rise to "posthumous scandal." (We remember the rumor Henry Tenby rejects in *Tumatumari*.) But this aspect of the myth, Dr. Wall insists, can also be taken seriously as

a remarkable omen signifying the barren living (feuds of the living) and the fertile dead, a metaphysical projection into the future of indestructible mankind despite the suffocating hordes of tyranny, even genocide, through a vicar of lighthouse. (p. 103)

Rundle-Clark explains the profound and perhaps universal significance of the Osirian myth:

The ancients thought of death as the essential prelude to life. The two form a polarity; one is meaningless without the other. . . . Death is a passing from one kind of time to another. . . . Life can be seen, becoming is hidden. . . . the Dat [underworld] is . . . the place of the formation of the living out of the dead and the past. . . ." [10]

Thus the answer to the question that haunts the Judge—why did Adam burn bed and board?—can be understood as a mythical equivalent to the death of Osiris. By first destroying himself in destroying his livelihood, he creates the fertile soil out of which he rises at the end of the novel in Victor's gaze to incorporate not only his own power but also the "power of Isis," represented by the petticoat, and puts out the fire he presumably started. The future comes out of the ruin of the past and can come from nowhere else—whether a personal, a cultural, or an organic past. Death is essential, and death is not an end but a profound passivity, a true passion or "victimization" that not only will be ended by the "great shout" (the high point of the Osirian rites, signaling and celebrating the stirring of the dead god) but that is also absolutely essential to the activity that succeeds the passivity in conventionally temporal terms. "Osiris is the past, Horus is the present," the Egyptian writings say. But the ancient story goes on to show that Horus cannot live without his rootedness in and continual respect for the truly "living-dead" parent, Osiris—an expression of the African community of "the living and the dead" that Harris evokes in *Omai* by a complex, sophisticated symbolic system rooted in African, Christian, and scientific sources:

. . . Limbo dancer. . . . Empty tomb. . . . Cross of the telescope. . . . *Spider transubstantiation. Trickster transubstantiation.* Metamorphosis of the Fall. *Deliverance and protection.* (p. 26)

8
The Epoch of Light:
Genesis of the Clowns

Perhaps fate and freedom are mixed immortal tenses or twins one meets
afresh, sees afresh in the womb of self-knowledge of selves other than
oneself.

Genesis of the Clowns, p. 81

In *Palace of the Peacock*, Harris achieves much of his effect by the
technique of plurisignation. In *Tumatumari*, his characteristic technique
is the use of systems of metaphor. In *Ascent to Omai*, he uses what I
call cross-association of images. In *Genesis of the Clowns*, his most
notable technique is interrelation of codes.

By code I refer to the meaning attributed to words or phrases in
intellectual systems organizing our understanding of the world. The
following paragraph offers an illustration from *Genesis*. It is organized
around the major symbol of the paytable and uses the codes of
economics, alchemy, and geology. Thus the English narrator
Wellington's reevaluation of his experiences in Guyana bring him a
new understanding of his relations with his surveying crew. The image
of the paytable comes to have expanded meaning for him in his
recollections:

I was becoming conscious of the paytable as capital genesis moving sometimes,
floating sometimes, within an erosive and accretive sentiment, a breath and a
breathless tide by which I was compounded to grope upon a datum line of
harlequin fire. . . . (p. 108)

Here, in this single brief passage, we have an excellent example of what I call the dissolution of codes into each other: the paytable as capital; water ("floating," "tide"); earth (erosion and accretion); air ("breath" and "breathless"); and fire/sun (harlequin/clown fire). We also have the scientific instrument, the measuring pole, transmuted into a datum line.

Although Harris's versatility in the literary use of language is shown by the differences in the four novels I consider, his concern with certain themes remains constant. These themes include: doubling, both in the relationship between the Caribbean and the West and in connection with the nature of the individual psyche; the nature of community; and the nature of time, especially in its relation to individual identity and memory and to communal history.

Genesis differs in several important ways from the three novels I discuss earlier in this book. Structurally, the novel adheres more closely to certain conventions of the classical realist novel. The characters and the narrative line are more unambiguously delineated. In *Palace* Harris indicates through such techniques as changing perspective on a single event, which I illustrate in analyzing the two versions of the death of Donne, that Donne/Narrator/Mariella may be construed as a single psyche. In *Genesis,* the narrator learns of the event that sets the novel in motion by a letter from an anonymous author. By novel's end, however, it is evident that this anonymous author may well be a region of the narrator's own psyche. The way Harris conveys the multiplicity of psyche in *Genesis* differs from the way he conveys it in *Palace.* In *Genesis,* the characters, although identifiable as individuals, also function as representatives of codes. The technique Harris uses for establishing equivalences among different orders of experience is the establishment of relations between codes.

Another very striking difference between *Genesis* and the other novels I discuss is the sense of distance, both temporal and spatial, between the narrator and his narrating present on the one hand and his recollection of the events he recollects on the other.

First, a conventional temporal structure is clearly indicated: the narrating present is Midsummer's Day, 1974; the most important events recounted occurred in 1942, in 1948 and at Christmas of 1946. Second, a conventional spatial location is clearly delineated: Frank

Wellington lives in Holland Villas Road, London. The events in Guyana occurred on the Cuyuni River, the Abary River, and in Albuoystown.

The three earlier novels plunge the reader into situations of immediate or imminent crisis. In *Tumatumari*, Prudence's breakdown effectively obliterates the time that has passed since her childhood. The imminent crash in *Omai* and the danger and stress of the river journey in *Palace* likewise precipitate insights that the reader experiences as contemporaneous with the characters' experiences of them. By contrast, *Genesis* does not convey a mood of crisis or of breakdown. At no point is the narrator threatened with loss of self-control or psychological dislocation or by physical danger.

Unlike any of the other narrators discussed here, Wellington is distanced from Guyana on several counts. He is not Guyanese; he is White. He has left Guyana definitively long before the novel begins, or so he thinks. It is essentially a finished chapter in his life. He is not in Guyana when the psychic reevaluation that constitutes the novel occurs. The entire "narrating present" of the novel is a flashback. The narrator is in his home in Holland Villas Road. Thus there is no "Guyanese present," and this fact alters the nature of the "Guyanese presence."

Something is lost with these changes of narratorial perspective and novelistic structure. Genesis strikes me as less emotionally intense, a less immediate experience, than the other novels; the complexity, the richness, and the difficulty of Harris's writing is less immediately evident, though if the reader readjusts expectations and realizes that Harris is not trying to write the way he did in the earlier works, the beauty of his writing is as strong here as elsewhere.

From another point of view, something is also gained. The novel is more accessible than some of his earlier work. One of its most successful aspects is that the characters are to some extent real "personalities," which heightens their still more important function as symbols of codes. More than in any of the other novels, the speech of the crew conveys both individuality and the particular flavor of the colloquial speech of certain sectors of the Guyanese population. Yet the crew members are also, explicitly and deliberately, symbols that constitute the interrelation of the codes, as shown in the next passage.

Wellington remembers that he and the crew members Moseley, Cummings Day, and Hope were all present on a certain occasion—"that other noon"—with the tools of their trade: measuring poles marked off in red and black. In Wellington's eyes, the poles acquire significance in terms of other associations than the scientific, as shown in this iridescent passage:

Cummings Day stood beside her [Ada] with a twelve-foot-tall staff, black and red decimal numbers on a white background; he leaned his forehead upon it so that it possessed him like an elongated mask, a vertical pole. . . . "I wonder," I thought to myself, . . . "how deeply rooted are we in a datum line of space to which we remain in part unconscious within the black/red land and the sea's harlequin fire."

The strinking image of the harlequin figure, standing with his surveyor's rod that is also phallus and harlequin's pole, is among the most vivid in Harris's work, and it also shows very well how the figure of Cummings Day functions symbolically.

In uneducated, working people's language, very different from the scholar Henry Tenby's formulation of the same situation in *Tumatumari*, the character Hope tells Wellington this truth of the Guyanese past when explaining the use of the term "Miss" instead of "Mistress" in referring to Moseley's wife, Ada:

Miss is no disrespect, Skipper, for common law wife in this part of the world. . . . When we say mistress we usually put the stress on the way a woman may be decked out big with responsibility. . . . Sometimes a mistress left to care for a whole family . . . especially when she god of a man can't find work on the coast and he left for Devil Hole rapids and gold-and-diamond field in the bush to see if he luck would take a turn. Sometimes he don't come back, he turn into skeleton hand on a drum. (p. 97)

Yet Ada is also presented strikingly as an African carved figure, an important symbolic image in the book:

I was astonished by the impression Ada made on me of vacancy and fullness, solidity and hollowness, exaggerated contours one associated with a kind of fertility goddess set upon a rein of economic malaise, erosion and accretion, that riveted a threatening sea into the dance of a threatened wall. (pp. 94-95)

Genesis of the Clowns is written as a first-person narration. The White narrator, Frank Wellington, formerly a land surveyor in Guyana and now living in London, has just received an anonymous letter from Guyana. It informs him that his old crew foreman, a Black man named Hope, has killed another Black man in a quarrel over a woman and then turned the gun on himself, fatally.

Wellington's recollections of Guyana relate principally to two surveying expeditions and an unplanned visit to Hope's Albuoystown home at Christmas Carnival Time 1946. The events in Guyana become symbolic terms for Wellington's reevaluation of the nature of historical and psychological experience.

Harris's central concern is what lies in store for the human community as a whole as we "move into a new century." Harris discusses the relation between what he believes is an essential revolution in consciousness and the social and political revolutions that have characterized the twentieth century and whose focus, in this last third of the century, moves increasingly to the Third World. This theme is expressed in one of the quotations that prefaces the book in which Stuart Hampshire speaks of a "Copernican revolution of the sentiments."

Wellington's reevaluation, like most revolutions whether psychic or social, has deep roots in the past. Indeed, in a sense it actually took place there, although it comes to conscious awareness only much later. In other words, it is a question of a temporal twinning or doubling, which in effect abolishes time.

Wellington's Guyanese surveying crew included three Black men: Hope the foreman, Moseley Adams the mechanic, and Cummings Day the meter reader. Moseley is married to Hope's cousin, Ada. The other members of Wellington's crew are Marti Persaud Frederick, of East Indian origin; Chung, of Chinese descent; and Reddy, an Amerindian, with whose sister Wellington apparently has a sexual encounter. These men belong to one or another of the principal ethnic groups of Guyana. Chung's wife, Lucille, who might have been sexually involved with Wellington as well as with Hope, also has symbolic import; so does Ada, as I have already shown.

On expeditions, Wellington's habit is to have Hope pitch the tent he, as surveying leader, will occupy, at a distance from the sleeping quarters of the crew. Wellington knows they are, "after a day's work, as purely technical bodies . . . [inclined] to become boisterous, a boisterousness that carried the threat of ineffectual violence." This ineffectuality, this threat, "reveals the ironic texture of uneasiness and uncertainty within the weight of confrontation or impending storm," for "at the heart of bodies manqué, violence manqué, lies a suppressed charisma or epidemic legend of fire" (p. 83).[1]

One midnight, on the Cuyuni expedition in 1942 (the "midnight" of the event parallels the "midsummer's midday" in England on which Wellington receives the letter), a storm cracks the ridgepole of the tent Hope has erected for his expedition chief. Wellington is nearly killed by the falling splintered shaft; its collapse rings out like a shot from a gun. Looking at Hope in the threatening midnight, half dazed with shock and sleep, Wellington sees his Black foreman in Wellington boots—standing in his own shoes—and realizes that the two "know," but have no real knowledge of, each other.

In Wellington's psyche, the shot—the cracked ridgepole at midnight—functions to start the movement, unconsciously, that the letter brings to consciousness thirty years later. Wellington describes the result of this experience as "the sense of a deeper confrontation than I had ever known . . . between myself and violent bodies manqué" (p. 86).

Wellington's reaction is to reject and repress this beginning psychological revolution he experienced at Cuyuni by a still more intense immersion in "the complex industry of fact," the scientists's equivalent of the crew's boisterousness; they are equally "technical bodies manqué," out of touch with the "charasmatic fire." He throws himself wholeheartedly into his surveying work. Yet he also begins to doodle obsessively on the margins of his field book, behavior similar to that of the Judge in *Ascent to Omai*. These doodlings, this comical play on the margins of the serious technical business of labor and life, seem to him in retrospect to be a beginning:

Across the years looking back now from the Thames to the Abary I feel myself riveted into a breathless tapestry of revolving continents, landscape and rivers I once possessed that may have started then. . . . As though the wheel of empire began to turn anew when for many it had already stopped, began to return to me as to a moving threshold of consciousness. (p. 86)

Harris speaks of the bodies and the violence of the crew as "manqué." This inadequacy or defect exists because neither in the individual nor in the social realm, neither in physical nor intellectual activity, have people succeeded in coming into contact with the "suppressed charisma," the "fire." The "legend of the fire" can be apprehended by human beings only in and through each other, both as individuals and as social aggregations. To be effective, both societies and individuals must activate their relationality, their reciprocity, and overcome the delusion of self-sufficiency. Otherwise, the charisma remains suppressed, the individual is untouched by "fire." Without reciprocity both charisma and the mundane "technical fact" of the body and the intellect remain in stasis, and individual and society remain imprisoned in a conceptual world of sterile dichotomization.

Like other Harris novels, *Genesis* is organized around sets of oppositions expressed as "characters" and "events" in the external world. On the other hand, the novel's language is organized around the interplay of several sets of linguistic codes: economic, political, and psychological. Although codes are useful as intellectual paradigms according to which people organize their reality, they are static categories that constitute a mental equivalent to the "technical bodies" of the physical plane. They become touched by the "suppressed charismatic fire" only when they touch each other, that is, linguistically dissolve into each other, whether through grammatical manipulation or metaphor. At such moments it becomes clear that they are constructs, not realities.[2]

Bringing the different codes into relation with each other comes to symbolize the manner in which the physical world—the world of "technical bodies" and "complex industry of fact"—comes into relationship with the "suppressed charisma." Harris indicates this textually in two ways. One is when the narrator gains an insight into the necessity of reciprocity to activate the suppressed charisma. The insight is expressed by dissolving the rigid phrasing or units of words used to describe reality according to one code, into the constituent verbal components of that code, then reorganizing them to convey reality according to another code. The second way of indicating reciprocity of experience is by bringing ideas from the text into association in the "reading present." In these cases, the reader must note this juxtaposition without assistance from the narrator.

These two techniques of associating adds to narratorial complexity. Thus, at times Wellington becomes the medium whereby the reader enters into relationship with "the suppressed charisma"; at other times the reader may make the connection although it seems to remain latent for the narrator. In the second case, the reader becomes in a sense the medium whereby Wellington enters into relationship with the charisma, since all the language of the text is presented as coming from Wellington's mind in the first-person narration. Thus reader and narrator are brought into relationship by the author. This dual technique increases the impression of movement in process of contemporary revolution. Wellington's "revolution of the sentiments," like the social and political revolutions in the historical world, is a process.

As Wellington evokes the past, he brings the economic code in *Genesis* into linguistic association with the geological and geographical code. This evocation is also a literal association, for the economic and social structures of Guyanese society derive from its historical past as shaped in part by its geography and by the economic possibilities deriving from it. Wellington comes to understand his Guyanese experience in terms of "erosion" and "accretion," and the novel sets up two principal contexts: the geological, geographical situation of Guyana and the economic code as played out in Guyanese society. In modern economic parlance, the Third World, of which Guyana is a part, is commonly regarded as having serious problems of "underdevelopment," inadequate "capital accumulation" and various kinds of population excesses and imbalances. Among other things, the phrasing expresses a continued perception of Caliban as deviation from a Western norm, while burying from consciousness the historical relationship that created both West and *América mestiza*.

Harris couches the discussions between Wellington and his crew members, and among the crew members, in these terms but relates the economic to other codes. Wellington notes that his relating of codes to each other began while he made marginal notations in his notebooks at Cuyuni:

I cannot even now after all these years brush them aside as fantasies, evasions or statistical doodles. They related to economic codes, were as pertinent or impertinent as sheer technical fact often is. And the more thorough, the more specific and comprehensive my scientific work became, they—on the other hand—seemed all the more to stand in the light of a buried sun that possessed a spatial reason deeper than all apparent unreason. As though they were the shadowplay of a genesis of suns—the shadowplay of interior suns around which I now turned whereas before they had turned around me in processional sentiment. (p. 86)

The interpenetration of codes is evident in Harris's use of two key symbols: the sun and the paytable. The paytable is the central symbol of the economic code. In his Guyanese days it was across the paytable that twice a month White Wellington doled out the wages to his crew with his Black assistant, Hope, functioning as witness. When Wellington receives the letter in London, that same crew returns, this time rising up in his memory, to collect their "real wages" (a phrase both indicating the reevaluation to a truer level of experience that is occurring and playing on the economic meaning of the term). It was in conversations over the paytable that Wellington became aware of relations between East Indians and other ethnic groups, through a crew member of whose "origins" the novel tells us that, ten years before the Abary expedition:

. . . a bullet/sun had been fired into the air and a breathless stroke/body was created out of instrumental dust, which began its collective subsistence upon nothing as the accumulative asset of the future. That was the genesis of Marti Persaud Frederick and Brothers, Guyanese capitalists. (p. 105)

Black and East Indian populations recognize that their fates are inextricably shared; a Black crew member, Moseley, underlines this awareness in a comment about the folly of joining in a strike, allegedly communist led: "They going cut their black nose to spoil their brown face." This was a "folk proverb" shared by East Indian and African alike within a capacity for subtle and naive "exaggeration or distortion of features as the shadowplay genesis of clowns." (p. 90).

As the history of the country shows, the shared relationship has frequently been bitter. The Blacks have often regarded the Indian willingness to "fast"—to live in abject poverty, to "do without" and save—as degrading. Of the Indian crew member we are told: "Frederick worked as a common laborer even as he and his brothers were achieving the uncommon task of creating capital out of their fast" (p. 104). Hope calls him "Poor Man's Capitalist."

Wellington spoke of "the unreality of capital for his trusted crew member Black Hope":

[He] remained spendthrift or dormant since he could not fast, could not build upon a commanding fast of numbers. . . . His desires were planted in the quarrels of the flesh, the beauty of the flesh, the enigma of the flesh, and this made him a supreme victim to the enterprise of others whose asceticism ran deeper than his plight. . . . (p. 100)

This is a classic, almost stereotypic presentation by Wellington of what he preceives as the attitude of the Black masses in the Caribbean, descendants of former slaves, toward the accumulation of capital.

The Indian family enterprise eventually comes to include M. M. Frederick and Brothers, Pawnbrokers and Money Lenders; M. M. Frederick and Brothers, Soft Drinks and Groceries; M. M. Frederick and Brothers, Lodging House Proprietors, Albuoystown to Bartica. In one of those lodging houses in Albuoystown Hope has his rooms, and it is there that the third major episode Wellington recollects, many years later in London, takes place.

Hope "saw in the industrious fast of others towards the accumulation of capital the collective death-mask of his day and age . . ." (p. 100). East Indians, Amerindians, and Blacks all came from preindustrial societies—the "Masked Societies"—whose people are now seeing their "death mask"—in Amerindia and Africa, under imperialism and industrialization. The living masks of traditional societies have become death masks, lethal as the Sleeping Rocks in *Tumatumari*.

Reddy, the Amerindian crew member, experiences the death of Masked Societies in a different way from the East Indians, Chinese, or Blacks. During his reevaluation Wellington comes to understand how the Amerindian's experience at the coastal campsite in 1948 constituted for him the equivalent of a Copernican Revolution:

The sun rolls across the paytable . . . and Reddy's turn to receive his pay has come around. As he advances to the paytable I consult the loom of light into which I threaded my inquiries about him, his background, his gods, his people in 1942. (p. 112)

That was in Cuyuni when the survey crew was working among Reddy's own hinterland people. Six years later, in 1948, he requested and was granted permission to join Wellington on the Abary expedition near the coast. He saw something then that he regarded with terror and awe: Objects that moved *upstream*—"logs and trees moving of their own accord in unison with heretical tides against the falls" (p. 115). His ancestors had been "born into a world of eternally descending waters . . . falling water was to them an instinctive guarantee of light . . ." (p. 113). They knew nothing of incoming Atlantic tides that could reverse the flow of the river below the falls. Now, Reddy saw the reversal at Bartica (location of Sorrow Hill, where the crew of *Palace of the Peacock* drowned), where Wellington's parents drowned and were buried. Here three rivers sacred to Reddy's people joined: The Essequibo, the Mazaruni, and the Cuyuni. All the resulting changes of currents and the tidal countercurrents that Reddy observed and that to Wellington simply supplied scientific data represented to the Amerindian the overthrow of his cosmology:

For the first time Reddy felt he possessed no medium of exchange, in coin or kind, to understand the inroads of the conception of a stranger universe. (p. 116)

Other members of the crew were more affected by other codes. The experiences Wellington had and the insight he gained during his time in Guyana are cast in terms of another aspect of that "stranger universe": the society and economy of the country, with its underpaid sugar workers, its men who cannot support themselves in the frail economy, and its deep-rooted ethnic tensions. The crew members talk of the high price of food and its scarcity in the markets, of the strike on a nearby sugar plantation; they argue with one another about whether those whom they call the "communist" organizers indeed have the answer to how to better the condition of the working people. These conditions also increase the strain on relations between men and women.

Like many men in the distressed and dislocated Guyanese economy, Moseley, the Black mechanic, is working away from home. Chung, the crew member of Chinese descent, succumbs to another form of stress. In London, Wellington remembers the time when Chung had a breakdown, although he himself says he was only "ashamed of his fear." Significantly, he pronounces "fear" as "fire." When Wellington arrives to rescue him in a remote surveying spot, Chung is near "the last series of rapids in the river before it descends under the plane of the sea and is subject to tides. . . . [In] the region of the gauging station, where Chung was, one enters the ancient isolation, the reign of the bush" (p. 129).

Chung, in this "ancient isolation," has fallen under the spell of the place, as have others in earlier novels by Harris. As Schomburgh tells the narrator in *Palace of the Peacock* after a similar experience, "Is a risk everyman tekking in this bush" (p. 28).

One day, Chung tells Wellington the bush had lighted up, with a "sound of voices like a forest fire," and Wellington thinks

here was a capitalization upon fear raised to the right level . . . on which an alchemisation of comedy of divinity had begun to happen . . . that would serve to invest an absurd watchhouse at the heart of the bush . . . with the stilted outlines of the future. . . . (p. 134)

Chung is removed from his "ancient isolation" to resume life in Albuoystown. He returns to the world of bodies manqué and the industry of fact, rescued from his brush with the charismatic fire.

The phallic symbolism of the surveying pole is a counterpart to the image of the fertility goddess, and the description of the woman calls to mind those representations of human beings in African art that characteristically possess "altered proportions." Wellington calls these "exaggeration or distortion of features as the shadowplay of genesis of clowns" (p. 80). Like the images evoked so dramatically in a passage posing a question about the remote past:

"Did ancient Adams and Adas sleep in the soil of time, larger than life, huge-limbed, phallic, huge-bodied, breasted?" (p. 95)

Further associations are immediately made with these recollections of Ada standing there with the surveying party as Harris writes:

. . . complex veils of inheritance, economic and historic fate, an erosion of fortunes within whose trench her [Ada's] shadow moved across tides and lands, across oceans and up rivers into arrested [i.e., static] bodies and institutions. (p. 95)

Moseley and Hope quarrel over Ada's affections, and Wellington understands this, too, in terms of Guyana's past and the imbalance in numbers between men and women.

Although the paytable is important, the sun, symbol of "charismatic fire," is the central image of the novel. The sun's complex significance is indicated in various passages. Wellington interprets the marks he began to make in his field book as standing "in the light of a buried sun" and as "the shadowplay of interior suns." These "buried suns" are the source of the upsurge representing the "Copernican revolution of the sentiments":

It all seemed to confirm . . . the hidden functions of erosive and accretive suns planted in all landscapes, functions of buried sunrise and sunset within the cultures of seas and rivers. (p. 87)

The code that threads the others together derives from Taoism. We see this in the invocation of the four elements: Earth, air, fire, and water. At one point it also informs the description of Ada in terms of "vacancy and fullness, solidity and hollowness," the emphasis on breath and breathlessness (Taoism teaches the yoga of breath control as a principal discipline in the search for Truth). The Taoist code is recognizable, too, as Wellington recalls a moment when he spoke as if he were on "an infinite scale of numbers occupied by a seed pearl that gazed upon extinction as if all nature were a full yet vacant womb" (p. 94). Most revealing, however, is Harris's choice of a subtitle, "The Epoch of Light," a phrase used in Taoist philosophy to refer to the attainment of insight. In *Genesis,* the "buried suns," source of fear and fire, are also the source of this light.

Of the four novels I discuss in detail in this book, *Genesis* may be read most clearly, although obliquely, as an intervention in the complex, ongoing intellectual, political, and artistic debate among the contemporary Caribbean intelligentsia. The debate concerns ramifications of the themes broached in Chapter 1 of identity and relationship to Europe, identity and doubling, and the stasis of victor and victim. It is significant that one of the dedications of *Genesis* is to C. L. R. James, Trinidadian scholar and doyen of the political Left in the Caribbean. Genesis reveals Harris's sensitivity to an issue that continuously challenges James and many other Caribbean intellectuals, artists, and political leaders, among them Walter Rodney of Guyana, Maurice Bishop, Eric Williams—all three now deceased—Aimé Césaire, and René Depestre. This is the question of how to synthesize Black Conciousness and solidarity with some aspects of Marxist-

Leninist theory and practice and with other, more traditional values. In this connection, it is interesting that Harris's "Fate and Freedom," those "mixed immortal tenses or twins," represent a possible literary formulation of the famous dictum associated with the philosophies of Hegel, Marx, and Engels, "Freedom is the knowledge of necessity." The anonymous letter writer, after saying that it was through Hope that he first heard of Wellington, continues:

And then I began to read your articles on "the encounters of cultures in the Guianas." (These are banned by the way in Albuoystown. I am told in fact that they do not exist. So how could they be banned? They smack it is said of a marriage between EBONY and MARX FATHER AND BROTHERS). . . .

(p. 144)

Harris is taking a courageous step in making fictional use of the political dilemmas of the contemporary Caribbean, as he has used its history and geography, to explore themes of wider applicability; an insufficiently careful reading might suggest that he is joining not in the Caribbean debate but in the activity fashionable in some circles of presenting the problems of the Caribbean as evidence of "unreadiness" for independence. Such a reading will not stand up under close textual scrutiny, though; the entire structure of the novel emphasizes that the basic dilemmas involve the West as well. This is to be seen in the doubling of Black Wellington/White Wellington and in the reciprocal identity White Wellington has felt for Hope ever since the midnight of the shattered ridgepole during the Cuyuni expedition. When in his London apartment on Holland Villas Road Wellington sees blossoms blowing like "a sudden swirl, like ghosts of the past, circles and counter-circles," sees them rising "into a pit of newspapers . . . with rumours of rigged elections across the Atlantic sea . . . democracies manqué," these democracies manqué, like the violence manqué, represent a failure to contact the charismatic fire, a failure that is, Harris indicates, by no means peculiar to the Caribbean.

Also, Harris is speaking not just of the Third World,but of the world as a whole. This point is underscored by making his narrator a White man and locating events of the narrative present in England. Thus, his concern with "democracies manqué" or "desires of the flesh" or "accumulation of capital" cannot be taken as referring to the Third World alone. So when the narrator speaks of the "price mixed societies must pay," although the terms of the novel are concretely Guyanese, the mixed society to which reference is made is ultimately the entire world. This global mixed society must learn to "displace a self-sufficient character, a self-sufficient destiny," for self-sufficiency is a destructive illusion. The point is clear when the narrator speaks of "this irony of revolving and counter-revolving potentials to which we begin to relate . . . [the] new quarrel between fate and freedom signalling us towards a heightened and deepened parallel to the gods in the dangerous childhood of mankind" (p. 108).

Such a displacement, from the illusion of a self-sufficient character, a self-sufficient destiny, to a "knowledge of ourselves in selves other than ourselves," represents humanity's hope for escaping from the stasis of "bodies *manqué*." It begins with reflection "upon the complicated activities of a civilization with head in the clowns if not the clouds, feet in subsistence as much as substance" and where "perhaps as hopeless as one's time is, there is a new movement, a new genesis of the clowns . . . perhaps it will take another age or two . . . " (p. 102).

As in other, earlier works, *Genesis* expresses this general human situation in Guyanese terms. With a telling irony, Harris discusses central philosophical and practical problems in terms of the difficulties of a small country, remote from centers of political and economic influence, in desperate social and economic straits. *Genesis*, however, introduces a significant new dimension in the figure of Wellington's assistant, Hope. In fact, as the closing of the anonymous letter (which is also the closing of the novel) indicates, Hope is presented as the reason and the ground on which an escape from stasis and victimization may be accomplished, and all the failures signaled by the reiteration of the word "manqué" may be transfigured.

That the novel's narrative present is in the period of Guyanese formal independence is particularly significant. Although the final major episode, Wellington's visit to Hope in the latter's Albuoystown home, takes place in 1946, Hope's words to the White Wellington on that occasion are clearly meant to apply to the dilemmas and developments of the Guyana of the narrative present, 1974.

The role Hope plays in the novel thus illustrates a subject that will be explored in the next chapter, namely Harris's suggestion that the experience of the Caribbean, because of its particular historical position and configuration, may offer a solution to dilemmas facing the world as a whole. The Caribbean person represents the "grassroots" of a fruitful and meaningful individuality. However, the character of Hope seems an unlikely candidate for this role. Throughout the novel we see in him that "consolidation of character" that Harris discusses in terms of the literary code, the "novel of persuasion," the novel of classical realism. He is a Black Guyanese, a working man without formal education or high social standing. With his scarred face, he is not physically prepossessing. Furthermore, his personality is that of "an incipient dictator of the flesh"; he has been "a staunch supporter of the regime." When he visits Hope in his home, White Wellington observes a collection of newspaper cutouts pasted on the wall, photographs of men Hope admires: Joe Louis, Rommel, Bustamante, Papa Doc Duvalier:

"Men of deeds," said Hope sullenly, resenting perhaps something stilted, uneasy, disapproving in my conversation. . . . It [the meaning suggested by these pictures] was the mixture of action on which he subsisted, allied to demagoguery and death that pulled me up short like a cloud under a sun overshadowing a frozen genesis. . . .

"Since I was a child," said Hope as if he had regained a measure of confidence in my apparent disorientation, "I always believe a man is chained to his deeds. We buy one another, we sell one another in chains. Call it love, call it labour."
(p. 141)

This is recognizably the same Hope as the one speaking during the expedition:

Hope gave a slight guffaw. . . . "Revenge is a sweet mistress. . . . Is so it was from the very beginning I believe. Revenge for the past, new upon old, old upon new, minority upon majority, majority upon minority. . . ." (p. 99)

Here we have a contemporary, ordinary Black Caribbean man who, in relating to his personal and cultural past, has chosen to escape from the role of victim in the stasis of victor and victim by seeking to become a victor in those same terms. This is the significance of the "men of deeds" Hope admires and his understanding of personal relations as chains of possession. Love is equated with slavery and with labor.

The anonymous letter writer, however, is able in the end to sign his letter "Yours in hope, F. W." He can do so because of the "picture" he is able to suggest Hope finds in the execution/nonexecution of his last deed of revenge: The apparent murder of Black Frank Wellington (because of jealousy over Lucille, Chung's widow) and his own suicide (real or imagined). Hena Maes-Jelinek perceptively points out:

Hope's aggression towards the other is now turned against himself, so that, as both assailant and victim, he has encountered as his own the fate he has imposed on the other and by so doing has obliterated the tyrant in himself.[3]

Yet even this formulation is perhaps a bit too static to convey in full the nature and import of Hope's transformation. Hope merits his name, despite the tyrannical aspect of his personality that was dominant throughout his life, despite his admiration of "men of deeds"—men consolidating stasis and perpetuating the interpretation of human personal relations and human history in terms of victor and victim—because, in this final act, he opens himself to alternative possibility.

This alternative possibility gives significance to the last paragraph of the anonymous letter, where, speaking of Hope's murder and suicide, the writer says:

Perhaps you [White Frank Wellington] were there in the shadows of that last paytable midnight and he [Hope] did not fire. Then history may possess an unwritten anecdote, an eclipsed but naked spiritual fact. (p. 146)

The writer notes that earlier, during the expeditions, Hope had never fired on the paytable where the Wellington-who-reads-and-writes doled out the wages to his crew or when Wellington lay with "the mother Lucille," the Chinese crew member's wife who was Hope's mistress. That abstention was, in fact, a latent reality capable of representing alternate possibility in another time. It becomes a "spiritual fact" entered into "history" as "unwritten anecdote" and thus represents the "charismatic fire" touching bodies previously "manqué" and breaking the stasis of victor and victim. The bodies are "manqué" because they, like Hope, rigged "the emotions as a dictator rigs votes to make them conform to the blood-statistic or alignment of opposite models, fatherland and motherland, until a tyranny of affections rules" (p. 147). This rigging, this dishonesty, possessiveness, competitiveness, exclusiveness, resulting in stasis, is the rigging that Hope finally manages to break, in favor of its "opposites," freedom, love, openness, mutual participation in "fields" and "currents" of being rather than in systems of closed delineations.

The anonymous letter from Guyana provided the impetus for Wellington's reevaluation of his experiences. The letter is signed "F. W."—the initials of both the narrator and the murder victim. This coincidence raises the possibility for the reader of the novel that the letter is, in fact, *from* the narrator as well as *to* him—a message to himself, from himself. In other words, a reevaluation, with this message from the double, the unconscious/alter ego, of the experiences buried both spatially (in an image of consciousness and in the geographical circumstance of having left Guyana behind for England) and temporally, since the events occurred twenty-five or thirty years before they are being recalled.

The idiom of twinning and doubling pervades the letter and raises questions in the reader's mind of who was actually shot and when, or whether anyone was shot and killed at all. "F. W." in Guyana writes to Frank Wellington in England, discussing the latter's old assistant Hope:

Perhaps on the last, the very last, really last imprinted occasion of which I now write he pulled the trigger but saw another head among the clowns and turned back from a grave of confused bargains to the coolness of another shadow, the gift of life without strings . . . the gift of life to you. . . . Twin Wellingtons, black and white, twin Lucilles, fantasy and beauty, father, son, mother, daughter all rolled into one carnival, into past and present personae, into known and unknown masks, into the fading memory of collective self abuse, into frailty and affection as other than a jealous right to possess properties of flesh-and-blood. . . . (pp. 147-148)

The link between present and past, Black and White, London and Guyana, slavery and sexual possessiveness ("to possess properties of flesh-and-blood"), pre- and post-independence, murder/suicide and mercy, life and death, and finally between technical fact and charismatic fire, is Hope. The anonymous letter writer says to Wellington, "It was through him [Hope] that I first heard of you" (p. 144). Or, in other words, Hope provides the link between the two alter egos or between the conscious and unconscious minds of White Frank Wellington. Hope constitutes the psychic ground joining the two Wellingtons: "Yours in Hope, " one F. W. offers as final address to the other at the end of the letter.

The name of the solicitor whose letter to Wellington arrives the same day as the one from F. W. is Burness, a circumstance Wellington immediately associates with the small burn scars he recalls around the mouth of his former foreman. (I take the burns to represent the result of Hope's then-incomplete relationship to the buried suns of revolutions.)   Burness's Dumferline address is in Hope Street. Although Wellington dismisses these phenomena as "accidents of an imperial and colonial legacy," their psychological significance to him is meaningful.   By the association thus engendered, his own monetary legacy, about which Burness is informing him, becomes Hope—or, reciprocally, Hope becomes the legacy.   This is an implied reformulation very characteristic of Harris's use of linguistic ambiguity to express intended multiple layers of meaning.

In addition to the continuities already noted between Harris's earlier books and *Genesis*, certain interesting new developments mark this later novel. The most important is the delineation of Hope.

The despair represented by the "boisterous technical bodies" and the "complex industry of fact" of the crew of which Hope is chief, and of their leader Wellington, and the crew's "violence manqué," are interpreted as a function of the short-circuiting of their development such that they are not in touch with the "charismatic fire." The result is that they live in a state of dichotomy, of unconsciousness, of impotence, of stasis, and finally of victimization. Their situation constitutes a continuity with the dichotomy of "victor-victim" of historical and psychological stasis, discussed in previous chapters in relation to Harris's earlier fiction.

As in his other books, Harris conveys in *Genesis* the idea that entities usually conceived of as opposites are better considered as dialectically related. He uses a linguistic metaphor to describe their relationship: They are "tenses." A "tense," grammatically speaking (and in this quotation Harris clearly intends the grammatical sense), refers to language usage that discriminates temporality and repetition. Tenses, the novel suggests, are "twins." As one "sees oneself" in others—especially, human beings widely believe, in one's twin—one sees the twins "fate" and "freedom" in different "times" or "spaces"; they are not opposites but aspects of each other. Remembering—thinking in terms of past and present—Wellington feels, will "affect the very grain of recollection . . . as though each present illumination shifts the debris of the past a little; or as if the life of the present never ceases. . ." (p. 82). Thus related, fate and freedom both "renew the appointment with ultimate clarity, ultimate love" (p. 81).

The novel's structure expresses the temporal aspect of the linguistic metaphor of tense. For Frank Wellington, the narrator, recalls the "past tense"—past time—of his experiences as leader of the surveying expeditions so many years earlier.

The potentialities of the Word as ultimate repository of human alternative are expressed in the anonymous letter writer's concluding passage:

All day I had relived the past, recorded the past on my own inner page, in my own mind but in each letter, each word. . . .

He [Hope] emigrated into the telling silences secreted in the family of the Word.

Yours in hope,
F. W.   (p. 148)

In my final chapter I investigate Harris's adaptation of the Arawak concept of the *zemi* as expressive of his crucial idea of alternate possibility. I also explore the relation of Harris's contrast of static history and "charismatic fire" in the light of chiliastic belief in the coming of "the New Jerusalem" that appears repeatedly in human history, and of the relation of history and hope in the philosophy of Ernst Bloch. Lastly, I explore Harris's adaptation of African and Amerindian ideas of the nature of linguistic power—the power of the Word—to his view of the power of verbal art.

9

Language and Revolutionary Hope as Immanent Moment

So our campaign slogan must be: reform of consciousness, not through dogma, but through the analysis of that mystical consciousness which has not yet become clear to itself. It will then turn out that the world has long dreamt of that of which it had only to have a clear idea to possess it really. It will turn out that it is not a question of any conceptual rupture between past and future, but rather of the *completion* of the thoughts of the past.

Marx, Letter to Ruge (1843)

Each of us now held at last in his arms what he had been forever seeking and what he had eternally possessed.

Palace of the Peacock, p. 152

Yours in hope,
    F.W.

Genesis of the Clowns, p. 148

In the preceding chapter I discussed the figure of Hope as an embodiment of the possibility of breaking the stasis of victor and victim. He is presented as a "self-sufficient character" in the sense in which Harris applies that term to characters in the novel of classical realism. Hope worships "men of deeds"—mostly military and political figures who are latter-day conquistadors—Rommel, Bustamante, Duvalier.

I also pointed out that it is precisely this unpromising character who, as his name indicates, becomes the symbol of the possibility of breaking the stasis of victor and victim. The novel ends, "Yours in hope, F. W." He is also the link between conscious and unconscious mind, for the F. W. who writes the letter to the narrator Frank Wellington (F. W.) may be taken as the narrator's double. The "letter," then, is a message through spatial distance (Guyana to England) that overcomes the temporal distance of more than a quarter of a century. It also overcomes the "spatial" distance from unconscious to conscious mind that is the temporal distance of past to present in a person's life.

This concluding chapter is devoted to the nature of hope in Harris's fiction, moving into the discussion through the character "Hope" in *Genesis*. I connect Harris's idea of hope (possibility) in human affairs with his theory of language as possessing inherent possibility (hope). This theory of hope is related to the possibilities of doubling, alterity, and alienation as both positive and negative, depending upon whether they are conceived as part of a centered, hierarchical structure or a decentered, nonhierarchical structure. I relate Harris's idea of hope to Ernst Bloch's theory of the immanent moment. And I discuss Harris's sophisticated adaptation of the ancient Arawak Indian symbol of the *zemi* as a representation from a Third World culture of a Third World Modernism. In Harris's work, the *zemi* is a Third World decentered structure.

But in concluding my study with an examination of Harris's idea of hope and its relation to language and to literature and history, it is necessary to return to the beginning of this book, to the terms of the discussion laid out in Chapter 1.

I spoke there of the ancient dichotomy in Western philosophy identified by Derrida as the dichotomy between Nature and Culture. I spoke of the way that, from the beginning of contact between the West and *América mestiza*, the West saw itself as the bearer of culture and *América mestiza* as embodying nature. I spoke of Caliban on his island under the tutelage of Prospero as emblematic of this relationship of alterity, of the Other.

The dichotomy of Nature and Culture is itself an alterity, a doubling. The West projects onto Caliban that part of itself it does not wish to recognize and deals with it as an attribute of the Other.

I introduced my subsequent examination of Harris's fiction as an exploration of his use of doubling, in the context of the relationship of the West and *América mestiza* .

I would like now to consider this alterity as alienation and examine Harris's views on various kinds of alienation, considering it under three aspects. First, I will consider alienation in its relation to the doubling and hierarchy of the centered structure of traditional Western thought, within which the encounter between the West and *América mestiza* was inserted. Second, I will consider alienation as opacity, or, in a Marxian sense, as false consciousness. Both of these aspects of alienation Harris considers destructive. A third aspect of alienation is the perception of the Other in her or his own right. This alienation can be the positive alienation of identity. To borrow Todorov's terms, this alterity is the alterity that does not equate difference with inferiority.[1] For our discussion, the most important point is that it is not a function of hierarchy.

Modernism represents the decentering of traditional Western-centered structures. With this decentering, represented in the West by ethnology, with its emphasis on cultural relativism, comes the potential for dissolution of hierarchy, of rankings of inferiority and superiority.

The following passage from *Capital* is important to our discussion for two reasons. It is a presentation of a kind of alienation that in itself is not pernicious but has roots in the profoundly social nature of human beings, in their dependency upon that "imperilled community," the fate of which concerns Harris so deeply. Yet this alienation, which is in fact the condition of identity, is distorted under certain social-economic conditions so that people fail to see themselves in the Other or in their own creations.

Marx develops the concept of commodity in the first chapter of Capital. Here he discusses the concepts of reification of human relations, fetishization of the commodity, and the opacity deriving from false consciousness as organized by particular social structures. Several students of Marx's writing have made the point that the great significance of his intellectual breakthrough was in the creation of new concepts for viewing what had been accepted as facts. Jameson considers Marx's formulation of the concept of "commodity" to be a creative innovation.[2] Althusser calls attention to the fact that in analyzing determinate structures, "Marx . . . uses at least a dozen different expressions of a metaphorical kind in order to deal with this specific reality, unthought before him. . . ."[3]

Using a coat and linen as an example to explain the difference between "relative form" and "equivalent form," Marx writes that the two are

intimately connected, mutually dependent and inseparable elements of the expression of value; but at the same time, are mutually exclusive antagonistic extremes—i.e., poles of the same expression. . . . The value of the linen can therefore be expressed only relatively, i.e., in some other commodity. . . . The linen expresses its value in the coat; the coat serves as the material in which that value is expressed. The former plays an active, the latter a passive, part. . . .

He goes on a few pages later to say:

In a sort of way, it is with man as with commodities. Since he comes into the world neither with a looking glass in his hand nor as a Fichtian philosopher, to whom "I am I" is sufficient, man first sees and recognizes himself in other men. Peter only establishes his own identity as a man by first comparing himself with Paul as a being of like kind. And thereby Paul, just as he stands in his Pauline personality becomes to Peter the true type of the genus homo. . . .[4]

The interplay between Peter and Paul is, as Marx observes, at once an alienation and a self-recognition. The terms of alterity, the "projection" of qualities, the assigning of terms such as "active" and "passive" to various manifestations of human production, are echoes of the alterity of the Nature-Culture dichotomy, of "activity" and "passivity," of male and female—of Donne and Mariella, for example.

Harris's conception of history—the past of the "imperilled community," the ancestral seedbed, Osirian source of energy for the present generations of characters about whom he writes—is connected with his theory of language. To him, as to Marx, history is not a compilation of discrete events that, simply by being fitted together in temporal sequence or in a logical way, reveal truth about the past. Histories, as written or told, are, rather, meaningful conceptions of the past. They are patterns or structures, and they articulate not only internally but also with other structures. An example is Prudence's psyche as nexus of two generations of Guyanese historical and personal dilemmas. Literature is invested with a function in the creation of history. Its distinctive type of conceptualization is metaphor, a technique identified by Althusser as Marx's innovation in his theory of society and history, which constitutes literature's characteristic articulation with other explanatory systems.

"To discover the various uses of things," says Marx, "is the work of history."[5] This can be rephrased as "history is the discovered uses of things." In itself, this is a dialectical notion. History is both the uses of things (which, as Marx goes on to demonstrate in *Capital*, reside in their relationship) and the *discovered* uses, that is, the concious conceptualization of those uses. Thus the act of constructing fiction becomes a historical work, not in the sense of using historical material or treating historical themes but in the sense of exploring the organization of conceptualizations about human existence.

Just as for Marx the "facts" were not truth, just as for him truth lay in understanding relationship and a meaningful history was a history of patterned relationships, so Harris writes of history and fiction. In understanding this conception of history and of literary style, it is helpful to remember from Harris's fiction, for instance, the ambiguous hairline-horizon along which the "alteration" occurs in the "settled fabric" of Prudence's psyche in *Tumatumari*.

Harris relates the inadequacy of the historical interpretation of the relation of the West and *América mestiza* as that of victor and victim to the inadequacy of the novel of classical realism in portraying the reality of the Caribbean; the novel of classical realism, as I have observed, was the characteristic genre of the trimphant Western bourgeoisie that consolidated the European empire following the voyages of conquest.

Some Western Modernist writers, from their side of the dichotomy, have reacted to the same social and historical situation. Robert Scholes observes:

The extraordinary differences between Joyce's early and late work are not the results of idiosyncratic stylistic experimentation so much as they are aspects of a radical redefinition of the world itself and man's place in it. This redefinition has been summed up neatly and vigorously in a recent collection of essays by Gregory Bateson called *Steps to an Ecology of Mind* (New York, 1972):

In the period of the Industrial Revolution perhaps the most important disaster was the enormous increase of scientific arrogance.

We had discovered how to make trains and other machines. . . .
Occidental man saw himself as an autocrat with complete power over a
universe which was made of physics and chemistry. And the
biological phenomena were in the end to be controlled like processes
in a test tube. Evolution was the history of how organisms learned
more tricks for controlling the environment; and man had better tricks
than any other creature. But that arrogant scientific philosophy is now
obsolete, and in its place there is the discovery that man is only a part
of larger systems and that the part can never control the whole.

Scholes goes on to say: "The intellectual position Joyce arrived at
has much in common with that of Lévi-Strauss, or Piaget, or
Bateson."[6] Wilson Harris certainly belongs in this company as part of
the Modernist tradition. For Scholes and Bateson are discussing a
rejection of the dichotomy and hierarchy of conquest, of victor and
victim, in whose terms *América mestiza* was both subjugated and
conceptualized by the West. But Harris brings to Modernism a Third
World perspective on history, and Third World resources as a writer.
One of these, the more general, I will discuss in its African and Afro-
Caribbean and American manifestation, the idea of *bwanga*. The other,
more specific, and a manifistation of the first, is the ancient Arawak
Indian idea of the *zemi*; Harris makes a sophisticated adaptation of it.[7]

Anthropologists would classify *zemi* and *bwanga* as aspects of
cosmologies that are sometimes called animistic. An animist believes
that gods or spirits reside in, and indeed animate, natural objects and
forces. This idea is very ancient and very widespread; it was found also
in pre-Christian Europe.

Like Christianity, animist beliefs had their popular and their subtler
theologies. The profound belief, of which the water spirits and wood
sprites of the animist pantheon may be a popular interpretation, is often
an understanding of the universe as a "play of forces." This is called
bwanga in certain West African societies and in some cultures in the
Americas, including Afro-American communities in the Carolinas.
Human beings, other animals, and inanimate objects are all influenced
by this play of forces; the forces are in turn susceptible to influence.
The forces or powers may be personified, as for instance in the *loas* of
Haitian Vaudoun. They may be used for either good or ill, to help or to
harm other individuals or a community as a whole. But the forces and

the play of forces is neither good nor evil; though how it is manipulated or treated may hold the universe together or blow it apart.

This view is not congenial to the Western mind, at least not since the triumph of Christianity. One of the great difficulties for the Christian world view is the moral neutrality of such forces. The idea is more similar to the Buddhist idea of karma and its effects, for karma, despite the way the term is popularly used in English, is not the result of an action but the will or volition to act, whether for good or ill. The results of karma are not themselves a punishment or a reward meted out by a deity. They are rather the result of what Western scientific philosophy might call a natural law.[8]

In Chapter 3, I discussed why for similar reasons, a Christian belief system was less useful in understanding *Palace of the Peacock* than was a Buddhist one. The important point I am making here is that the Christian belief system as it dominated Western thought is much more profoundly a centered system, much more profoundly a hierarchical system, and much more profoundly a system of inferiority and superiority than is an animistic one.

The Arawak Indians, from whom Harris takes the idea of the *zemi*, inhabited many regions of South America and the Caribbean before the coming of the Caribs and the Europeans. They treasured certain objects, often stones or shells, that they called *zemis*. These objects possessed "power," or, in an Afro-Caribbean idiom, *bwanga*.

In Harris's development of this idea, anything may be a *zemi*. It might not be too much to say that everything is a *zemi*. For the Arawak, the *zemi* existed not only in itself, as it could be experienced in the physical world as a stone or a shell, but it also contained and generated other possibilities of itself. These might be other shapes, other forms, other existences in parallel universes of possibility. Harris extends the idea beyond objects to persons and events. The *zemi* secretes possibility and dissolves stasis. By qualifying certain events and series of events as facts of history, facts of personality—what Wellington in *Genesis* refers to as "the whole complex industry of fact"—we reify "truth" and "reality." In Harris's thought, the idea of the *zemi* represents structure of personality, of history, of cultural configurations, of the physical universe, and it may be described as asymmetrical—that is, decentered. This is the source of all creative potential.

Harris's literary style makes *zemis* of novels. The fiction I discuss in this book refuses to accord a finished, settled status to the "true" and the "real"; it refuses to exclude alternative. It is here that by looking at Harris's theory of language we can see how it articulates with his theory of history. The parallel possibilities that make language itself a *zemi* are "the telling silences secreted in the family of the Word" (*Genesis*, p. 148); Hope has "emigrated" into these silences.

Harris writes of the role of language in enabling us to perceive alternative:

A mental landscape is a field of authentic discovery—a field where "new" things are "seen" as though language itself is the ground of an interior and active expedition through and beyond what is already known—because language itself . . . carries an inverse factor, an unsuspected revolutionary pressure which stands in inverse proportion to obsessive centrality. . . .

As a decentered system, language permits exploration of alternative, including, notably, alternative to "obsessive centrality."

The passage quoted above reveals the relationship Harris establishes among history, psychology, and language. His description of language itself as "the ground of an interior expedition through and beyond what is already known" recalls the metaphorical equation he makes in *Tumatumari* between Prudence's expedition into the interior in joining Roi at the Tumatumari work site and her expedition into the interior of her own and her family's psyche (and thereby into Guyanese society and history).

Through his literary style, Harris seeks to raise the question of whether, if we listen to our own speech—to the alternative not only possible but inseparable from the very construction of human language—we may not find the revolutionary potential to understand alternative, to find watershed instead of escarpment:

. . . the innate life of the word . . . may in itself resist ready-made patterns of exploitation, may in itself resist predetermined objects or biases of truth.[9]

The concept of parallel possibility as the way to break what Harris calls "obsessive centrality," attain a decentered system, and break the idea of history as the "stasis of victor and victim" finds expression on several linguistic levels in the novels I have examined.

The shot fired/not fired in Genesis raises the question of parallel possibility, with the doubling of Frank Wellington Black and White. In *Ascent to Omai* the conception of change in repetition is expressed in the conflation of characters and events over time. In *Tumatumari* the conception is expressed through the "re-conception" Prudence achieves, an alternate possibility of her own life and the lives of others. As Comrade Block says in that novel, "History never repeats itself but it never outlasts itself either." In *Palace of the Peacock* the idea of parallel possibility is expressed on the most general structural level, on the level of plot in the two voyages of the crew. The two versions of the death of Donne that I examined in Chapter 3 furnish an excellent example of parallel possibility in history and in psychology—that is, on both the individual and the social planes. The first version tells the story of the conquest of America by Europe and the terms of the Western Nature-Culture dichotomy that placed *América mestiza*—Nature, female, subjugated, in opposition to Europe; Culture, male, conquistador—and warns of the destructiveness inherent in all such formulations. The second version of the death of Donne represents what Harris called in the passage quoted in Chapter 1 the "subjective alteration" without which "the community is doomed to perpetuate an endless reinforcement of conflict." And the characteristics of his fiction that I am now pointing out are the changes in the "texture of the novel to allow these juxtapositions to play" in a way that allows the "creation of a vision through and beyond stasis."

This alteration constitutes a fundamental change in the experience of the Self and the Other—a change in the understanding of the nature of alterity. Todorov describes a system in which otherness is not hierarchized in inferiority and superiority. Harris goes beyond this, for, as I show in the analysis of the two versions of the death of Donne, victor-victim, active-passive, Nature-Culture not only come to understand and value each other as difference but also come to understand that the poles of difference are integral parts of self. Mariella's experience is an alienated experience shared with both the narrator and Donne.

Other characteristics of Harris's writing that have sometimes mystified commentators also become comprehensible. His use of "and . . . and . . . and," of "or . . . or . . . or," is not an expression of ambiguity but rather grammatical expression of parallel possibility.

Importantly, this is not hierarchized explanation but nonhierarchized parallel possibility. In Scholes's terms, it is appropriate to speak of Harris's exploitation of the paradigmatic resources of language; that is, the way a word "is . . . defined . . . by all the words which might have filled its place but have been displaced by it"[10] In Scholes' system paradigmatic sets include synonyms and antonyms, other words with similar sound patterns, and other words with the same grammatical function. Harris establishes reverberations of all the other possibilities inherent in the structure of language, temporarily displaced by the "reality" of what is present, but not definitely excluded; these parallel possibilities are in fact present in their very absence.

Derrida writes of the anxiety that can arise when people accustomed to centered, hierarchical structures are no longer able to defer responsibility to, and look for safety in, a confirming center outside the structure. They must look to themselves—in Derrida's words, they are "implicated in the game."

But such a nonhierarchized structure also offers the possibility of freedom from the stasis of victor and victim, people achieve an adequation to Reality in its many manifestations, and not just to the various Reals (again in the Lacanian sense where the Real is a social, symbolic construct permitted by language). They can emerge from the sequence of human-made disasters issuing from domination and subjugation. From acceptance of total "implication in the game" of a decentered system analogous to Lacan's decentered linguistic system and opposed to a centered, hierarchical structure, a new, fluid, creative, living, and nondevastating conception of the human personality and human society emerges. "Language has always been the companion of empire," Todorov writes; Harris's use of language undermines it as supportive of empire.

Psychologically speaking, such a result constitutes an end to alienation as opacity but not to alienation as identity. This is contact with the real, no longer mediated by Reals; or, perhaps better, the mediating symbolic structures of the Real become transparent so that they are perceived even as they are used. Therefore, they are taken less seriously as absolute measure and lose their power to dominate the psyche.

The "individual ego," no longer suffering an internal doubling and hierarchy, no longer tyrannizes but functions integratively, as a kind of psychological rudder. This final accomplishment that heals the interior and exterior was inherent in the hierarchy of dominance and subjugation; if achieved, it goes beyond Lévi-Strauss's "undertaking to reintegrate culture into nature . . . and finally, to reintegrate life into the totality of its physiochemical conditions," to become the fully self-aware human psyche.[10]

To sum up this part of the discussion: Harris proposes the possibility for change inherent in a decentered structure like the Lacanian linguistic model, expressing the idea in his fiction as parallel possibility. In doing this, Harris develops the Arawak Indian idea of the *zemi* as a sophisticated metaphor for a Third World decentered structure, symbolizing the possibility of ending alienation as opacity and as false consciousness in the Marxian sense and of ending the hierarchy of conquest and subjugation, of the stasis of victor and victim.

Again, certain Marxian formulations express very well the Herculean effort to reconceive the world beyond the ancient Western dichotomy of Nature-Culture, body-spirit, matter-mind.

Christopher Caudwell, the British Marxist literary critic (who died in the Spanish Civil War before he was thirty and whom Robert Scholes among other literary critics considers underrated) wrote:

Thought is a relation of matter; but the relation is real; it is not only real but determining. It is real *because* it is determining. Mind is a determining set of relations between the matter in my body and in the rest of the Universe.[11]

Harris's fiction is thought attempting to express linguistically that "set of relations between the matter in my body and in the rest of the universe."

Indeed, in several places in Marx's own writing one encounters an emphasis on the transindividual nature of products of the mind and on the nexus where matter and mind in the universe manifest themselves in human physical and ideational forms. I discussed earlier Marx's elaboration of the concept of commodity in Chapter 1 of *Capital*.

In the same chapter, he discusses the related concepts of reification of human relations and fetishization of commodities and the opacity deriving from false consciousness as caused and organized by particular social structures. In Harris's hands, the Arawak Indian idea of the *zemi* becomes a symbol of the possibility of ending alienation as opacity and as false consciousness in the Marxian sense. It becomes a symbol for the possibility of decentered structures, as a way of thinking that ends the hierarchy of conquest and subjugation, of the stasis of victor and victim.

I come now to the final part of my discussion, the nature of hope in Harris's fiction. Clearly he is concerned with social, historical, and political issues. His idea of hope is not one that can be conveyed in the novel of classical realism. From the point of view of a critic like Pierre Macherey, the argument could be advanced that despite Harris's critique of colonialism and imperialism, despite his critique of those colonial classes that refuse *América mestiza* for the West, his own fiction remains caught, not as regards its content but actually in its structure, in the toils of the same kind of class assumptions. Such an analysis would see Harris's limitations in the structural limitations of his fiction, not in that which Harris does as a writer or of which he speaks but in that which is absent and about which he is silent. From this standpoint, one of the most serious objections to the novels I discuss is the almost constant association between insight into the nature of society and death, the ultimate absence. Indeed, it seems almost as if death is the likely, if not inevitable, result of such insight. Insight becomes failure, with the final failure, death, as its consequence. Where then is the basis for asserting that Harris proposes a philosophy of revolutionary hope?

This seems to me a very important question, one that Harris invites by organizing his fiction around social concerns and around the relation between individual and society. The answer lies in his understanding of the relation between the categories of nature, death, and hope. Not surprisingly, we find ourselves back at the dichotomy Derrida identifies as fundamental to Western philosophy, the dichotomy between Nature and Culture, body and mind.

Earlier in this chapter I analyzed Harris's fiction as linguistically structured around the idea of parallel possibility. This parallel possibility and the hope such a perspective engenders offers a Third World resolution of the ancient Western dichotomy.

Again, it is useful to consider aspects of the Western tradition that throw light on Harris's approach. C. L. R. James, in a perceptive essay, has pointed out the affinities of Harris's thought with Heidegger's, especially the emphasis upon language as crucial in man's experience of Being and Time.[12] In considering the specific question of hope, a close affinity also exists between Harris's thought and that of Ernst Bloch. Bloch, an intellectually eccentric German-Jewish scholar, first exercised an impact upon the English-speaking world indirectly, through his influence upon Karl Mannheim's theories of chiliastic religion developed in the latter's book *Ideology and Utopia*.[13] Later he was introduced through the interest of New Wave Christian theologians.

Bloch ultimately seeks an adequation of subject and object that will permit the realization of a genuine self-consciousness. Such self-consciousness eludes us in known societies, where experience necessarily comes to us fragmented. A similarity to Harris's ideas is apparent. The deepest similarity, however (I do not suggest direct influence), is in their emphasis on the category of hope.

Hope would seem to be time bound. In conventional terms it always implies a future. What, then, is the nature of hope in Harris's world, where linear time is called into question as a valid category? It is useful to consider the concept of "immanent moment" developed by Bloch.[14]

To Bloch, the "immanent moment" was stated in terms of the religion of his own ethnic group. It was the awareness of an "opening" in consciousness, allowing the advent of the Messiah. In other words, it is a future experienced as a pull toward something lying beyond a horizon. Yet it can be experienced "now." Only certain rare individuals, whose contemporaries usually define them as eccentric, report experience of the "immanent moment." Among those who have convinced great numbers of its reality are individuals as diverse in culture and temperament as Mohammed, Joseph Smith (founder of the Church of Jesus Christ of Latter-day Saints, or Mormons), and Thomas of Munster, the sixteenth century Anabaptist to whom Bloch devoted a careful and detailed study.

Bloch objected to existentialism because he felt it left human beings invalidated in the face of death as a natural catagory. In fact, Bloch makes the important point that the very idea of an unchanging "nature" runs counter to Marxist theory. Human beings and nature reciprocally alter and redefine each other; consider the interactive process Caudwell describes in the passage I quoted earlier. Bloch writes:

For dialectical materialism . . . no preestablished natural order, valid for all eternity, exists . . . and in this sense materialism does not exclude the possibility of a victory over death.

The French scholar, Laënnec Hurbon writes regarding this enigmatic statement that

Bloch proposes to Marxists that they rethink the concept of history (*Geschichte*) in accordance with a cosmology that considers matter as a totality open to surprises and novelties, and that renders possible the confrontation with death other than as a submission to fate.

This is what Harris's idea of the *zemi* as alternative, parallel possibility, proposes. Hurbon then introduces into his discussion the expression "extraterritorial to death," a rendering of Bloch's "Exterritorialität zum Tod."

... the true being-there (*das Da-Sein*) has not yet been realized and will not yield itself up except in the future. If this be so, one cannot affirm that death holds power over the essential kernel of human existence; all it can do is bring us as close as possible to this kernel which, itself, is extraterritorial to death![15]

It is this "extraterritoriality to death," this possibility of finding a meaning in immortality, which unfolds to Harris's characters. It is conditional upon an understanding of the limitations of the individual body and psyche as usually conceived. In literary terms, it involves abandoning the limitations of the novel of consolidation of character and of seeking a way to convey an understanding of the "extraterritoriality to death." For Harris's novels are as much experiments in trying to communicate the ineffable as are the classic writings of Christian, Islamic, and Buddhist mystics; they are akin, too, as we have seen, to certain trends in Western Marxist thought.

Bloch's immanent moment, itself potent and fraught with potential, is the moment that fascinates Harris and constitutes the spatial-temporal locus of his fiction. Hope exists in a realization or reperception of *what is* rather than in experiencing an alteration of *what is*. In the dialectical process as Marxists view it there comes a moment when the new is fully developed and coexistent with—and within—the old. It is a moment when truth—reality—becomes a question of state of consciousness, of perspective, of whether the view is understood, in Harris's words, as being "watershed" or "escarpment." This moment also involves movement. Jameson's discussion of the moment is useful in considering, for instance, the psychic and historical process depicted in *Tumatumari*. His minimal definition of the dialectical moment is

moment in which thought rectifies itself, in which the mind, suddenly drawing back and including itself in its new and widened apprehension, doubly restores and regrounds its earlier notions in a new glimpse of reality. . . .[16]

The stasis of victor and victim finds literary expression in the novel of persuasion, with its insistence upon the self-sufficient, consolidated character—one true version of events—and its exclusion of all parallel possibilities. Harris, I believe, has rejection of such conventional history in mind when he asserts that conquest is the greatest evil that human beings can commit. For conquest solidifies stasis, absolutizes opacity, and exiles alternative—which is to say, it forbids hope.

The Harrisian idea of opacity seems akin to the Marxian position that the commodity form of production conceals the true relation between human labor and alteration of the world and thus creates alienation.[17] For Harris, all objects, events, relations—including his own fiction—are in a sense *zemis*; but to perceive them as such requires penetration of the opacity of stasis. He uses painting as a metaphor for our profound resistance to the perception that the whole world we know, including our "selves" (physical and psychological), is a palimpsest, containing not only the record of the "forgotten Siberian pilgrimages" that we—like the enigmatic member of the "folk" held captive in *Palace*—have all taken, as cultures and as individuals, but also the record of all possible alternative pilgrimages. Marxian "opacity" can be seen as a manifestation, in a certain social formation and at a certain historical juncture, of the larger opacities Harris discusses.[18] In our time the commodity may be the densest, most characteristic, and most potent of our culture's *zemis*, could we learn to see it so. This learning might be described as the undoing of a false consciousness, which is essential if the world is to survive the legacy of the voyages of European conquest. For the first time, we live in what can be truly understood only as "one world." Bloch writes:

Columbus, in any case, firmly believed that the islands which he had discovered were those of the Hesperides, and that behind the land at the mouth of the Orinoco, Eden lay concealed. And this paramount basic goal, when one believed that it had been attained, gave the world such completely different shades of coloring that it was, in a fundamental manner, wrenched out of its old status. Columbus goes so far as to speak of Heaven and the New Earth which had been reached through him.[19]

In the novels I treat in this study, Harris writes from a Caribbean perspective on this historical movement. From that perspective, the "New Heaven and the New Earth" are expressed in his version of *lo real maravilloso americano*. The "different colorings" of the world, to which Bloch alludes, become in Harris's fiction the patternings, textures, and orderings suggested by an American landscape, an American psyche, an American history. He seeks to "wrench the world out of its old status" through uses of language, discussed in this study, that are intended to enable us to perceive proportions that are alternatives to those of conventional Western history, psychology, and literature.

Language, the most precious of our *zemis*, is structured; yet its singular value derives from its unpredictability and its plenitude, from its profound asymmetricality. To understand language in this way is to understand the potential at the heart of the universe. For Harris, it is only in understanding this potential that humanity may find the capacity to overcome its recurrent self-inflicted conquests and catastrophes. Because he writes in such a way as to undercut the opposition of Nature and Culture, in the name of which *nuestra América mestiza* was subjugated, Harris's work is profoundly revolutionary and liberating. Because that conquest was fundamentally and ultimately as devastating for the West as for *nuestra América*—as the quandaries of the modern era eloquently demonstrate—the possibility of liberation is equally relevant for Euro-America. Throughout a writing career that now spans over three decades, the conviction of the power of language and imagination has remained central to Harris's fictional vision; and so has what he calls in his most recent critical work, *The Womb of Space*, "the pursuit of enduring cross-cultural spirit" (p. xx). Of this cross-cultural spirit, he wrote at the beginning of his literary career in 1951:

... the impact of the human mind and body on the hard world, in constructing something and destroying something, has a unity or combination that is both secret and plain; ... the new architecture of the world must be a profound understanding and revelation of all factors that combine into the phenomenon of effort and achievement not for one race of men but for all mankind together.[20]

Harris's art reveals his faith in the resources of language both to express and to create an understanding that will constitute such a "new architecture of the world."

Notes

Chapter 1

1. Gordon K. Lewis, *The Growth of the Modern West Indies* (New York: Monthly Review Press, 1968), p. 257.

2. David Halliburton, *Poetic Thinking: An Approach to Heidegger* (Chicago: Univ. of Chicago Press, 1981), p. 211. Derrida, to whom Halliburton refers, states, "The event I called a rupture . . . would presumably have come about when the structurality of structure had to begin to be thought, that is to say, repeated, and this is why I said that this disruption was repetition in all senses of this word." From "Structure, Sign, and Play in the Discourse of the Human Sciences" in *The Structuralist Controversy: The Language of Criticism and the Science of Man,* edited by Richard Macksey and Eugenio Donato (Baltimore: Johns Hopkins Univ. Press, 1972), p. 249. For an interesting discussion of this article, see Halliburton, especially pp. 202-10.

3. Jaques Derrida, "Structure, Sign and Play" in *The Structuralist Controversy*, p. 251.

4. I deliberately do not address in this book the vexed question of a distinction between Modernism and post-Modernism (see, for example, Ihab Hassan, *Paracriticisms* (Urbana: Univ. of Illinois Press, 1975), pp. 40-44. However distinguished—if at all—they are merely aspects of the larger shift in cultural relations of which the relation between the Third World and the West is my principal concern here.

5. Anonymous review, *Times Literary Supplement*, 5 December 1965.

6. The phrase "language of crisis" that Gilkes uses in "Hidden Densities," *Times Literary Supplement,* 25 March 1977, p. 334, and "art of extremity," title of Part 3 of his book on Harris's fiction, *Wilson*

Harris and the Caribbean Novel (London: Longman Caribbean, 1975), are both apt in identifying Harris's ties to a Modernist sensibility.

7. See Gordon K. Lewis, *The Growth of the Modern West Indies*, p. 258. He stresses the point that contemporary forays into the interior represent a twentieth-century repetition of the conquistadorial impulse.

8. See Hena Maes-Jelinek, "The Myth of El Dorado in the Caribbean Novel," *Journal of Commonwealth Literature* (June 1971), p. 113, on the compulsively repetitious quality of the European assault on *América mestiza* in pursuing El Dorado. Harris writes of this conquistador myth that it constitutes the potential for a fiction of ambiguity, "the substance of this adventure, involving men of all races, past and present conditions, has begun to acquire a residual pattern of illuminating correspondences. El Dorado, City of Gold, City of God." From *Tradition, the Writer and Society, Critical Essays* (1967; reprint, London: New Beacon Press, 1973), p. 35.

9. "Wilson Harris", in *Contemporary Novelists* (New York: St. Martin's Press, 1982), p. 292.

10. Wilson Harris, "Fossil and Psyche," in Wilson Harris, *Explorations: A Selection of Talks and Articles, 1966-1981*. Edited with an Introduction by Hena Maes-Jelinek (Mundelstrup, Denmark: Dangaroo Press, 1981), p. 77.

11. Harris, *Tradition, the Writer and Society*, pp. 28-30, for the terms "novel of consolidation" and "novel of persuasion," contrasted with another kind of realism he identifies as akin to that of Garcia Marquez's fiction and Merleau-Ponty's philosophy (pp. 24-25).

12. Derrida, "Structure, Sign and Play," in *The Structuralist Controversy*, p. 250.

13. Ibid., p. 252.

14. Kas-Kas: *Interviews with Three Caribbean Writers in Texas*. (Austin: Univ. of Texas Press, 1972), p. 44.

15. See Ian Watt's *The Rise of the Novel: Studies in Defoe; Richardson and Fielding* (Berkeley and Los Angeles: Univ. of California Press, 1962), esp. Ch. 3 on the development of individualism and the individual character in the novel.

16. On Modernism, see Albert J. Guerard, "Introduction," *Stories of the Double* (Philadelphia: Lippincott, 1967) and Richard Ellman and Charles Feidelson, Jr., *The Modern Tradition* (New York: Oxford University Press, 1965), esp. p. vi.

17. Jacques Lacan, *The Language of the Self*, translated with notes and commentary by Anthony Wilden (Baltimore: Johns Hopkins Univ. Press, 1968), pp. 161-63.

18. Jacques Lacan, "Of Structure as an Inmixing of an Otherness Prerequisite to any Subject Whatever," in *The Structuralist Controversy*, p. 192.

19. R. D. Laing, *Politics of the Family and Other Essays* (New York: Vintage Books, 1972), pp. 3-10.

20. M. M. Bakhtin, "Discourse in the Novel", in *The Dialogic Imagination*, edited by Michael Holquist, translated by Caryl Emerson and Michael Holquist. (Austin: Univ. of Texas Press, 1981), p. 332.

21. Ibid., p. 326.

22. For the meaning of "Guyana," see the front quotation to *Tumatumari*. See J.H. Perry, *The Discovery of South America* (New York: Taplinger Publishing Co., 1979) for the impression the Americas made on the first European explorers.

23. Hena Maes-Jelinek, "'Inimitable Painting,' New Developments in Wilson Harris's Latest Fiction," *Ariel* 8, no. 3 (July 1977): 63-80.

24. "Wilson Harris," in *Contemporary Novelists*, p. 292.

25. For a comprehensive discussion of maronnage, see "Introduction," Richard Price, comp., *Maroon Societies; Rebel Slave Communities in the Americas,* 1st ed. (Garden City, N. Y.: Anchor Press, 1973) and "The Guiana Maroons: Changing Perspectives in 'Bush Negro' Studies," *Caribbean Studies* 11, 4 (1972): 82-105.

26. For a brief account of Guyanese history, see Lewis, *The Growth of the Modern West Indies*, Chapter 10; see also *Encyclopaedia Britannica* (1963), vol. 10, "Guiana." For population figures, see *Collier's Encyclopedia* (1981), vol. 11, "Guyana." In 1970 (about the time of Prudence's breakdown in *Tumatumari*), total population was 699,848. About fifty percent of this number was Indian, thirty-three percent was Black, twelve percent was mixed Black and White, and the remainder Amerindian and "other".

27. Lewis, *Growth of the Modern West Indies*, pp. 257-58.

28. Ibid., pp. 257-8.

29. For Harris's strong interest in Latin America, see his statement in "The Making of Tradition, " *Explorations*, pp. 88-96. Gilkes, *Wilson Harris* (p. 22), discusses Harris's intention of writing a novel set in Brazil.

30. See C. L. R. James's *The Black Jacobins: Toussaint L'Ouverture and the San Domingo Revolution.* This is a classic account; James, a Trinidadian, is one of the foremost scholars and political activists of his generation. Also: Eric Williams, *Capitalism and Slavery* (New York: Russell and Russell, 1961; reissue of Univ. of North Carolina Press, pp. 194-95 and Wallace K. Ferguson, *The Renaissance* (New York: Holt, Rinehart and Winston, 1940) esp. pp. 96-103.

31. See Guerard, *Stories of the Double*. Although, as Guerard notes on p. 14 of his introductory essay, the word "double" is often "embarrassingly vague" and therefore requires contextual flexibility in its application, it is useful in both literary and psychological studies. Harris's "revenants," or characters from one novel that reappear in a later one, are another of his versions of multiple personalities. I discuss doubling and *América mestiza* at greater length in Chapter 2.

32. Tzvetan Todorov, *The Conquest of America,* translated by Richard Howard (New York: Harper and Row, 1985), p. 70. Translation of *La Conquête de l'Amérique* (Paris: Editions du Seuil, 1982). Todorov seems rather to downplay Las Casas's negative views of Blacks.

33. Stephen Jay Gould, *The Panda's Thumb: More Reflections in Natural History* (New York: W.W. Norton and Co., 1982), p. 289.

34. V. S. Naipaul, *The Mimic Men* (New York: Macmillan, 1967).

35. See Winifred K. Vass, *The Bantu-Speaking Heritage of the United States* (Los Angeles: Center for African and Afro-American Studies, University of California, 1979); Margaret E. Crahan and Franklin W. Knight, eds., *Africa and the Caribbean: Legacies of a Link* (Baltimore: Johns Hopkins Univ. Press, 1979); Ivan van Sertima, *They Came Before Columbus: The African Presence in Ancient America* (New York: Random House, 1972); and Wilson Harris, *Explorations*, p. 25.

36. See my "Alejo Carpentier's *Los Pasos Perdidos,*" in *Escritura: teoría y crítica literarias* (Journal of the University of Venezuela, Caracas), año 4, 7 (enero-junio 1979): 93-108, for implications of the perception of the Caribbean as a double of the Mediterranean. Much of what Edward Said discusses in his book *Orientalism* (New York: Pantheon Books, 1978) is relevant to my concept of Euro-America and *América mestiza.* Thus the Orient "is one of [Europe's] deepest and most recurring images of the Other . . . the Orient has helped to define Europe [or the West] as its contrasting image, idea, personality, experience" (pp. 1-2). Said's discussion of Orientalism as a discourse in Foucault's sense has similarities to my discussion here, as does his stress on the discourse of Orientalism as a "unifying set of clues" (p. 42) that developed as ideological justification coinciding with the "unparalleled expansion" that from 1815 to 1914 extended European colonial dominion from 35 to 85 percent of the earth's surface. The process occurred in the Caribbean considerably earlier.

37. Guerard, *Stories of the Double,* p. 14.

38. From a conversation between the author and Wilson Harris in April 1983.

39. Michael Gilkes discusses Harris's attitude not only toward accepting his own mixed ancestry but also in seeing the process of

miscegenation as a natural one for races in contact and cultural blending as a source of great richness. See *Wilson Harris and the Carabbean Novel*, p. xii.

40. For a very important contemporary development of this idea from a Caribbean perspective, see the Cuban theoretician Roberto Fernández Retamar's *Calibán: Apuntes sobre la cultura ennuestra América*, 2d ed. (México: Editorial Diógenes, S. A., 1974).

41. Derrida, "Structure, Sign and Play," in *The Structuralist Controversy*, p. 252.

42. Frantz Fanon, *Black Skin, White Masks* (New York: Grove Press, 1967), pp. 160-61. For similar investigations in the United States see work by the Afro-American pyschiatrist Alvin M. Pousraint of Harvard University, including *Why Blacks Kill Blacks* (New York: Emerson Hall Publishers, 1972). Fanon engages the controversy of Prospero and Caliban in his.critique of D.O. Mannoni's *Prospéro et Caliban: Psychologie de la Colonisation* (Paris: Editions du Seuil, 1950); English version, London: Methuen, 1956.

43. Jacques Lacan, "The Mirror Stage as Formative of the Function of the I as Revealed in Psychoanalytic Experience," paper delivered at the Sixteenth International Congress of Psychoanalysis, (Zurich, 17 July 1949. English version is in is in Jacques Lacan, *Ecrits: a Selection*, translated by Alan Sheridan (New York: W.W. Norton and Co., 1977), pp. 2-3

44. Fanon, *Black Skin, White Masks*, p. 161.

45. Todorov, *Conquest*, p. 35, on Indians as "naked" and "dark"; p. 130 on Spanish views of them as occupying a place in a natural series.

Chapter 2

1. Todorov, *The Conquest of America*, p. 25.

2. Roberto Gonzalez Echevarria, *Alejo Carpentier: The Pilgrim at Home* (Ithaca, N.Y.: Cornell Univ. Press, 1977), p. 252.

3. Ibid, pp. 25, 26.

4. Todorov, *The Conquest of America*, p. 5.

5. Ibid., p. 25.

6. Derrida, "Structure, Sign and Play," in *The Structuralist Controversy*, pp. 247 ff.

7. For discussions of the concept of Negritude, see W.A. Jeanpierre, "Negritude" (pp. 32-50), and Lilyan Lagneau, "The Negritude of L. S. Senghor" (pp. 124-39), in *Présence Africaine*, vol. 2, no. 39 (1962), English edition, vol. 2. For an emphasis on Aimé Césaire, see *Non-Vicious Circle: Twenty Poems of Aimé Césaire*, translated and with an introduction and commentary by Gregson Davis (Stanford, Calif.: Stanford Univ. Press. 1984). Davis stresses the important point, applicable also to Harris's work, that in considering Césaire's writing, the "mythic universality must be tempered by . . . another set of concrete facts: the origins of the concept of négritude within a specific historical situation." Davis quotes Césaire from a 1971 interview with Depestre: "It [négritude] was really a form of resistance to the politics of assimilation" and continues, "Thus . . . for Césaire the concept of négritude is a countermyth created in a concrete intercultural situation (colonization)" (Circle, p. 20). The changes in this "concrete intercultural situation" during the nearly thirty years that separate the emergence of Négritude and the first publication of Harris's fiction may account for some of the differences I note between Négritude and Harris's thought.

8. See Frederic Jameson, *Marxism and Form* (Princeton, N.J.: Princeton Univ. Press, 1971), pp. 131-32.

9. Arthur O. Lovejoy, *The Great Chain of Being: A Study of the History of an Idea* (Cambridge: Harvard Univ. Press, 1936).

10. Charles Bonnet, *Contemplation de la nature*, (Amsterdam: Marc-Michel Rey, 1764), p. 27. Quoted in Stephen Jay Gould, *Ontogeny and Phylogeny* (Cambridge, Mass., and London: the Belknap Press of Harvard Univ., 1977), p. 23.

11. Derrida, "Structure, Sign and Play," in *The Structuralist Controversy*, p. 249.

12. Ibid., p. 248

13. The idea of "falling outside of history" is very useful in considering the Caribbean situation.

14. Ibid., p. 134

15. Naipaul, *The Loss of El Dorado*, p. 16.

16. Jameson, *Marxism and Form*, pp. 131-32.

17. Ernst Bloch, *Verfremdungen*, 2 vols. (Frankfurt: Suhrkamp Verlag, 1963), vol. 1, p. 58. Quoted in Jameson, *Marxism and Form*, p. 131.

18. Wilson Harris, *Tradition, the Writer and Society*, p. 29.

19. Ibid., p. 28.

20. Richard O. Boyer and Herbert M. Morais, *Labor's Untold Story* (New York: UE, 1980), p. 193.

21. Derrida is speaking of this in "Structure, Sign and Play" in *The Structuralist Controversy*.

22. Derrida writes: "One can say in total assurance that there is nothing fortuitous about the fact that the critique of ethnocentrism--the very condition of ethnology--should be systematically and historically contemporaneous with the destruction of the history of metaphysics. Both belong to a single and same era ("Structure, Sign and Play," in *The Structuralist Controversy*, p. 252). Todorov calls ethnology "at once the child of colonialism and the proof of its death throes" (*Conquest*, p. 250).

23. Bakhtin's ideas on carnival and on caricature are interesting in this connection. A prominent sociological and anthropological interpretation of carnival has been functional; that is, it is seen as an escape valve for oppressed social strata. For example, this interpretation would explain the license given slaves during Caribbean carnival to mock their masters. This perspective sees carnival as ultimately tending to stasis and maintenance of the political and social status quo. In contrast, Bakhtin proposes carnival as an eruption of socially nonprivileged voices that enter creatively and actively into the pluriverse of discourse, creating new linguistic and imaginative forms that can also lead to thinking in new ways that facilitate social change. Bakhtin's approach is more useful in thinking about Harris's writing. I discuss Harris and carnival in more detail in Chapter 7 of this book.

Bakhtin's discussion of caricature is also useful; see, for instance, *Rabelais and His World*, Ch. 5, "The Grotesque Image of the Body," translated by Hélène Iswolsky (Bloomington: Indiana Univ. Press, 1984). It is noteworthy, however, that he accepts the figure of Dido, "a blunt-nosed African Negress" (p. 304), as appropriate to "degrade" high art (Scarron's example of burlesque) and finds childbirth an appropriate example of the "clownish" (p. 304, after Scheegans). He writes: "In the clownery example, no one is mocked, neither the stutterer nor Harlequin" (p. 306). How about women? "In the example of the burlesque the high style of the *Aeneid* and classicism in general are the object of mockery ..." (p. 306). How about Black people, specifically Black women? The mockery is so deep rooted in Western culture that Bakhtin misses it. It is below the level on which he conducts his analysis. He does not see women as one of his oppressed strata; and he sees Blacks as those others who form the category appropriate to symbolize the degradation of the West's classical culture. Thus, although Krystyna Pomorska writes that Bakhtin was concerned all his life with "the danger of European cultural 'centrism,' the recognition of the multiplicity of cultural strata, their relative hierarchy, and their dialogue" (*Rabelais and His World*, p. x), these passages suggest that he remained caught in some of Europe's most basic imperialistic and patriarchal assumptions. With regard to both imperialism and patriarchy, and their connection, Harris is far more aware of these underlying assumptions.

24. Wilson Harris, *Tradition the Writer and Society*, p. 34.

25. Todorov, *Conquest*, p. 248. This statement is especially puzzling because his book documents the Western *refusal* to know the Other as its dominant tendency; such a sweeping assertion has something of the flavor of the conqueror about it! How would one demonstrate that the Third World does not "know" the West? Furthermore, it seems odd not at least to qualify this assertion with an acknowledgment of the role superior Western fire power, rather than "knowledge," often played. See Fanon's *Black Skin White Masks* for a critique similar to the one I make here. Fanon objects to the interpretation of natives' dreams using Freudian categories rather than as dreams of the guns that destroyed their autonomy. Are both of these examples of a tendency to miss an especially ugly aspect of the relation of alterity between the West and the Third World?

26. J. Hillis Miller raises a number of intriguing questions about language, realist and modernist fiction, and doubling. Speaking of Dickens's *Sketches by Boz* he writes: "Each character lives as a sign referring not to substance but to another sign" and sees the work as concerned with "the collective creation of meaning and value" (p. 29). And, he continues, "the sketches are not *mimesis* of an externally existing reality, but the interpretation of that reality according to highly artificial schemas inherited from the past" (p. 32). He writes of Roman Jakobson's concepts of metonymy and metaphor: "Jakobson . . . comes close to formulating the covert identity of metonymy and metaphor as two versions of the necessary displacement involved in all language" (p. 42). He thus suggests that realist fiction is no more mimetic than Modernist fiction and that the reason for this lies in the very nature of language. What distinguishes Harris's writing from such writing as Dickens's in the *Sketches*, in my view, is the level at which the "collective creation of meaning and value" is foregrounded in the fiction. As I discuss in Chapter 1 of this book, Harris's emphasis, to borrow Bakhtinian terminology, is less on individuals and social context than on the play of social (and psychological) heteroglossia.

Hillis Miller's discussion of Jakobson also has significant implications for my analysis of psychological and historical doubling and its relation to language and psyche. He writes that "the view of literary language I am presupposing would not see a work of literature as able ever to be self-contained, self-sustaining, in its referential purity."

Rather, it is "a link in a chain of transformations and substitutions" (p. 39). This chain is open to the extra-literary world; we must remember Gregson Davis's warning to take account of the "specific historical situation" of the Caribbean. Thus, as I discuss in the text, the implications of contesting the conventions of the realist novel are different from a Third World than from a Western perspective. Hillis Miller continues: "One might even argue that the metonymic displacement, in its movement from presence to absence, is even more fundamental than metaphorical transference or superposition" (p. 40). For Lacan, the very foundation of the psychological Subject/I is linguistic and conceived according to the "displacement involved in all language."

The defining and confining mark of the relation between the West and *América mestiza*, affecting América mestiza's relation to centers and origins, was its function as negation, absence. From the Western point of view, the double or shadow Other was the denied (negated) embodiment of rejected characteristics of the Self; the Other, Caliban, stands for the self in possessing what must not be part of the self. This operation constitutes a psychological movement of metonymy, from "presence" to "absence." In adopting the conqueror's view, *América mestiza* is left only a (non)existence as a negative.

In terms of contiguity (the mark of metonymy) and similarity (the mark of metaphor), *América mestiza* and the West stand in charged relationship literally and symbolically. Prospero and Caliban function as they do only because of a perceived similarity nevertheless marked by a disjunction that Prospero must at all costs maintain, for Caliban is the dark side of the self, similar (metaphorical) but other, not-self and also elsewhere, not contiguous (metonymical). Thus the peculiar charge miscegenation has carried in America, for, though parents and children may always stand in both metaphorical and metonymical relation, the children of miscegenation threaten the maintenance of the psychological otherness necessary to guarantee Western identity as not-Caliban. All quotations are from J. Hillis Miller and David Borowitz, *Charles Dickens and George Cruikshank: Papers read at a Clark Library Seminar on May 9, 1970* (William Andrews Clark Memorial Library: Univ. of California Press, 1971).

Chapter 3

1. V. S. Naipaul, *The Loss of El Dorado: A History*, pp. 43-44.

2. Gilkes and Harris himself have both discussed the cauda pavonis (peacock) as the alchemical symbol of spiritual progress. The parrot was believed to announce the proximity to El Dorado, and so functions in *Palace of the Peacock*. See also Harris, "History, Fable and Myth," in *Explorations*, p. 31, on *nigredo* (blackness) and *albedo* (whiteness). These colors represent, respectively, the unknown and the discovery of the unknown and are therefore aspects of each other. Which is which depends on psychological perspective. See also Herbert Silberer, *Hidden Symbolism of Alchemy and the Occult Arts* (New York: Dover, 1971).

3. Gilkes, *Wilson Harris and the Caribbean Novel*, p. 66, n.22. Gilkes here describes the mandala as a symbol of psychic integration. Edward Bernbaum, from lecture notes taken at the California Academy of Sciences, San Francisco. See also his *The Way to Shambhala* (Garden City, N. Y.: Anchor Press, 1980).

4. *The Diamond Sutra and the Sutra of Hui Neng*. Translated by A. F. Price and Wong Mou-Lam. (Boulder, Colo.: Shambhala, 1977), p. 21.

5. See entry for "Swastika," *Webster's New World Dictionary of the American Language*, p. 1437, David B. Guralnik, Editor in Chief, Second College Edition (New York: Simon & Schuster, 1982).

6. A collection of over 100 Anancy tales was collected from 60 story tellers in Jamaica just before World War I. They were published as Vol. XVII, 1924, of Memoirs of the American Folklore Society, Martha Warren Beckwith's *Jamaica Anansi Stories*. Twenty years later, a distinguished West Indian educator published a group of Anansi stories as currently told to children. He stressed differences between Anancy stories as told in West Africa and those told in the Caribbean, the result of centuries of separation between Africans and New World black populations. (Philip M. Sherlock, *Anansi the Spider Man*, New York; Thomas Y. Crowell, 1954.) A very attractive illustrated presentation of Anancy stories as told today among the Ashanti of Ghana is available in Peggy Appiah, *Ananse the Spider* (New York: Pantheon Books, 1966).

7. Charles Darwin, *The Voyage of the Beagle* (Garden City, N. Y.: The Natural History Library, Anchor Books: 1962), p. 35.

8. R. D. Laing explains "coinherence" thus: "As Sartre would say, the family is united by the reciprocal internalization by each (whose token of membership is precisely this interiorized family) of each other's internalizations." From *Politics of the Family and Other Essays*, p. 5.

9. Quoted by Frank Collymore in a review of *Palace of the Peacock*, *Bim* 9, (July-December 1961): 76.

10. Walpola Rahula, *What the Buddha Taught* (New York: Grove Press, 1974).

11. Hena Maes-Jelinek, *The Naked Design* (Aarhus, Denmark: Dangaroo Press: 1978), p. 35 ff.

12. Two excellent discussions may be found in Raphael Patai, *The Hebrew Goddess* (New York: KTAV Publishing House, 1967), and Gershem Scholem, *On the Kabbalah and Its Symbolism* (New York: Schocken Books, 1965).

Chapter 4

1. Laing, *Politics of the Family*, p. 91.

2. The Diamond Sutra, Section 25, "The Illusion of Ego," p. 64.

3. Gregory Bateson, *Steps to an Ecology of Mind: Collected Essays in Anthropology, Psychology, Evolution and Epistemology* (New York: Ballantine Books, 1972), p. 206.

4. W. J. Howard, "Guiana Quartet: From Personal Myth to National Identity," *Ariel* 1 (January 1970): 46-60. In "Inimitable Painting" (cited in n. 4, Ch. 1), Maes-Jelinek speaks of Harris's double-edged perception of human interactions, as in this passage from *Palace*: "survival through another . . . or another's predicament . . . is a further development of Harris's concept of community. . . ." For a general discussion of this topic, see, *The Naked Design: A Reading of Palace of the Peacock*, esp. pp. 37-39.

5. Lacan, "Of Structure" in *The Structuralist Controversy*, pp. 104 and 192. See the bottom of page 192 for a diagram of "the Lacanian torus" mentioned on p. 86 of this book.

6. Laing, *Politics of the Family*, p. 57.

7. For a discussion of Harris's work in the context of mystical traditions as varied as St. Teresa's "swoon," "the cloud of unknowing," and the Buddhist "void" as well as in terms of Keat's "negative capability," see Nathaniel Mackey's penetrating analysis in "The Unruly Pivot: Wilson Harris's *The Eye of the Scarecrow*" [*Texas Studies in Language and Literature* 20, 4 (Winter 1978): 633]. A Sri Lankan critic, who knew Wilson Harris as a fellow participant in activities of the Commonwealth Literature Association, writes of the Guyanese author's "mythic history" from the perspective of another Third World culture whose philosophies have long accepted such ideas as central. He notes that "the Eastern man has always been wary of linear definitions of any kind." James Goonewardene, "Nationalism and the Writer in Sri Lanka and the West Indies," *Savacou* 11-12 (1975): 12-17.

8. Lacan, "Of Structure," in *The Structuralist Controversy*, p. 194.

9. In connection with this passage, Howard's observation (in "Guiana Quartet," n. 8 above) seems appropriate: "Harris is consciously playing a variation on the well-known passage from Section Five of 'Little Gidding,' the last of Eliot's 'Four Quartets':

> We are born with the dead;
> See, they return, and bring us with them.

The truly striking thing is the success with which Harris, while writing within Eliot's tradition, writes also within a tradition of far different imagery than the rose and the yew-tree that Eliot mentions a little later in the poem.

Chapter 5

1. Hena Maes-Jelinek discusses other aspects of the important image of the Rock in *Wilson Harris* (New York: Twayne World Authors Series, 1982), p. 100; and Michael Gilkes considers the relation between the Rock and the Eye in Prudence's vision in *Wilson Harris and the Caribbean Novel*, esp. p. 125. Ivan van Sertima recognizes their import in titling his article "The Sleeping Rocks: Wilson Harris's *Tumatumari*" in *Enigma of Values*, edited by Kirsten H. Petersen and Anna Rutherford (Aarhus, Denmark: Dangaroo Press, 1975), p. 109. The Sleeping Rocks are explicitly associated with the figure of the Gorgon in classical mythology. Throughout Harris's writings—in his poetry and essays as well as his fiction—classical allusions occur. Poseidon in *The Secret Ladder* is a case in point, as are references in his volume of poems published in 1954, *Eternity to Season*. Harris recasts these themes and figures from classical mythology as he takes on the role of novelist instead of poet. They become important symbols and metaphors within an indigenous cultural tradition of *América mestiza*.

Chapter 6

1. Laing, *Politics of the Family*

2. Joyce Adler observes that Tenby's withdrawal from social struggles results in a "purely abstract conception of a 'model' of purity or innocence, of perfection supposedly" and that Pamela's name is probably inspired by Richardson's *Pamela, or Virtue Rewarded*. From "Tumatumari and the Imagination of Wilson Harris," *Journal of Commonwealth Literature*, 7 (July 1969): 29.

3. Harris's use of this ubiquitous Guyanese folk rumor demonstrates the significance he accords folk culture. He discusses the tale at length in "The Unresolved Constitution," *Caribbean Quarterly* 14; 1, 2 (March-June 1968): 43.

Chapter 7

1. For another approach to this novel, see Ch. 4 of Maes-Jelinek's *Wilson Harris*, "A Novel-Vision of History: *Ascent to Omai*." Emphasis upon still another aspect will be found in Nathaniel Mackey's "The Imagination of Justice: Ascent to Omai" in the Spring 1983 issue of *World Literature Written in English*, "Symposium on Wilson Harris," edited by Jean-Pierre Durix of the University of Dijon, France. Even their perceptive insights do not exhaust the possibilities of interpretation offered by this novel.

2. See Michael Gilkes, "The Art of Extremity, a Reading of Wilson Harris's *Ascent to Omai*," in *Caribbean Quarterly* 17 (September-December 1971): 83-90, and Part 3 of Gilkes's book *Wilson Harris*.

3. Carnival is a customary observance found in various forms throughout *América mestiza*. See, for one area, Ernst Mirville, *Considérations ethnopsychanalytiques sur le carnaval Haïtien* (Port-au-Prince, Haiti: Collection Coucoille, Série Anthropologie, 1972). For a more general discussion, see *Caribbean Quarterly* 4; 3, 4, which contain several articles on carnival. In "History, Fable and Myth in the Caribbean and the Guianas," Harris includes a complex discussion that is illuminating for considering all his work and in some respects especially useful in considering *Ascent to Omai*. Thus Harris develops the idea of "spider limbo," drawing on the local Caribbean dance and the folk figure of the spider Anancy. For discussion of African folk elements in New World cultures, see Lawrence W. Levine, *Black Culture and Black Consciousness: Afro-American Folk Thought from Slavery to Freedom* (London: Oxford Univ. Press, 1977), pp. 103, 105, 373, 463 n. 7; and

Roger D. Abrahams and John F. Szwed, eds., *After Africa* (New Haven: Yale Univ. Press, 1983), Ch. 3, pp. 108-38.

4. Mircea Eliade, *The Forge and the Crucible*, translated from the French by Stephen Corrino (New York: Harper, 1962).

5. R.T. Rundle-Clark, Myth and Symbol in Ancient Egypt (London: Thames and Hudson Ltd., 1959). See also A. Derrick, who comments on the "notion of 'death in life' and 'life in death,' of an inalienable nexus between the dead, the living and the unborn" in Harris's fiction and states his opinion that this conception "is responsible for most of the apparent obscurity of Harris's work." From "An Introduction to Caribbean Literature," *Caribbean Quarterly* 15; 1, 2 (June-September 1969): 65, 76.

6. E.A. Wallis Budge, *Osiris and the Egyptian Resurrection* (London: Medici Society, 1911), vii, xxv.

7. John S. Mbiti, *African Religions and Philosophy* (Garden City, N.Y.: Anchor Books). Mbiti writes: "We have repeatedly emphasized that the spiritual world [of African peoples] is a unit with the physical ... it is not easy, or even necessary, at times to draw the distinction ... " and "it is through the living-dead . . . that the spirit-world becomes personal to men . . . they are the guardians of family affairs, traditions, ethics, and activities" (pp. 97, 108).

8. Rundle-Clark, *Myth and Symbol*, p. 106.

9. Ibid., p. 109.

10. Ibid., p. 165.

Chapter 8

1. The French word *manqué* means defective; falling short of the intended.

2. Hena Maes-Jelinek, in *Wilson Harris*, pp. 158-61, presents an interpretation of the title "Genesis of the Clowns" as well as interesting interpretations of other symbolism in the book.

3. Ibid., p. 160. For further ramifications of *Genesis*, described as an "exploration of modern existence," complementary to another of Harris's novels, *Da Silva da Silva's Cultivated Wilderness*, see Michael Gilkes, "Hidden Densities," in *Times Literary Supplement*, 25 March 1977, p. 334. For an explicatory diagram of dynamic movement associated with Harris's concept of the sun, see p. 91 of *Genesis*. On pp. 113 and 115 are additional diagrams that elaborate his own interpretations of "clown of light" and Amerindian cosmology.

Chapter 9

1. Todorov, *Conquest*. Todorov discusses the Western conception of alterity as seeing the Other as (1) potentially equal but only if Westernized, assimilated, or (2) as different and inferior but never as different and equal (*Conquest*, p. 42). As he points out, Christian doctrine potentially provides for a genuine equality (e.g., p. 192) Giordano Bruno's rejection of a centered universe, an interesting example supporting my association in this book of decentered structures with nonhierarchy and equality). But in fact the dominant mode adopted by the West vis-à-vis the Third World was Todorov's "different and inferior"—that is, a centered hierarchical world-view.

2. Jameson, *Marxism and Form*, pp. 335-36.

3. Louis Althusser, "Marx's Immense Theoretical Revolution," in Richard De George and Fernande De George, eds., *The Structuralists from Marx to Lévi-Strauss* (Garden City: Anchor Books, 1972), 239, on Marx's use of metaphor in developing concepts for analyzing structures.

4. Karl Marx, *Capital: A Critique of Political Economy*, edited by Frederick Engels, translated form the 3d German edition by Samuel Moore and Edward Aveling, to form text of English-language 1887 edition (New York: International Publishers, 1967), vol. 1, 48, 52

5. Marx, Ibid., p. 35.

6. Robert Scholes, *Structuralism in Literature: An Introduction* (New Haven: Yale Univ. Press, 1974), 181-82. For his discussion of de Saussure and the paradigmatic aspects of language, see pp. 18-19.

7. For his insight into the significance of *zemis* and his development of the concept, see Wilson Harris's "History, Fable and Myth," in *Explorations*, pp. 25, 38-41. I am also indebted to the author for discussing his ideas with me when he was teaching at the University of California, Santa Cruz, in 1983.

8. Walpola Rahula, *What the Buddha Taught*, p. 32.

9. Harris, "Fossil and Psyche," in *Explorations*, p. 77.

10. Scholes, *Structuralism in Literature*, p. 19.

11. After giving this quotation, Scholes writes that Caudwell, who "remains undervalued as a thinker . . . had an appropriately dialectical response to the problems of mind/matter dualism" (*Structuralism in Literature*, p. 2). Cedric J. Robinson calls the idea systems that have underlain social revolt in the Caribbean part of a "tradition [whose] . . .

ideological, psycho-social, cultural and historical currencies were more charismatic than political." He states, further, "When its actualization was frustrated, it became *obeah, voodoo, myalism, pocomania*—the religions of the oppressed, as Vittorio Lanternari put it. When it was realized, it could become the Palmares, the Bush Negro [maroon] settlements, and at its heights, Haiti." Robinson emphasizes: "*But always its focus was on the structures of the mind. Its epistemology granted supremacy to metaphysics. . . .*" From *Black Marxism: The Making of the Black Radical Tradition* (London: Zed Press, 1983), p. 244 (my emphasis). Robinson's use of "metaphysics" suggests a conception within the Western dichotomization of body and mind. If his statements on Caribbean "currencies" are considered in the context of the quotation from Caudwell, his formulation suggests, rather, an interesting analysis of a Caribbean "determining set of relations between the matter in my body and in the rest of the universe."

12. See C.L.R. James, *Wilson Harris—A Philosophical Approach*, General Public Lecture Series, West Indian Literature I, 1965. (Trinidad: University of the West Indies, College of Arts and Science, Extramural Department, E. D. Rameswar).

13. See Karl Mannheim, *Ideology and Utopia* (New York: Harcourt Brace and Co., 1936), pp. 190-97. For analysis of a chiliastic sect's bizarre quest for El Dorado in the modern Guyanese interior, see Gordon K. Lewis's *"Gather With the Saints at the River," The Jonestown Holocaust of 1978: A Descriptive and Interpretive Essay on Its Ultimate Meaning from a Caribbean Viewpoint* (Rio Piedras: Institute of Caribbean Studies, University of Puerto Rico, 1979).

14. Bloch's main work is *Das Prinzip Hoffnung [Hope, the Principle]* (Frankfurt/Main: Suhrkamp, 1959). See p. 908 for Bloch's comments on the Orinoco region as the locus of El Dorado. For Bloch on "Exterritorialität zum Tod" ("Extraterritoriality to Death"), see *Das Prinzip Hoffnung*, pp. 1385-91.

15. Laënnec Hurbon, *Ernst Bloch: Utopie et Espérance* (Paris: Les éditions du Cerf, 1974).

16. Jameson, *Marxism and Form*, p. 372.

17. Alienation is a difficult concept, and the word is often used without precision. István Meszáros has attempted to relate it to other concepts. He writes, "Hume, paradoxically, helps to confirm Marx's contention that the 'need of possession' is an *abstract* and *artificial* need. Every abstract need—since it abstracts from man—is, by implication, artificial. And thus 'abstract,' 'artificial,' and 'alienation' become equivalent, in relation to both *needs* and *powers*. . . .[such] needs can only generate *abstract powers* which are divorced from the human being

and even set up against him." From *Marx's Theory of Alienation* (New York: Harper and Row, 1972); see esp. p. 177. This passage is useful when thinking of conquest and desire in Harris's fiction—for instance, the alienation Donne experiences when he cries "Rule the land" early in the book, contrasted with what he feels when he watches the carpenter in "Paling of Ancestors" near the end.

18. The question arises here, as elsewhere, of the relation of alternative to social reality. Writing on the relation of biology, social reality, and psychological realities, Bateson provides a useful analogy when he writes that: "The unfertilized [frog's] egg . . . embodies an *immanent question* to which the entry point of spermatozoon provides an answer. . . . The message must come into an appropriate *structure*. But structure alone is not enough . . . [the] meridian must be *ready* for the activating messages. . . . Readiness . . . is precisely *not-structure*. . . . In terms of the economics of flexibility . . . this readiness is *uncommitted potentiality for change* , and . . . must be appropriately located in a structural matrix. . . ." From *Steps to An Ecology of Mind*, p. 395. The structural matrix would correspond to the parameters of possibility in any given society and any given psyche at any given time. The uncommitted potentiality for change would correspond to the parallel possibilities I have attempted to describe for Harris's fiction, the available answers to our immanent questions implicit in his work.

19. Ernst Bloch, *Das Prinzip Höffnung*, p. 879 (selection translated by Raymond Meyer, Ph.D.).

20. Harris, "Art and Criticism," in *Tradition, the Writer and Society*, p. 9.

Bibliographic Essay

Wilson Harris was born on 24 March 1921 in the colony of British Guiana, now the Cooperative Republic of Guyana, and educated in that country as an engineer. While working as a supervisor of government land surveying expeditions in the interior during the 1950s, he published two volumes of poetry and a number of articles on art and literature in the Guianese journal *Kyk-over-al*. In 1959 he moved to London, where his first novel was published in 1960 by Faber and Faber. (All my quotations and citations from Harris's novels are from Faber editions.) By 1982 he had published seventeen novels, and two collections of his essays had been compiled: *Tradition, the Writer and Society* and *Explorations*. In 1983 the publication of *The Womb of Space: The Cross-Cultural Imagination* reaffirmed his reputation as a literary critic as well as an outstanding novelist.

Palace of the Peacock appeared in 1960. This first novel and first volume of the *Guiana Quartet* was swiftly followed by the other three, *The Far Journey of Oudin* (1961), *The Whole Armour* (1962), and *The Secret Ladder* (1963). Harris's literary output since has been sustained at a remarkable level for a writer of his quality and complexity. Between 1964 and 1983 he published a major fictional work at intervals of one, two, three, and—only once—five years. In 1964 *Heartland* appeared; *The Eye of the Scarecrow* came out in 1965. Two years elapsed between that novel and *The Waiting Room*, but this latter was followed in 1968 by *Tumatumari* and, in 1970, by both *Ascent to Omai* and *The Sleepers of Roraima*. In 1971 came *The Age of the Rainmakers* (sometimes classified, like *Roraima*, as a collection of short stories based on Amerindian folklore). In 1972 *Black Marsden* appeared. An unusual three years intervened before the publication in 1975 of *Companions of the Day and Night,* but in 1977 Harris published two novels, *Genesis of the Clowns* and *DaSilva daSilva's Cultivated Wilderness*. These were

followed in 1978 by *The Tree of the Sun; Angel at the Gate* appeared in
1983. All were published by Faber and Faber of London. During this
period, Harris also published numerous essays and articles; many are
gathered in two collections: *Tradition, the Writer and Society* (1967,
reprinted 1973, by New Beacon Press, London) and *Explorations*
(Dangaroo Press, Aarhus, 1981). In 1983 came *The Womb of Space*
(Greenwood Press), a volume of literary criticism and reflections.
Harris's novels were reviewed regularly, on publication, in the *London
Times,* the *Times Literary Supplement (TLS),* and occasionally in the *New
Statesman, Time and Tide,* and other British magazines. The consensus
was that his work was significant and perhaps "brilliant" but also
"difficult" (e.g., *London Times,* 1 September 1960). The critical
response to the *Guiana Quartet* was ambivalent, but the *TLS* review was,
on balance, favorable. ("Journey's End," *TLS,* 16 February 1963). Those
who registered negative reactions to the *Quartet* frequently objected that
Harris's prose "resembled poetry" (e.g., *TLS,* 20 October 1961, 7
September 1962, and 16 February 1963). Critic-novelist Anthony
Burgess, however, deemed this style appropriate and effective in treating
Harris's material. (*The Novel Now,* 1967, p. 163). (Burgess later
included a post-*Quartet* novel, *Heartland,* in his list of the 99 best novels
written in English since World War II published in the *New York Times).*
    With regard to Harris's entire oeuvre, some critics objected to his
frequent use of myth (e.g., *New Statesman,* 31 August 1962, and *TLS,* 19
May 1978); others considered his symbolism too "complex" and
"bewildering" (e.g., *New Statesman,* August 1960, and *TLS,* 17
September 1964). Even one of the critics who approved of Harris's
unconventional use of language and his rejection of linear plot structure
(and who compared him favorably with Joyce) accused him, in a
patronizing manner, of being "too ambitious" and "too ebullient" *(TLS,*
5 December 1965. See also *TLS,* 27 August 1960 and 17 September
1964).
    West Indian critic Kenneth Ramchand pointed out in the *Journal of
Commonwealth Literature* (vol. ix, no. 2, December 1976) that English
reviewers seemed more comfortable with the fiction of V. S. Naipaul and
George Lamming, who had presumably overcome what they considered
Caribbean stylistic weaknesses and dealt with more popular themes in a
more conventional manner. During the late 1970s the *Times Literary
Supplement* published one signed review by Professor Louis James (10
October 1975) and another by Professor Michael Gilkes (25 March 1977)
that treated Harris's work in a serious, scholarly fashion and avoided the
prevalent tendency to prescribe appropriate topics and treatments for

Caribbean writers; but this level of reviewing appeared late in that periodical's treatment of Harris's work.

Between 1965 and 1975 an international group of scholars, critics, and creative writers associated with the Commonwealth Literature Association published a small body of critical articles on Harris's work. (Most of these are cited in the notes to the chapters of this book.) Also, Professor Louis James included a critical analysis of the *Guiana Quartet* in his 1968 anthology of Caribbean writing, *The Islands in Between* (Oxford University Press, pp. 140-53), and in 1970 a new Canadian literary quarterly carried an article placing the *Quartet* in the symbolist tradition of Blake and Yeats (W. J. Howard, "Wilson Harris's *Guiana Quartet*: From Personal Myth to National Identity," *Ariel* 1 (January 1970, pp. 46-60). In 1979 Bruce King included a chapter on Harris in a volume edited for MacMillan of London, *West Indian Literature*.

Despite the criticism in journals, until 1982 only one book was available that dealt with Harris's work in a comprehensive manner: Michael Gilkes's *Wilson Harris and the Caribbean Novel* (London: Longman Caribbean, 1975). Gilkes included a chapter on Harris's career as a poet, preceding the publication of *Palace of the Peacock*, and considered Harris's fiction from a perspective deriving from Jungian psychology and alchemical metaphor. He also offered insightful comparisons with other Caribbean writers.

In 1982 G. K. Hall brought out in its Twayne World Authors Series a volume entitled *Wilson Harris* by Professor Hena Maes-Jelinek, a member of the faculty at the University of Liège, Belgium, and one of the most prolific critics in the Commonwealth Literature Association circle discussing Harris's work. Her extensively annotated book integrates summaries of seventeen of Harris's fictional works with perceptive interpretation in a symbolist frame of reference, commenting that she had "tried to keep close to the text and to explain it in its own terms" and making the modest claim that she "only offers one possible reading of the novels among many." However, in her book, as in her articles, Maes-Jelinek is not averse on occasion to combining Harris's own interpretations with her own. She also presents an analysis of stages in Harris's literary development that discerns an increasing concern with psychological problems of characters in settings away from Guyana and with the relation between painting and writing.

The first comprehensive bibliography of Harris's work, compiled in 1972 at the University of Texas at Austin, by Reinhard Sander, now of the University of Bayreuth, was published in Maes-Jelinek, ed., *Commonwealth Literature and the Modern World* (Brussels: Didier, 1975). Her section "Articles" in *Wilson Harris*, taken with Sidney Singh's section on Harris in his "Bibliography of Critical Writing on the West Indian Novel" in *World Literature Written in English* (University of Guelph, Guelph, Ontario, Canada, Spring, 1983, Vol. 22, No. 1), constitute the most complete bibliography of Harris's oeuvre. Both are annotated.

Whereas a few scholars have speculated about the literary and social influences on his poetry and fiction, Harris himself from time to time has published explicit or implicit comment on these subjects. In "Art and Criticism," written in 1951 and printed in *Tradition, the Writer and Society*, he expresses hope for "a new architecture of the world" (the subtitle I have chosen for this book) and refers to particular writers who had "displayed a wonde ul energy and spirit" and "a natural daring"—characteristics he _arly admires. Editor Maes-Jelinek notes of the essays in *Explorations* that "together they represent an imaginative writer's effort to express theoretically the vision to which he has intuitively given shape in his fiction" (p. 1). In "A Talk on the Subjective Imagination" (1973), Harris states that imaginative writers have a duty to speak out in defense of what they are doing because "there is a signal lack of imaginative daring to probe the nature of roots beyond fixed or static boundaries" (*Explorations*, p. 57).

Harris's own continuing exploration is evident from the essays appearing in *The Womb of Space: The Cross-Cultural Imagination*. A hint of ideas he develops fully there may be found at several points in *Explorations*—a well-chosen title—and especially in "Fossil and Psyche," one of his most important theoretical articles, written between 1972 and 1974.

In *The Womb of Space*, Harris opens new perspectives on work by Ralph Ellison, Jean Toomer, William Faulkner, and Edgar Allen Poe in the United States: Jean Rhys, Aimé Césaire, Derek Walcott, Paule Marshall, and Edward Brathwaite in the Caribbean; and Wole Soyinka and Christopher Okigbo in Nigeria. He compares them with authors from Australia, Pakistan, India, and Mexico. Gates and Blassingame, editors of the Greenwood Series in which the book appears, write in their introduction to the volume that it "will be especially useful for students and scholars of comparative literature and especially black literature" (p. xii).

Harris's earliest reputation was gained as a poet in his native Caribbean. With his move to England in 1959 and his subsequent, almost exclusive, publication by Faber and Faber, he came to the attention of the British literary world and the Commonwealth nations. His reception by Caribbean writers and critics has remained largely favorable.

During the 1970s and 1980s, Harris visited various academic institutions in the United States as guest lecturer or writer-in- residence, especially the University of Texas at Austin and Yale University. During the early 1960s, *Palace of the Peacock* and *The Eye of the Scarecrow* were published in France. Professor Jean-Pierre Durix of the University of Dijon translated them and subsequently edited the proceedings of a 1983 conference in Dijon devoted to Harris's work as a special issue of *World Literature Written in English* ("Symposium on Wilson Harris," vol. 22, no. 1, 1983). It includes valuable articles on his poetry and fiction by scholars from France, Germany, and the United States.

Two works by Harris appeared in 1985: Faber and Faber's new one-volume edition of the *Guiana Quartet*, with a preface by the author, and Harris's latest novel, entitled *Carnival*.

Index

About the Author

SANDRA DRAKE is Assistant Professor of English, Comparative Literature, and African and Afro-American Studies at Stanford University. Her articles and reviews have appeared in journals in the United States and abroad.